TURNING AROUND

What Happened When I Discovered
the Other Side of the Cross

MARK SHAFER

TURNING AROUND: *What Happened When I Discovered the Other Side of the Cross*

© 2019 by Mark Shafer—For educational purposes only

Published by Upper Room Fellowship Ministry (URFM)
Livonia, MI 48150
www.urfm.org

ISBN-13: 978-1-930529-40-3

DEDICATION

With love and appreciation to my family: Jason, Justin, Lauren, Andrea, and all grandchildren.

CONTENTS

Introduction

It was out of desperation that I became involved in Advance Discipleship Training (ADT). My marriage had just crumbled due to many lies and unfaithfulness on my part. I was living a secret life of homosexual activity and fantasy as well as an addiction to drugs. The *methamphetamines* helped to deaden the reality of what I was involved in. The drugs enabled me to do things well beyond what I thought I was capable of. The Lord clearly spoke to me in choir one Sunday morning. As I walked onto the platform the Lord said, *"Be sure your sins will find you out"*. This soon became a devastating reality. Within a week my wife discovered her worse fears were true.

We went to see our church counselor as a couple. However, despite his best efforts to salvage what was left our 34 year marriage the church counselor could not do it. The trust between my wife and I was completely destroyed. Out of desperation the only option I felt in my heart was to assume my responsibility and start working on my personal walk with the Lord and to know Him in a real way. The good thing was that the counselor could sense my sincerity. He recommended to get in touch with a mentor with special calling in the area of Discipleship. I took his advice to heart and that was is exactly what I did.

Over the course of the ADT program I discovered who I truly am in Christ. Not only that but I was able to understand why I had embraced the destructive path I had taken. Moreover, I began to discern why I was so powerless in my Christian life. That was in 2014. Praise God! It has been more than three years that I have been free from the cycle of sexual sin and drug addiction. The process was grace-based, non-judgmental and non-threating. Because the pastoral counseling and discipleship training was offered in a personal and loving approach, it enabled me to experience profound changes and radically transformed my life.

Advanced Discipleship Training (ADT) covers various topics over eight modules from *The Bible* to *Fruits of the Spirit*. These modules are woven together to form a tapestry of biblical and spiritual knowledge and truth. Throughout the training God gave me so many aha moments; I call them spiritual golden nuggets. The interesting part is that when those nuggets of truth are applied, it literally transformed my weak and failed spiritual life into a life of freedom, joy, and power in the Holy Spirit. Praise the Lord! Not only that my life was changed, but I experienced healing and empowerment to live the Christian life in ways I never dreamed been possible.

I thank God for the Advanced Discipleship Training (ADT). Thousands of thanks to God for the spiritual formation and personal transformation He worked in my life.

The book you hold in your hands is my graduation paper called, "The Capstone Project." While working on my final written paper, I reflected back and revisited a lot of good memories and important aha moments I received during my training and equipping time. I worked diligently to complete my project. Towards the end of my Capstone Project, my mentor and I begin to entertain the idea of turning this paper into a book. Both of us got excited and, moving forward, we took this direction.

I can confess that I was not even dreaming that towards the end of my life, not only that God graciously redeemed me, but He empowered me to come up with this book.

I hope that you will be touched by the concepts and ideas contained in this book. In everything and for everything I give all the glory to the Lord, my Redeemer, my King, and my Leader in life.

1. The Bible—The Foundation for Spiritual Growth & Maturity

In a few paragraphs please provide an overall evaluation of **Module I.** Please explain what you liked the most about this important module. Explain also what you disliked the most about this module. How do you suggest we can make Module I even more helpful and appealing for future disciples/students?

I found the first module: **The Bible**—*The Foundation for Spiritual Growth and Maturity*, to be very exciting as well as enlightening. The choice of authors and reading, and video materials were spot on and complete. Each author used great care to educate us with sound doctrine and teaching, backed up by rock solid scripture and spiritual resources.

I felt that every aspect of this module, from how the Bible was canonized, to how to correctly study, interpret, and apply the Scripture was very well blended together. The icing on the cake of this study, for me, was the excellent historical DVD's that explained how the Bible came to be and how God preserved it over the years.

What I liked most about this module was its completeness. Any questions on various subjects of the Bible that I had limited understanding before were answered during this module. It was a picturesque journey: from the languages employed into the Bible, to the hermeneutics of the biblical text, and from the correct way to study the Bible to practical applications of the Scripture in one's life.

I did not find anything of a negative nature in the module. Maybe, I was coached at a very accelerated pace, and, at times, I was immersed in many readings and studies. My humble recommendation, for future students/disciples, would be to implement a more relaxed coaching pace.

Please provide an overview about the Bible based upon the information and experiences you accumulated during **Module I.** Explain about the process of learning. Please elaborate.

3

The Bible is reliable and true. Paul writes: "*All scripture is inspired by God and is profitable for teaching, for reproof, for correction, for training in righteousness so that the man of God may be adequate, equipped for every good work.*" (2 Timothy 3:16). This fact permeated throughout the entire module. The inerrancy of the Bible, is the very foundation for everything we do in our Christian growth: *observation, interpretation, correlation,* and *application.* These facts were explained at the very beginning of the module.

This part of my training contained various lessons. Each lesson consisted of multiple questions. This format encouraged me to search various authors and Bible verses for answers on how to correctly study the Holy Scriptures in a sound manner. Among the main materials required, besides the Bible, were various DVD's, books, brochures, and some audio files. I was also required to practice at least one personal retreat, plus complete a mini-project. All the authors and historians I studied during this module were biblically sound in their teaching and points of view.

In terms of the process of learning, let me share just a few aspects. Kay Arthur, in her book, "How to Study Your Bible", recommends the Inductive approach to Bible study. This method is about letting the Bible interpret the Bible. The main approach in Bible Study, as suggested by her, has four important components: OBSERVATION, followed by INTERPRETATION, then APPLICATION, and, finally ORGANIZATION.

In case you are wondering, her book is divided into six parts:

Part 1 –Observation–*Discover what it says.*
Part 2 –Interpretation–*Discover what it means.*
Part 3 –Application–*Discover how it works.*
Part 4 –Organization–*Broaden your skills.*
Part 5 –Practical helps–*Tools for further study.*

Let me briefly explain the Part 1–Observation–*Discover what it says.* Because the Bible has a complete message, Kay is suggesting studying the Scriptures book by book. How? Begin observing the text as a whole. This way you will get the complete message of the Bible. Let's look now at some of the *nuts* and *bolts* employed into this section of the book.

1. The Rule of Context—*Context Rules*

First of all, start the process of OBSERVATION, with PRAYER. In other words, relay on the guidance of the Holy Spirit not just the METHODS.

Secondly, in any Bible study it is vitally important to identify the *context*. The process of *observation* requires to pay close attention to the *words, phrases,* and *sentences* surrounding a particular passage of study. This will give meaning to that particular part of the chapter or book of the Bible you are studying, and it will ensure a correct interpretation of what the author is saying.

The third step is to observe the *obvious*. Begin by looking for things that are easier to spot: *people, places,* and *events.* Keep your focus on the self-evident, and you will discover significant or repeated ideas.

Fourth, deal with the text *objectively.* **In other words, let the text speak for itself.** Observing the text in order to establish the context must be your primary objective.

Fifth, read with a *purpose.* Ask questions like these: ***Who*** *wrote it?* ***What*** *are the main events?* ***When*** *it was written?* ***Where*** *it was this done?* ***Why*** *was there a need for this to be written?* ***How*** *was it done?* This is referred as: **5 Ws and H.**

When it comes to biblical interpretation the *context* always rules. When studying the Bible inductively, this principle, is one of the most important principles of handling the Word of God.

2. Getting the Big Picture

Firstly, the key is to start with *prayer.* Secondly, *read* and *re-read* the book. As you re-read the book you have chosen to study, you will become very familiar with the text. **There is no substitute for reading and meditating on the word of God.** (See Joshua 1:8). Thirdly, identify the *type of literature.* The type of literature determines the way you will handle the text. Is it *historical, biographical, proverbial, prophetic, an epistle,* or a *combination*? Fourthly, let the *text speak for itself.* Come to the Word of God *objectively,* not with any preconceived ideas, so God can teach you what you need to know. Fifthly, use the **5 Ws and H.** See the explanation I provided above. Number six, discover *facts* about people and events. Number seven, *mark key words.* You'll want to mark each key word, along with synonyms and pronouns in a distinctive color. Eighth, discern the *main theme* of the book. Now that you've worked through the previous instructions you are in a better position to discern the statement that best summarizes the book. **Come up with a summary statement.** Ninth, develop an *'At a glance chart'*. This kind of chart is such a helpful tool for future reference, as well as giving you a quick synopsis of the book. Tenth, discover t*he theme of each chapter*. What is the *main subject* the author dealt with in that chapter? Ask yourself: Does the theme relate to the overall theme of the book? **Record your findings.** Finally, number eleven, *identify clearly defined segments*. A group of verses or chapters that deal with the same subject, doctrine, person, place, or event.

3. Focus on the Details

We are still in the OBSERVATION part of the process. The steps in part three are:

First, remember to *pray* and to rely on the Holy Spirit's to reveal God's thoughts and ideas. Next, (number 2), keep the *context* in mind. Don't forget that each chapter must be considered in the context of the whole book. Thirdly, remember, as you read the text, to keep on asking the **5 Ws and H**? Who? What? When? Where? Why? Fourth, look for and *mark key words and phrases*. Marking the text helps you slow down and soak in the context of the chapter. This way you allow the Holy Spirit to minister truth to you. Fifth, *list* what you have learned about each word. Be on the alert for topical lists. Not all lists are formed from key words, but they are the basis for a list. Sixth, look for *contrasts, comparisons, terms of conclusion,* and *expressions of time*. Seventh, with historical or biographical books, *record the location* or *timing* of the chapter. Any significant changes in location or time. Also record major characters, doctrines, and events in the chapter. Eighth, check the chapter's *theme*. Does it adequately describe the main teaching of the chapter? Finally, (number nine), *develop a memorable paragraph's themes*. **You may like to write themes or statements that summarize the content of each paragraph in the chapter.** This is the only way to let the paragraph speak for itself.

Explain and elaborate regarding the *'general guide'* of studying the Bible. Present and briefly explain the *'key principles'* and practices in biblical hermeneutics (i.e., interpretation).

The four major essentials or parts of Bible study, as outlined by Walter A. Henrichsen in his book, "Layman's Guide to Interpreting the Bible," are: *observation, interpretation, correlation,* and *application.* To become versed in the Bible requires a combination of methods of studying the Scriptures: *analytical, synthetic, topical,* and other methods. As in any other field, time and patience are absolutely necessary. There is no limitation to the concepts and methods of Bible study, you just have to be creative. We have to remember that **creativity follows structure**.

In interpreting the Bible or hermeneutics it is important to apply several ***key principles and practices.*** First of all, we need to assume that the Bible is *authoritative:* being accurate or true, reliable, dependable, trustworthy, valid, attested, verifiable, and accurate.

According to Walter Heinricksen's, (see chapter 14 of his book), there are about **nine general principles of interpretation**.

Principle One, states: *"Work from the assumption the Bible is authoritative."* When it comes to studying and interpreting the Bible, most Christian traditions submit to one of the following:

– Tradition,
– Reason, or
– The Scriptures.

The Bible contains ***its own laws or principles of interpretation.***

According to the ***first principle*** of interpretation sounds like this: *'The Bible is the final court of appeal.'*

It is also important to understand that Bible authority is expressed in different ways:

1. A person acts in an authoritative manner, and the passage explains whether the act is approved or disapproved (Gen. 3:4).

2. A person acts in an authoritative manner, and the passage does not indicate approval or disapproval. In this case the action must be judged on the basis of what the rest of the Bible is declaring. If it is inconclusive. Example: Abraham lied about Sarah as being his sister, not his wife (Gen. 12:10–20).

3. God or one of His representatives states the mind and will of God (John 13:34–35).

Principle two states: "*The Bible interprets the Bible, or Scripture is best explained by Scripture.*" When you study the Bible, there should be no additions or omissions. **Let the Scripture speaks for itself.** Neither add to it nor subtract form it. Let the Bible be its own commentary, and when you are at a fork in the road so to speak, **compare Scripture with Scripture**.

A future application of this principle is the use of cross-reference. Make sure you use a very good Bible Concordance for this task. Look for thoughts rather than just words or phrases.

Principle Three stipulates: "*Saving faith and the Holy Spirit are necessary for us to understand and properly interpret the Scriptures.*" People have two sets of eyes and ears. One set operates in the physical realm, the other set operates in the spiritual domain. The dedicated Christian reads a passage and it's truth is self-evident to him. Seeing things from God's point of view is a ministry of the Holy Spirit to those who have not only trusted Him for salvation, but for enlightenment as well.

Principle Four sounds like this: "*Interpret personal experiences in the light of Scripture and not Scripture in the light of personal experiences.*" Your personal experiences, whatever they may be, must be taken to the Scriptures in order to be properly interpreted, and not the other way around.

Principle Five states: "*Biblical examples are authoritative only when supported by a command.*" Are you obligated to follow examples in Scripture? Not necessarily. But, when it is supported by a command we have to obey it. In other words, in those particular cases, the believer is free to do anything that the Bible does not prohibit. For example: The Christian Church in the first century observed Communion every day of the week. Does this mean that churches today have to meet and observe communion in the same manner. I don't think so. Why? This is not supported by a command. Therefore, the answer is no.

Principle Six stipulates: "*The primary purpose of the Bible is to change our lives, not increase our knowledge.*" The Holy Spirit intends that every time we read the Scriptures, we should not only learn but apply what the Bible teaches us.

When we apply what this Scripture teaches, we should remember two things:

– Some Scriptures are not to be applied in the same way they were applied at the time they were written, and
– When you apply a passage, it must be in keeping with a correct interpretation.

Principle Seven states: *"Each Christian has the right and responsibility to investigate and interpret the Word of God for himself."* The reality is that the presence of the Holy Spirit and your ability to read, write and think about the TRUTH contained in the Bible, gives you all you need to study and interpret the Bible for yourself.

As R.C. Sproul once said, when it comes to studying the Bible, our problem is laziness. He writes:

> *Here, then, is the real problem of our negligence. We fail in our duty to study God's Word not so much because it is difficult to understand, not so much because it is dull and boring, but because it is work. Our problem is not a lack of intelligence or a lack of passion. Our problem is that we are lazy.*[1]

Principle Eight sounds like this: *"Church history is important but not decisive in the interpretation of Scripture."* *Reason* and **tradition** must yield to Scripture, not the other way around. When there is disagreement among the three types of authority, **Scripture must be the final court of appeal**. The Bible holds the final authority. In addition to this the Church does not determine what the Bible teaches. The Bible determines what the Church should teach.

Principle Nine states: *"The promises of God throughout the Bible are available through the Holy Spirit to all believers from all generations."* The promises of God found in the Bible equal the means by which God reveals His will to men. In saying this we must acknowledge that claiming promises is a subjective thing. The promises are given to help us respond properly. If we desire to be truthful to what the passage is saying, we cannot claim a promise outside it's historical context. We have to be aware of teachings that states: *"Name it and Claim it."* Proper attitude is extremely important and should be used with the objective to do God's will, not your will or mine. A promise is God's commitment to do something if you respond in faith based obedience.

Theology is the study of God and His relation to the world. The source book for this study is the Bible. Theological principles are those broad rules that deal with the formation of doctrine. Henrichsen gives us **four theological principles of interpretation.**

Principle One: *"You must understand the Bible grammatically before you can understand it theologically."* You must understand what the passage says before you can expect to know what it means, or draw any doctrinal conclusions from it.

Principle Two: *"A doctrine cannot be considered biblical unless it sums up and includes all that the Scripture says about it."* It is foolish to come to a conclusion before hearing all of the arguments, just as it is in all of life. To come to conclusions regarding all the Bible says on a subject is a mistake. This is where a topical Bible study is useful, studying all the passages on the subject. Words, ideas, and doctrinal parallels. You must dig into the Scriptures yourself and get your own convictions, for if they have been formed by what others have told you, you cannot count on remaining faithful during times of adversity on the basis of hearsay.

Principle Three: *"When two doctrines taught in the Bible appear to be contradictory, accept both as Scriptural in the confident belief they will resolve themselves into a higher unity."* Scripture may sometime seem contradictory, but it is not. Man cannot comprehend the infinite mind of God. Do not lose biblical balance by wrenching the Scriptures apart in an attempt to force two conflicting doctrines into compromise. When you interpret the Bible, don't allow human logic to make it say any more or any less than it in fact IT says. Where the Bible teaches two conflicting doctrines you must follow it's example and hold to both. Keeping each in perfect balance with the other.

Principle Four: *"A teaching merely implied in Scripture may be considered biblical when a comparison of related passages supports it."* This can be practiced through deductive reasoning and could be charted in the form: *First Premise–Second Premise–Conclusion.*

Don't be afraid to use deductive reasoning in your Bible study. Think back on the number of times you have deduced something to be true on the basis of certain facts, or how someone implied something to be true even though he did not specifically say so.

If you would be required to teach others this module, **please provide a *written plan* how you would do it.**

If I were to be required to teach this module, I would begin by showing the DVD's. In doing this I aim to demonstrate through reliable authors, the authenticity and reliability of God's Master work—the Word of God (the Bible). After that, I will introduce the new student/disciple in the areas of: *How to study the Bible, How to Interpret the Bible, and How to Apply the Bible.* This will be accomplished through the various Lesson Plans already developed for this module. Other than that, I do not think I would want to change the structure of this Module.

2. Discipleship–The Heart of the Great Commission

In a few paragraphs please provide an overall evaluation of **Module II.** Please explain what you liked the most about this important module. Explain also what you disliked the most about this module. **How do you suggest we can make Module II even more helpful and appealing for future disciples/students?**

Module II was the first module that explained the *nuts* and *bolts* about discipleship. This was accomplished through successive lessons and readings. I learned a lot about what a disciple consists of and what his responsibilities are. I also learned where the discipleship path should lead Christians in the future.

It was the first module that caused me to question where I was in my own walk of faith. Sometimes the discoveries were somewhat painful. However, it enlightened me and caused a change the direction of my thinking and my walk of faith.

I was introduced to various written materials and DVDs that I really appreciated and enjoyed. I especially enjoyed. Dr. Juan Carlos Ortiz's seminars because of his way of teaching in a friendly, humorous way, but at the same time, right to the point.

The lessons, the questions, and the book summaries thoroughly covered all the materials. Sometimes it dug deep into my own misconceptions about discipleship. I realized that for a long time I held various wrong ideas and beliefs about discipleship. This module helped me discover that many of these '*spiritual teachings*' that I have been accepted as truth in fact were not biblically sound.

Thinking can be painful, especially if it challenges long held belief. If there was anything I didn't like about this module it was that I had to get used to spiritual introspection. **Growth and change take work.** The results can be tremendous. I would not change a thing about this module.

Please explain the main difficulties of discipleship. Please elaborate from your own heart. What was (or still is) the main obstacle in discipleship from your own prospective and in your own life? Please elaborate.

The main difficulties about discipleship is that it doesn't just happen overnight. Discipleship is a process. It is the work of the Holy Spirit which takes time. In my own life I found that clearing away the *cobwebs* or the *confusion* was the main difficulties. To fully understand where the real issues are is not always easy.

Please explain the main benefits of discipleship. Please elaborate from your own heart. What is, from your own prospective, the main benefit of discipleship? Please elaborate.

The main benefits of discipleship are: spiritual growth, real and visible change in my own life, and a more victorious spiritual walk. The more I am discipled the deeper my spiritual walk is. The more I grew spiritually, the clearer I was able to see God's hand in my life's circumstances. The more I experience victory in my own life the more effective I am with the people I am involved with on a daily basis.

Please explain the main characteristics of a genuine disciple. Imagine that you are traveling on the *discipleship road* and you hold a *spiritual map* in front of you. **Where are you on this *road*?** According to your *map* what are the main milestones you have to reach and how do you plan to do that.

Discipleship takes a decisive action. **Disciples are made not born.** A genuine disciple has to have the objective in life set forth according with the Scripture. He must be willing to pay the price to achieve it. Sincere love for the Word of God, and a disciplined life without any confidence in the flesh is a MUST. A disciple must not allow himself to become trapped in bitterness, but have a love for people and a servants heart.

I have moved greatly along the road from where I started with the help of my discipler, and I see that it is a continual journey. I continue to trust the work of the Holy Spirit, stay open and accountable. Keeping in the word of God and prayer.

Since discipleship is about <u>spiritual multiplication</u>, **please explain the concept of spiritual multiplication.** Since you are approaching your own graduation from the Advanced Discipleship Training (ADT) – *What is your plan and strategy for multiplication?*

This is a very deep question. I will attempt to answer it by referring to a couple of good resources I studied during this Module.

Dr. Billy Graham wholeheartedly recommends Dr. Robert E. Coleman's book, "The Master Plan of Evangelism."
He writes:

> Instead of drawing on the latest popular fad or newest selling technique, Dr. Coleman has gone back to the Bible and has asked one critical question: What was Christ's strategy of evangelism? In so doing, he has pointed us to the unchanging, simple (and yet profound) biblical principles which must undergird any authentic evangelistic outreach.[2]

As we can see, in his opinion, this book explains the importance of having the right strategy of evangelistic outreach and it's correct biblical application.

The following are some important quotes from Dr. Coleman's book:

SELECTION: *He chose from them twelve.* His thoughts are based on Luke 6:13.

> It all started by Jesus calling a few men to follow Him. This revealed immediately the direction His evangelistic strategy would take. **Men were to be His method of**

winning the world to God. The initial objective of Jesus' plan was to enlist men who could bear witness to his life and carry on his work after he returned to the Father. (The Master Plan...)

The next idea is clear: *In order to be used by God we have to be teachable.*

Coleman continues:

> What is more revealing about these men is that at first they do not impress us as being key men. For the most part they were common laboring men, probably having no professional training beyond the rudiments of knowledge necessary for their vocation. One might wonder how Jesus could ever use them. Not the kind of group one would expect to win the world for Christ. Yet Jesus saw in these simple men the potential of leadership for the Kingdom. They were indeed *"unlearned and ignorant"* according to the world's standard (Acts 4:13), but **they were teachable.** What is perhaps most significant about them was their sincere yearning for God and the realities of his life. Such men, pliable in the hands of the Master, could be molded into a new image. Jesus can use anyone who wants to be used. (The Master Plan...)

This is a key idea! It is clear to me that only transformed people can impact the culture and society. And, I may add, I would like to be part of this kind of people.

Coleman writes:

> One cannot transform a world except as individuals in the world are transformed, and individuals cannot be changed except as they are molded in the hands of the Master. The necessity is apparent not only to select a few helpers but also to keep the group small enough to be able to work effectively with them... It also graphically illustrates a fundamental principle of teaching: that other things being equal, the more concentrated the size of the group being

taught, the greater the opportunity for effective instruction. (The Master Plan...)

The author clearly conveys the fact that '*Jesus was not trying to impress the crowd, but to usher in a Kingdom.*'

He writes:

> Why? Why did Jesus deliberately concentrate His life on comparatively so few people? Had he not come to save the world? The answer to this question focuses at once on the real purpose of his plan for evangelism. **Jesus was not trying to impress the crowd, but to usher in a Kingdom.** This meant that he needed people who could lead the multitudes. His only hope was to get leaders inspired by His life who would do it for Him. Hence, he concentrated on those who were to be the beginning of this leadership he had to devote Himself primarily to a few men, rather than the masses, so that the masses could at last be saved. **This was the genius of his strategy.** (The Master Plan...)

Christ's work requires a solid foundation. Coleman continues his thoughts:

> Surely if the pattern of Jesus at this point means anything at all, it teaches us that the first duty of a church leadership is to see to it that a foundation is laid in the beginning on which can be built an effective and continuing evangelistic ministry to the multitudes. This will require more concentration of time and talents on fewer people in the church while not neglecting the passion for the world. It will mean raising up trained disciplers "*for the work of ministering*" with the pastor and church staff (Eph. 4:12). A few people so dedicated, in time, will shake the world for God. **Victory is never won by the multitudes.**
> ...
> But if we can't begin at the top, then let us **begin where we are** and train a few of the lowly to become the great. Anyone who is willing to follow Christ can become a

mighty influence on the world providing, of course, this person has the **proper training.** Here is where we must begin just like Jesus. It is necessary now to see how Jesus trained his men to carry on his work. (The Master Plan...)

The author goes on with the next phase used by the Master:

ASSOCIATION: Lo, I am with you always Matthew 28:20.

Christ's plan is genial! Basically, Jesus was both, the *School* and *Curriculum.* Pretty awesome, isn't it?

Coleman writes:

> Having called His men, Jesus made a practice of being with them. This was the essence of His training program—just letting His disciples follow Him. Amazing as it may seem, all Jesus did to teach these men His way was to draw them close to Himself, **He was his own school and curriculum.** His disciples were distinguished, not by outward conformity to certain rituals, but by being with Him, and thereby participating in His doctrine (John 18:19).
> ...
> Knowledge was gained by *association* before it was understood by *explanation.* At home with Jesus they could talk things over and there in private see intimately into His nature and work.
> ...
> In his presence they could learn all that they needed to know. This principle, which was implied from the start, was given specific articulation later when Jesus chose from the larger group **around** Him the Twelve *"that they might be with Him"* (Mark 3:14; see Luke 6:13). Jesus made it clear that before these men were "to preach" or "to cast out devils" they were to be "with Him. (The Master Plan...)

To emphasize the *principle of association* Jesus increased the time spent with His disciples.

Coleman writes:

> Contrary to what one might expect, as the ministry of Christ lengthened into the second and third years **He gave increasingly more time to the chosen disciples**, not less. Frequently He would take them with Him on a retreat to some mountainous area of the country where He was relatively unknown, seeking to avoid publicity as far as possible. These journeys were made partly because of the opposition of the Pharisees and the hostility of Herod, but primarily because Jesus felt the need to get alone with His disciples. The time which Jesus invested in these few disciples was so much more by comparison to that given to others that it can only be regarded as a deliberate strategy. He actually spent more time with His disciples than with everybody else in the world put together.
> ...
> One must not overlook that even while Jesus was ministering to others, the disciples were always there with Him. In this manner, Jesus' time was paying double dividends. They were thus getting the benefit of everything He said and did to others plus their own personal explanation and counsel.
> ...
> Such close and constant association, of course, meant that Jesus had virtually no time to call His own. They were his spiritual children (Mark 10:24; John 13:33; 21:5), and the only way a father can properly raise a family is to be with it...
> It would be wrong to assume, however, that this principle of personal follow up was confined only to the apostolic band. Jesus concentrated on these few chosen men, but also manifested concern for others who followed Him. Jesus did not have the time to personally give all these people, men or women, constant attention. He did all that He could, and this doubtless served to impress on His disciples the need for immediate personal care of new converts, but He had to devote Himself primarily to the

18

task of developing some leaders who in turn could give this kind of personal attention to others.

…

Really the whole problem of giving personal care to every believer is only resolved in a thorough understanding of the nature and mission of the church. Actually it was the church that was the means of following up with all those who followed Him. That is, the group of believers became the body of Christ, and as such ministered to each other *individually* and *collectively*. Again this meant that Jesus had to train them to do it, which involved his own constant personal association with a few chosen men. (The Master Plan…)

Personal attention and association is vitally important. The author continues with his thoughts:

When will the church learn this lesson? It requires constant personal attention, much like a father gives to his children. This is something that no organization or class can ever do. There is a lot of talk in the church about evangelism and Christian nurture, but little concern for personal association when it becomes evident that such work involves the sacrifice of personal indulgence.

Of course, most churches insist on bringing new members through some kind of a confirmation class that usually meets an hour a week for a month or so. With such haphazard follow-up of believers, it is no wonder that about half of those who make professions and join the church eventually fall away or lose the glow of a Christian experience, **and fewer still grow in sufficient knowledge and grace to be of any real service to the kingdom.** There is simply no substitute for getting with people, and it is ridiculous to imagine that anything less, short of a miracle, can develop strong Christian leadership. After all, if Jesus, the Son of God, found it necessary to stay almost constantly with His disciples for three years, and even one of them was lost, how can a church expect to do this job on an assembly line basis a few days out of the year?" (The Master Plan…)

Coleman continues:

> This means that some system must be found whereby every convert is given a Christian friend to follow until such time as he or she can lead another. The counselor should stay with the new believer as much as possible, studying the Bible and praying with him or her, all the while answering questions, clarifying the truth, and seeking together to help others. (The Master Plan...)

CONSECRATION: "Take my yoke upon you" (Matthew 11:29).

Jesus was looking (and still is) for loyal men who are going to be faithful to His mission—*The Great Commission.*

Coleman writes:

> Jesus expected the men he was with to obey Him. They were not required to be smart, but they had to be loyal. This became the distinguishing mark by which they were known. No one will follow a person in whom he or she has no trust, nor sincerely take the step of faith unless he or she is willing to obey what the leader says. (The Master Plan...)

To make sure that true obedience is being formed in the lives of the disciples, Jesus places the CROSS at the center of everything.

He continues:

> Following Jesus seemed easy enough at first, but that was because they had not followed Him very far. Perfection of love was now the only standard of conduct (Matthew 5:48), and this love was to manifest itself in obedience to Christ (John 14:21, 23) expressed in devotion to those whom He died to save (Matthew 25:31-36). There was a CROSS in it—**the willing denial of self for others**

(Mark 8:34-38; 10:38-45; Matt. 16:24-26; 20:17-28; Luke 9:23-25; John 12:25-26; 13:1-20). He was training leaders for the Kingdom, and if they were going to be fit vessels of service, they were going to have to pay the price. (The Master Plan…)

Those who would not go all the way thus in time fell by the wayside. They separated themselves from the chosen company by reason of their own selfishness. One simply could not follow Jesus through the course of His life without turning loose of the world, and those who made a pretense of it brought only anguish and tragedy to their souls (Matthew 27:3-10; Acts 1:18-19). Jesus did not have the time nor the desire to scatter Himself on those who wanted to make their own terms of discipleship. To sum up bluntly, Jesus said: "Therefore whosoever he be of you that renounceth not all that he hath, he cannot be my disciple" (Luke 14:33; see Mark 10:21 Matthew 19:21: Luke 18:22). (The Master Plan…)

Actually, when the opportunists left him at Capernaum because he would not satisfy their popular expectations, Jesus had only a handful of followers left. (The Master Plan…)

Their ability to grasp the deeper truths of the Lord's vicarious ministry was encumbered with all the limitations of human frailty. Not comprehending clearly the message of the cross, of course, they faltered at first in understanding their own place in the Kingdom. It was hard for them to accept the teaching of lowly servitude for the sake of others (Luke 22:24-30; John 13:1-20). Their capacity to receive revelation would grow, provided they continued to practice what truth they did understand. **Obedience to Christ thus was the very means by which those in His company learned more truth.** Hence Jesus did not urge his disciples to commit their lives to a doctrine, but to a person who was the doctrine; and only as they continued in his word could they know the truth." (John 8:31-32)

Supreme obedience was interpreted to be the expression of love. "This is my commandment, that ye love one another, as I have loved you. Ye are my friends if ye do whatsoever I have told you" (John 14:15, 21, 23, 24; 15:10, 12). (The Master Plan…)

Absolute obedience to the will of God, of course, was the controlling principle of the Master's own life. When Jesus therefore spoke about obedience, it was something that the disciples could see incarnated in human form. As Jesus put it, "Ye should do as I have done unto you. Verily, verily, I say unto you, as a servant is not greater than his lord; neither He that is sent greater than he that sent him. If ye know these things, blessed are ye if ye do them" (John 13; 15-16). (The Master Plan…)

Following are more golden nuggets from this book:

It must be remembered, too, that Jesus was making men to lead His church to conquest, and no one can ever be a leader until first he has learned to follow a leader. This required absolute obedience to the Master's will, even as it meant complete abandonment of their own. (The Master Plan…)

There is no place in the Kingdom for a slacker, for such an attitude not only precludes any growth in grace and knowledge but also destroys any usefulness on the world battlefield of evangelism."
"One must ask, why are so many professional Christians today stunted in their growth and ineffectual in their witness? Or to put the question in it's larger context, why is the contemporary church so frustrated in its witness to the world? (The Master Plan…)

The great tragedy is that little is being done to correct the situation, even by those who realize what is happening. It is high time that the requirements for membership in the church be interpreted and enforced in terms of true Christian discipleship. If this task seems to be too great, then we will have to start like Jesus did by getting with a few chosen ones and instilling into them the meaning of obedience. (The Master Plan...)

Coleman continues with the following section.

IMPARTATION: Receive ye the Holy Spirit (John 20:22).

Obedience is a key factor. But this type of obedience must be deeply formed in them by the power of the Holy Spirit.

The author writes:

> Jesus wanted His followers to obey Him. But in recognizing this truth, He realized that His disciples would discover the deeper experience of his Spirit.
> ...
> His was a life of giving—giving away what the Father had given him (John 15:15; 17:4; 8, 14). He gave all He had-- nothing was withheld, even His own life. Just as man by his sin had to die, so God by His love had to send His Son to die in our place. "Greater love hath no man than this, that a man lay down his life for his friends (John 15:13). (The Master Plan...)

Jesus led and modeled His men motivated by a deep and consuming passion. If we want to have a similar impact we have to be passionate for the Kingdom of God and loyal to our Master— Jesus Christ.

Coleman writes:

> That is why He lost no opportunity to impress on His followers the deep compulsion of His own soul aflame with the love of God for a lost world. **Everything He did and said was motivated by this consuming passion.** As they watched Him minister to the sick, comfort the sorrowing, and preach the gospel to the poor, it was clear that the Master considered no service too

small nor any sacrifice too great when it was rendered for the glory of God. They may not have always understood it, and certainly could not explain it, but they could never mistake it.

...

The constant renewing of His consecration of Himself to God through loving service to others constituted Jesus' sanctification. This was brought out clearly in His high priestly prayer when he said: "As thou didst send me into the world, even so sent I them into the world. And for their sakes I sanctify myself, that they themselves also may be sanctified in truth" (John 17:18–19). His whole evangelistic plan hinged on this dedication, and in turn, the faithfulness with which his disciples gave themselves in love to the world about them.

...

This was to be the measure by which they were to regard their own service in His name.

...

Such a demonstration of love through them was to be the way that the world would know that the gospel was true. How else would the multitudes ever be convinced? (The Master Plan...)

What follows is an extremely important principle. His discipleship PLAN is not based on human ingenuity, rather on the supernatural power and effect caused by the Holy Spirit.

He continues:

Let no one imagine, however, that this kind of an experience with Christ could be engendered by human ingenuity. Jesus made it abundantly clear that His life was mediated only through the Holy Spirit. "It is Spirit that quickeneth; the flesh profiteth nothing" (John 6:63)."

...

It is only the Spirit of God who enables one to carry on the redemptive mission of evangelism. Jesus underscored this truth early in relation to His own work by declaring that what He did was in cooperation with "the Spirit of the Lord." By His power the disciples were promised the very ability to do the works of their Lord (John 14:12). In this light, evangelism was not interpreted as a human undertaking, but as a divine project that had been going on from the beginning and would continue until God's purpose was fulfilled. It was altogether the Spirit's work.

...

From the standpoint of their own satisfaction, however, the disciples needed to learn in a more meaningful way the relationship of the Spirit to the person of their Lord Jesus, of course, recognized this need, and therefore He spoke more specifically about it as the days of his flesh came to a close.

Christ guided His men step by step during His earthly ministry. Even after His departure, the Master thought it through. The disciples will be guided by a divine Comforter who is going to be with them and in them.

It was at this time that Jesus told them about the Spirit as "another Comforter", an Advocate, one who would stand by their side, a person who would take exactly the same place with them in the unseen realm of reality that Jesus had filled in the visible experience of the flesh (John 14:16). After all, in His flesh, Jesus was confined to one body and one place, but in the Spirit these limitations were all removed. Looking at it from this perspective, it was better for Jesus, having finished His work, to return to the Father and send the blessed Comforter to come and take his place (John 16:7).

...

It is easy to see then why Jesus expected His disciples to tarry until this promise became a reality to them (Luke 24:49; Acts 1:4-5, 8; 2:33). **They needed an experience of Christ so real that their lives would be filled with His presence.** Evangelism had to become a burning compulsion within them, purifying their desires and guiding their thoughts. Nothing less than a personal baptism of the Holy Spirit would suffice.

...

"However, it is well to mention again that only those who followed Jesus all the way came to know the glory of this experience. Such a policy may seem strange until we remember that Jesus was deliberately investing all He had in these few men so that they could be properly prepared to do his work."
...
And so it must be with his followers. We must have His life in us by the Spirit if we are to do His work and practice His teaching. Any evangelistic work without this is meaningless. Only as the Spirit of Christ in us exalts the Son are people drawn unto the Father. It is also necessary for one to see in us a clear demonstration of the way to live His life. (The Master Plan...)

Everything that Jesus thought was demonstrated, one way or another, in front of His disciples. In the next section the author talks about that.

DEMONSTRATION: I have given you an example (John 13:15).
Coleman writes:

Jesus saw to it that His disciples learned his way of living with God and man. His disciples needed to know how His experience was to be maintained and shared if it were to be perpetuated in evangelism. Of course, in a technical sense, life precedes action, but in a thoroughly practical point of view, we live by what we do.

Take for example, His prayer life. Surely it was no accident that Jesus often let his disciples see Him conversing with the Father. Note that Jesus did not force the lessons on them, but rather he just kept praying until at last the disciples got so hungry that they asked Him to teach them what he was doing.
...
Thereafter He emphasized the life of prayer again and again when talking with his disciples, continually enlarging on its meaning and application as they were able to

comprehend deeper realities of his Spirit. It was an indispensable part of their training."

...

Another aspect of Jesus life which was vividly portrayed to the disciples was the importance and use of the Holy Scriptures. This was evident both in maintaining His own personal devotion and in winning others to the Way.

...

All this served to show the disciples how they, too should know and use the Scriptures in their own life. Furthermore, it was made clear to them that if they were to continue in His fellowship by the Spirit after He was gone from them in the flesh, they would have to abide in the Word (John 15:7).)

Through this manner of personal demonstration, every aspect of Jesus' personal discipline of life was bequeathed to His disciples, but what perhaps was most important in view of his ultimate purpose was that all the while He was teaching them how to win souls. (The Master Plan...)

In His discipleship approach Jesus did not let the *method* to obscure the *lesson*. Truth is more important than the presentation in itself.

Coleman writes:

Jesus was so much the Master in His teaching that He did not let His method obscure His lesson. **He let the truth call attention to itself, and not the presentation.** His method in this respect was to conceal the fact that He even had a method. **He was his method."** ... "Evangelism was lived before them in spirit and in technique. Watching Him, they learned what it was all about. He led them to recognize the need inherent in all classes of people, and the best methods of approaching them. They observed how He drew people to Himself; how He won their confidence and inspired their faith; how He opened to them the way of faith; how He opened to them the way of salvation and called them to a decision.

His method was so real and practical that it just came naturally.

...

"The disciples were always there to observe His word and deed. If the particular approach was not clear, all they had to do was to ask the Master to explain it to them." ... "When the disciples seemed reluctant to confess their bewilderment, Jesus often would have to take the initiative in clearing up the problem.

...

His training classes were never dismissed. Everything He said and did was a personal lesson in reality, and since the disciples were there to notice it, they were learning practically every moment of their waking day." ... "How else will His way ever be learned? It is good to tell people what we mean, but it is infinitely better to show them.

When it is all boiled down, those of us who are seeking to train people must be prepared to have them follow us, even as we follow Christ (1 Cor. 11:1). We are the exhibit (Phil. 3:17; 1 Thess.2:7, 8; 2 Tim. 1:13). They will do these things that they hear and see in us (Phil. 4:9)." ... "Yet, as we know, mere knowledge is not enough. There comes a time for action. To disregard this privilege can nullify all that has been acquired in the process of learning. Indeed, knowledge unapplied to living can become a stumbling stone to further truth. No one better understood this than the Master. He was training men to do a job, and when they knew enough to get started, he saw to it that they did something about it. (The Master Plan...)

To ensure that His men will take over the world Jesus progressively built them into the kind of leaders to whom He will delegate the remaining work of the Kingdom.

DELEGATION: I will make you fishers of men (Matthew 4:19).

The author continues:

"Jesus was always building His ministry for the time when His disciples would have to take over his work and go out into the world with the redeeming gospel. This plan was progressively made clear as they followed Him." ... "His method was to get the disciples into a vital experience with God, and to show them how He worked, before telling them they had to do it." ... "For that matter, even after they were formally ordained to the ministry a few months later (Mark 3:14-19; Luke 6:13-16), they still showed no evidence of doing any evangelistic work on their own. This observation perhaps should cause us to be more patient with new converts who follow us."
...

"They had seen enough at least to get started. They needed now to put into practice what they had seen their Master do. So "He called unto him the twelve, and began to send them forth" (Mark 6:7, see Matt. 10:5; Luke 9:1-2). Like a mother eagle teaching her young to fly by pushing them out of the nest, Jesus pushed His disciples out into the world to try their own wings."
...

Before letting them go, however, Jesus gave them some briefing instructions regarding their mission." ...
He first reaffirmed his purpose for their lives. They were to go and "preach the kingdom of God, and to heal the sick" (Luke 9:1, see Matt. 10:1; Mark 6:7). It also spelled out more completely the scope of their authority by telling them not only to heal, but to "cleanse the lepers, cast out devils, and raise the dead" (Matt. 10:8)." ... "Go not into any way of the Gentiles, and enter not into any city of the Samaritans; but go rather to the lost sheep of the house of Israel" (Matt.10:5, 6). It was as though Jesus was telling His disciples to go where they would find the most susceptible audience to hear their message." ... "As to their support, they were to trust God to supply their needs. As they were faithful to God, He would see to it that they were supplied their needs. "The laborer is worthy of food" (Matt. 10:10).
...

Into whatsoever city or village ye shall enter, search out who in it is worthy, and there abide till ye go forth" (Matt. 10:11; see Mark 6:10; Luke 9:4). In effect, the disciples were told to concentrate their time on the most promising individuals in each town who would thereby be able to follow up their work after they had gone. This principle of establishing a beachhead in a new place of labor by connecting with a potentially key follow-up leader is not to be minimized. Jesus had lived by it with His own disciples, and he expected them to do the same.

...

The fact that some people would refuse the disciples' ministry only accentuated Jesus' warning of the treatment they could expect to receive. "Beware of men: for they will scourge you; yea and before governors and kings shall ye be brought for my sake, for a testimony to them and to the Gentiles" (Matt. 10:17–18). They were sent "as sheep in the midst of wolves" (Matt. 10:16).

...

It is significant, too, that Jesus reminded them of the decisive nature of the gospel invitation. There could be no compromise with sin, and for this reason, anyone holding out on God was sure to be disturbed by their preaching. They were not hand shaking emissaries maintaining the status quo of complacency. They were going forth with a revolutionary gospel, and when it was obeyed, it effected a revolutionary change in people and their society.

...

The point Jesus made in all these instructions was that the mission of His disciples was not different in principle or method from His own. He began by giving them His own authority and power to do his work (Mark 6:7; Matt. 10:1; Luke 9:1), and He closed by assuring them that what they were doing was as though He were doing it Himself. The disciples were to be the actual representatives of Christ as they went forth. So clear was this association that if someone even gave a child a cup of water in the name of a disciple, that act of mercy would be rewarded (Matt. 10:42).

...

But before they went out, He teamed them up in pairs (Mark 6:7). Doubtless this plan was intended to provide for His disciples' needed companionship along the way. Together they could help one another, and when adverse circumstances greeted them as surely often would be the case, they could still find solace among themselves.

...

Not many months after this, "seventy others" were sent out again two by two to witness for their Lord (Luke 10:1)." ... "Again the instructions given to this larger group were essentially the same as those delivered earlier to the Twelve (Luke 10:2–16). It merely indicated again that they all were to practice what they had learned to be their Master's strategy of evangelism.

...

The principle of giving evangelistic work assignments to His disciples was conclusively demonstrated just before Jesus returned to heaven after his crucifixion and resurrection. On at least four occasions as He met with his disciples he told them to go out and do His work." ... "Finally, before He ascended back to the Father, Jesus went over the whole thing again with his disciples for the last time, showing them how things had to be fulfilled while he was with them (Luke 24:44–45). Jesus went on to show His disciples "that repentance and remission of sin should be preached in His name unto all nations, beginning from Jerusalem" (Luke 24:47). They were to be the human instruments announcing the good tidings, and the Holy Spirit was to be God's personal empowerment for their mission.

...

Clearly Jesus did not leave the work of evangelism subject to human impression or convenience. To His disciples it was a definite command, perceived by impulse at the beginning of their discipleship, but progressively clarified in their thinking as they followed Him, and finally spelled out in no uncertain terms. No one who followed Jesus very far could escape this conclusion. It was so then; it is so today" ... "Evangelism is not an optional accessory to our life. It is the heartbeat of all that we are called to be and do. It is the commission of the church that gives meaning to all else that is undertaken in the name of Christ.

…

But it is not enough to make this an ideal. It must be given tangible expression by those who are following the Savior. The best way to be sure that this is done is to give practical work assignments and expect them to be carried out. When the church takes this lesson to heart, and gets down to business with evangelism, then those in the pews will soon start moving out for God." … "Certainly the assignments that Jesus gave His followers, at least at first, were no discharge from His school of training. They had much more to learn before they could be considered ready for graduation, and until that time came, He had no intention of turning them loose from His personal direction. (The Master Plan…)

SUPERVISION: Do ye not yet perceive? (Mark 8:17)
The author continues:

Jesus made it a point to meet with His disciples following their tours of service to hear their reports and to share with them the blessedness of His ministry in doing the same thing. His questions, illustrations, warnings, and admonitions were calculated to bring out those things that they needed to know in order to fulfill his work, which was the evangelization of the world.

…

Accordingly, not long after the Twelve were sent out, they gathered themselves "together with Jesus" to tell "what things they had done" (Mark 6:30, Luke 9:10).

…

The regrouping of the disciples following their evangelistic tour, of course, provided them some needed rest in body and soul." Similarly, after the seventy went out, Jesus called them back to report on their work during the visitation. "And the seventy returned with joy, saying, Lord, even the devils are subject unto us in thy name" (Luke 10:17).

...

Nothing could have given Jesus more joy than this. This was what Jesus had been working for all these long months, and now He was beginning to see His labors show fruit. Yet, to show how Jesus was alert to make experiences teach truth, even this occasion was used to caution the disciples against pride in their accomplishments. As He put it, "Howbeit in this rejoice not, that the spirits are subject unto you; but rejoice that your names are written in heaven" (Luke 10:20).

...

What is seen here so vividly in these checkup sessions following the disciples' visitation merely brings into bold relief a strategy of Jesus throughout His ministry. As He reviewed some experience the disciples had, He would bring out some practical application of it to their lives." ... "Take as an illustration, the way He responded to the futile efforts of some of His disciples to heal an afflicted boy. The case was too much for their faith, and when Jesus returned to see how things were, He found the distraught father with the sick child having a fit before the helpless disciples. Jesus, of course, took care of the boy, but He did not let the occasion pass without giving the frustrated disciples a much needed lesson on how they, through more prayer and fasting, should have laid hold upon God's faithfulness (Mark 9:17–29; Matt. 17:14–20; Luke 9:37-43).

...

One of the most penetrating of the Lord's correctional lectures following the disciples' activity was in connection with their attitude toward others in the work who were not members of the apostolic company. Doubtless Jesus' disciples felt they were doing the right thing, but when it was reported to the Master, He felt constrained to give them an extended discourse on the dangers of discouraging any sincere work on His behalf (Mark 9:39-50; Matt. 18:6–14). "Forbid him not," Jesus said, for he that is not against you is for you" (Luke 9:30).

...

He kept after them constantly, giving them increasingly more attention as his ministry on earth came to a close. He rejoiced in their success, but nothing less than world conquest was his goal, and to that end He always superintended their efforts. …

The important thing about all this super-visionary work of Jesus was that He kept the disciples going on toward the goal He had set for them. His plan of teaching—by example, assignment, and constant checkup—was calculated to bring out the best that was in them.

…

No less patient yet determined supervision is needed today among those who are seeking to train others for evangelism. It is thus crucial that those engaging in the work of evangelism have **personal supervision** and **guidance** until such time as they are mature enough to carry on alone.

…

When will we learn the lesson of Christ not to be satisfied merely with the first-fruits of those who are sent out to witness? **Disciples must be brought to maturity.** There can be no substitute for total victory, and our field is the world. We have not been called to hold the fort, but to storm the heights. It is in this light that the final step in Jesus' strategy of evangelism can be understood. (The Master Plan…)

REPRODUCTION: Go and bring forth fruit (John 15:16) Professor Coleman explains:

Jesus intended for the disciples to produce His likeness in and through the church being gathered out of the world. Thus His ministry in the Spirit would be duplicated manifold by His ministry in the lives of His disciples. By this strategy, the conquest of the world was only a matter of time and their faithfulness to His plan. It had started small like a grain of mustard seed, but it would grow in size and strength until it became a tree "greater than all the herbs" (Matt. 13:32; see Mark 4:32, Luke 13: 18-19). Jesus did not expect that everyone would be saved, (He recognizes realistically the rebellion of men in spite of grace), but He did foresee the day when the gospel of salvation in his name would be proclaimed convincingly to every creature.

This incredible confidence in the future was based on His knowledge of those who worshiped Him in the present. He knew that his disciples had learned at least the essence of His glory.

…

However, we must not fail to see the direct relation between bearing witness of Christ and the ultimate victory over the world. **One cannot come without the other.** Bringing these two dynamic facts together by the power of the Holy Spirit is the climactic genius of Jesus' strategy of evangelism.

…

It all comes back to His disciples. They were the vanguard of His enveloping movement. "Through their word" He expected others to believe in Him (John 17:20), and these in turn to pass the word along to others, until in time the world might know who He was and what He came to do (John 17:21, 23). This is the way His church was to win— through the dedicated lives of those who knew the Savior so well that His Spirit and method constrained them to tell others. As simple as it may seem, this was the way the gospel would conquer. He had no other plan.

…

Here was the acid test. Would his disciples carry on His work after He had gone? Or what might be even more to the point, could they do as good a job without His bodily supervision as they could with it? (The Master Plan…)

No wonder Jesus so indelibly impressed on His disciples the necessity and inevitability (for certain) of life reproducing its kind. As surely as they were participants in His life, even so they would bear His fruit (John 15:5, 8), and furthermore; their fruit would remain (John 15:16). **A barren Christian is a contradiction.** A tree is known by its fruit."

Coleman explains:

In various ways, and among all kinds of people, Jesus called men to evaluate the product of their lives. This was the revelation of what they were. In fact, where fruit bearing is seen in its larger context of reproducing the Christ life in human personality, first in ourselves and then in others, practically everything that the Master said and did pointed to this principle.

...

The Great Commission of Christ given to His church summed it up in the command to *"Make disciples of every creature"* (Matt. 28:19). The word here indicates that the disciples were to go out into the world and win others who would come to be what they themselves were—disciples of Christ. **Only as disciples were made could the other activities of the commission fulfill their purpose.**

...

Leadership was the emphasis. Jesus had already demonstrated by His own ministry that the deluded masses were ripe for the harvest, but without spiritual shepherds to lead them, how could they ever be won? *"Pray ye therefore the Lord of the harvest,"* Jesus reminded his disciples, *"that He will send forth laborers into His harvest"* (Matt. 9:37-38; see Luke 10:2). The only hope for the world is for laborers to go to them with the gospel of salvation, and having won them to the Savior, not to leave them, but to work with them faithfully, patiently, painstakingly, until they become fruitful Christians savoring the world about them with the Redeemer's love.

...

Here finally is where we must all evaluate the contribution that our life and witness is making to the supreme purpose of Him who is the Savior of the world. And those who have followed us to Christ now leading others to Him and teaching them to make disciples like ourselves? Our work is never finished until it has assured its continuation in the lives of those redeemed by the Evangel.

...

The test of any work of evangelism thus is not what is seen at the moment, or in the conference report, but in **the effectiveness with which the work continues in the next generation.** Similarly the criteria on which a church should measure its success is not how many new names are added to the roll nor how much the budget is increased, but rather how many Christians are actively winning souls and training them to win the multitudes.

...

We can be thankful that in those first disciples this was done. They gave the gospel to the multitudes, but all the while they were building up the fellowship of those who believed. The Acts of the Apostles is really just the unfolding in the life of the growing church the principles of evangelism that have already been outlined here in the life of Christ." ... "Suffice it to say that the early church proved that the Master's plan for world conquest worked. Had the momentum continued in the evangelistic outreach of the church that characterized its beginning, within a few centuries the multitudes of the world would have known the touch of the Master's hand.

...

But times have changed, and gradually the simple way of Jesus' evangelism was forced into a new mold. The costly principles of leadership development and reproduction seem to have been submerged beneath the easier strategy of mass recruitment. **Jesus' plan has not been disavowed; it has just been ignored.** It has been something to remember in venerating the past, but not to be taken seriously as a rule for conduct in the present. (The Master Plan...)

I like his point of view reflected below:

This is our problem of methodology today. Well intended ceremonies, programs, organizations, commissions, and crusades of human ingenuity are trying valiantly to do a job that can only be done by people in the power of the Holy Spirit. (The Master Plan...)

He continues:

> When will we realize that evangelism is not done by
> *something*, but by *someone*? It is an expression of God's love,
> and God is a person. His nature, being personal, is only
> expressed through personality, first revealed fully in
> Christ, and now expressed through His Spirit in the lives
> of those yielded to Him.
> …
> This is the new evangelism we need. This finally is the way
> the Master planned for His objective to be realized on the
> earth, and where it is carried through by His strategy, the
> gates of hell cannot prevail against the evangelization of
> the world. (The Master Plan…)

EPILOGUE: I am the Alpha and the Omega (Revelation 1:8)
In the last section of the book Professor Coleman concludes:

> What is the plan of your life? Everyone has to live by
> some plan. The plan is the organizing principle around
> which the aim of life is carried out.
> …
> Nevertheless, if the principles outlined here have any
> validity at all, they should be understood as guidelines for
> action. It is only as they are applied to the everyday work
> of living now that they have any real significance for our
> lives. To regard them as true means that they must be
> relevant.
> …
> Every one of us then should be seeking some way to
> incorporate the wisdom of Jesus' strategy into our own
> preferred method of evangelism. The Master gives us an
> outline to follow, but he expects us to work out the details
> according to local circumstances and traditions. A person
> unwilling to fail in the determination to find some way to
> get the job done will never get started, nor will the one
> afraid to try and try again make much progress.
> …

But whatever the particular form our methodology takes, Jesus' life would teach us that finding and training people to reach people must have priority. The multitudes cannot know the gospel unless they have a living witness.

…

It requires deliberate planning and concentrated effort. If we are to train people, we must work for them. We must seek them. We must win them. Above all, we must pray for them.

…

We should not expect a great number to begin with, nor should we desire it. The best work is always done with a few. Better to give a year or so to one or two people who learn what it means to conquer for Christ than to spend a lifetime with a congregation just keeping the program going.

…

In a deeper sense, of course, Christ is the leader, not ourselves. Let this be absolutely clear. So keep the focus on Jesus. He commands through the Spirit and the Word. In subjection to him, disciple and discipler alike learn at his feet.

..

The only realistic way to effect this is by being together. If our followers are to see through us what they are to become, we must be with them

…

A plan like this, of course, is going to take time. Anything worthwhile does. But with a little forethought we can plan to do many things together that we would have to do anyway, such as visitation, going to conferences, getting recreation, and even having devotions together.

…

To give a little stability to this system, however, it may be necessary to arrange special times when the group, or part of it, can meet together with us. During these informal gatherings we can study the Bible, pray, and in general share with one another our deepest burdens and desires.

…

This group idea is being rediscovered in many places today. As such it probably represents one of the most hopeful signs of awakening on the horizon.

…

In this connection, it is not without great significance that the leading evangelist in the world today, Billy Graham, recognizes the tremendous potential of this plan when used properly in the church. I know one or two churches that are doing that, and it is revolutionizing the church. Christ, I think, set the pattern.

…

But it is not enough just to involve persons in some kind of group association, of which the church is but the larger expression. They must be given some way to express the things they have learned. Unless opportunity is provided for this outreach, the group can stagnate in self-contentment, and eventually fossilize into nothing more than a mutual admiration society.

…

It is our business, then, to see to it that those with us are given something to do that requires the best that is in them. **Everyone can do something**.

…

Probably no more essential contribution can they make to the ministry of the church than in the area of follow up of new Christians. Those whom we train for this work thus become the key to the preservation of every evangelistic effort of the church, not only in conserving the forward advance but also in assuring its continuing outreach.

…

All of this is going to require a lot of supervision, both the personal development of these people, and in their work with others. This will mean seeking them out where they are with us in other activity.

…

The main thing is to help them keep growing in grace and in knowledge. We will need to exercise patience, for their development very likely will be slow and encumbered with many setbacks.

…

What perhaps is the most difficult part of the whole process of training is that we must anticipate their problems and prepare them for what they will face. We have to accept the burden of their immaturity until such time as they can do it for themselves. To take the attitude, at least in the early stages of their development, that they can handle completely on their own whatever comes along is inviting disaster. As their guardian and advisor we are responsible for teaching our spiritual children how to live for the Master.

…

Everything should be leading these chosen men and women to the day when they will assume by themselves a ministry in their own sphere of influence.

…

The crucial thing, of course, is their own spiritual experience. Before they should be turned loose from our control, they need to be thoroughly established in the faith that overcomes the world. Every inch of progress will have to be won by conquest, for the enemy will never surrender. Nothing less than the infilling of the Spirit of Christ will be sufficient to meet the challenge.

…

Everything that we have done then depends on the faithfulness of these workers. It does not matter how many people we enlist for the cause, but how many they conquer for Christ. If we get the right quality of leadership, the test will follow; if we do not get it, the rest have nothing worth following.

…

Probably many of those we start out with will think it is too much and fall by the way. We might as well face it now, Christian service is demanding, and if people are going to be of any use for God, they must learn to seek first the Kingdom.

…

We are not living primarily for the present. Our satisfaction is in knowing that in generations to come our witness for Christ will still be bearing fruit through them in an ever-widening cycle of reproduction to the ends of the earth and unto the end of time.

...

The world is desperately seeking someone to follow. That they will follow someone is certain, but will that person be one who knows the way of Christ, or will he or she be one like themselves, leading them on only into greater darkness?" "This is the decisive question of our plan of life. The relevance of all that we do waits on its verdict, and in turn, the destiny of the multitudes hangs in the balance. (The Master Plan...)

As you can see, I was very impressed by Coleman's book: "The Master Plan of Evangelism."

The flowing are some thoughts and ideas, (including quotes), from an important book titled, "Destined for The Throne", by Paul E. Billheimers.

God knows the end from the beginning, and He is in control of the entire history of humankind. I like the way the author explained this concept.

In **Chapter 1** of his book, Billheimers writes:

The average historian has no clue to the meaning of history because he ignores the only infallible source book, the Bible. Thus the Church, and only the Church, is the key to and explanation of history. The Church, blood washed and spotless, is the center, the reason, and the goal of all of God's vast creative handiwork. Therefore history is only the handmaiden of the Church, and the nations of the world are but puppets manipulated by God for the purposes of His Church (Acts 17:26). **Creation has no other aim. History has no other goal.** From before the foundation of the world until the dawn of eternal ages God has been working toward one grand event, one supreme end—*the glorious wedding of His Son*, the Marriage Supper of the Lamb... Therefore from all eternity, all that precedes the Marriage Supper of the Lamb is preliminary and preparatory. Only thereafter will God's program for the eternal ages begin to unfold, God will not be ready, so to speak, to enter upon His ultimate and supreme enterprise for the ages until the Bride is on the throne with her divine Lover and Lord. Up until then, the entire universe under the Son's regulation and control is being manipulated by God for one purpose—*to prepare and train the Bride.* Verily, God is the Lord of history.[3]

Adam was created in God's image. When Adam disobeyed God he became the slave of Satan. Christ became one of us. He took the form of a man. More than that, Jesus agreed to be made sin for us. By the Cross, Christ defeated Satan and redeemed us. After the initial salvation experience Christians are called to embrace, (by faith and prayer), the *training* and *preparation* program for the rulership with Christ.

In **Chapter 2** Paul E. Billheimers writes:

Created originally in the image of God, redeemed humanity has been elevated by means of a divinely conceived genetic process known as the new birth to the highest rank of all created beings. "*He took not on Him the nature of angels, but he took on Him the seed of Abraham*" (Heb. 2:16). However else He might manifest Himself in nature, God could not become incarnate in angels because they were not created in the full image of God. No other created being approaches the capacity of the human being to "*contain the utter God.*" **Only man has a nature in which God can become incarnate** God 'tipped His hand,' so to speak, in the Incarnation. By this He dignified the human race and elevated redeemed humanity beyond the highest ranking angelic star in the radiant canopy of the firmament. Here is a completely new, unique, and exclusive order of beings which may be called a "new species." There is nothing like it at all in all the kingdoms of infinity. This is the order of beings which God envisioned when He spoke the worlds into being. This is the order of beings which Paul called "*the new man*" (Eph. 2:15), the "*new humanity*" destined through the new birth to be the aristocracy of the universe. They form a new and exclusive royalty, a new ruling hierarchy who will also constitute the Bride, **The Lamb's wife.** This order is divinely designated to be co-ruler, co-sovereign, co-administrator and a judicially equal partner to the throne by virtue of redemption and wedlock with the King of Kings.

…

Perhaps some are wondering what is the relationship of the supreme rank of the redeemed to the subject of prayer and intercession. The explanation is that prayer is not primarily God's way of getting things done. It is God's way of giving the Church *"on-the-job"* training in overcoming the forces hostile to God. **This world is a laboratory in which those destined for the throne are learning,** by actual practice in the prayer closet, how to overcome Satan and his hierarchy, God designed the program of prayer as an *"apprenticeship"* for eternal sovereignty with Christ. Here we are learning *"trick of the tools"*—how to use the weapons of prayer and faith in overcoming and enforcing Christ's victory so dearly bought. "The crown is only for the conqueror" (Sauer). And the conqueror overcomes within the framework of God's program of *prayer* and *faith*. The prayer closet is the arena which produces the overcomer.[4]

For sure that prayer is a baffling mystery! God limits Himself to the level of the Church willingness to pray and intercede on God's behalf.

In **Chapter 3** the author writes:

Has it ever occurred to you that the design of prayer in the divine economy is a fantastically puzzling mystery? Why should there be a system or plan of prayer at all? Is not the God almighty self-sufficient? Then why did He devise the plan of prayer? Why and how did He become *"dependent"* upon the intercession of men? Why can He do nothing in the realm of human redemption apart from human cooperation through prayer and faith? He is "*helpless*" without a man, without an intercessor. Why should He be "*dependent*" upon the prayers of a man to defend the nation from the judgments which He, Himself, wishes to withhold?

...

Moreover, since God's will is supreme in all things, when He wills or plans certain divine purposes such as the salvation of a soul or a revival in a specific area, why doesn't He arbitrarily go over our heads and carry out His will? **Is this not a baffling mystery?** He not only invites us; He entreats; He importunes, He urges, He even begs us to exercise this privilege. He not only invites and exhorts us to pray, He also commands: "*Pray ye therefore the Lord of the harvest, that he will send forth laborers into his harvest*" (Matt. 9:38). It is as though God handed us His scepter and begged us to use it. God's offer of His scepter to redeemed humanity is, therefore, a bona fide offer. It is an offer in good faith. Through the plan of prayer God actually is inviting redeemed man into FULL partnership with Him, not in making the divine decisions, but in implementing those decisions in the affairs of humankind. Why did God choose to work within the framework of this system of prayer? God had something infinitely great in mind when He planned the system of prayer, **God's eternal purpose in the creation of the universe and the human race was to obtain an Eternal Companion for His Son.** Redeemed members of the human race, the only race in all creation that was made in the image of God, will constitute this Eternal Companion. Since this companion is to share the throne of the universe with her Lover and Lord she must be trained, educated, and prepared for her queenly role.

...

And many of us are too busy—watching television, following sports, hunting and fishing, bathing and boating, engaging in farming or business, moonlighting, etc., etc. We are so busy with the cares and pleasures of this life, trying to keep up with the trend in new cars, new homes, new appliances, new furniture, etc., that we do not have time to pray. Perhaps some may be thinking: Are we to have nothing at all for ourselves? The answer is, NO. **Christ is to be ALL and in all.** You are not your own. You are bought with a price (1 Cor. 6:19-20).

. . .

Whether therefore ye eat, or drink, or whatsoever ye do, do all to the glory of God" (1 Cor. 10:31). By our failure to pray we are frustrating God's high purpose in the ages. **We are robbing the world of God's best plan for it and we are limiting our rank in eternity.**[5]

The amazing thing is that God made the Church to be the trustee of the good news of Christ. In other words, when Christians pray, God moves. When the Church does not intercede, the Holy Spirit cannot work miracles.

This is exactly what the author is talking about in **Chapter 4.** He writes:

Behold, I give you power to tread on serpents and scorpions, and over all the power of the enemy: and nothing shall by any means hurt you (Luke 10:19). This is the Church's Magna Carta in her conflict with Satan. Here is a clear legal basis for deliverance from Satan's bondage and oppression, and for offensive action in the conflict with him. It is clear from this and other passages that God intends the true Church, not Satan, to be the controlling factor in human affairs. If there were nothing to hinder him, Satan would make a hell out of this world here and now. The only saving virtue in the howling deserts of human life flows from the cross of Calvary. From the womb of the gospel, then, are born all the principles, standards, and qualities of character which form the foundation of all moral, spiritual, social, and political well-being. **The Church is the trustee and steward of that gospel.** To the extent to which the Church has been faithful to that trust, to that extent she historically has been the saying and preserving influence in human affairs. If it were not for the Church, Satan would already have turned this earth into hell. The fact that it has been preserved from total devastation in spite of him, proves that at least a remnant of the Church is effectually functioning and already has entered upon her rulership in union with her Lord. She is even now, by virtue of the scheme of prayer and faith, engaged in "on the job" training for her place as co-sovereign with Christ over the entire universe following Satan's final destruction. This being so, then the Church, not Satan, holds the balance of power not only in world affairs but in the salvation of individual souls. Therefore a holy Church, by her intercession or lack of it, holds the power of life or death over the souls of men. Without violating a person's free moral agency (full moral responsibility), the Spirit can so powerfully persuade that soul that he will voluntarily yield. But He does this only in answer to believing prayer and intercession of a believing Church. May this not be why some are powerfully convicted and converted while others are lost? God can and does deal thus with any sinner when the Church learns to use these mighty weapons of importunate prayer and faith. It is my firm belief that wherever a soul has not crossed the deadline, a believing Church may pray in full assurance and faith for that soul's salvation. Hallelujah![6]

It is extremely important to comprehend that the victory obtained by our Lord at the Cross of Calvary has extraordinary ramifications. Not only that Satan was legally defeated, but the new human race has absolute power over Satan and his dominion.

I like the way the author explains this concept in **Chapter 5. He writes:**

It is vitally important for every believer to know with absolute certainty that Calvary was an unutterably glorious triumph. Unless the believer fully understands and is immutably convinced of the infallible basis of his faith, he will be hampered by misgivings and will be unable effectually to exercise his authority over Satan. Satan constantly seeks to persuade the Church and the world that he is almost, if not quite, as powerful as God. The entire universe is governed by laws. Redemption from beginning to end is based upon a system of divine jurisprudence. It has a legal foundation. Without doubt, Omnipotence had the power to void Satan's conquest of Adam and his heritage, but this would have violated His own moral principles of government. If God had gone over man's head and had forcibly repossessed the title to the earth from Satan, that would have been without due process of law. **When Adam chose to obey Satan, he became Satan's slave.** "Know ye not that to whom ye yield yourselves servants {slaves} ye are?" (Rom. 6:16). When Jesus died without failing in the smallest detail, His death resulted not only in defeating Satan's purpose to obtain a claim upon Him—it also canceled all of Satan's legal claims upon the earth and the whole human race. As a slave-owner, Satan had legal title to Adam and all of his offspring. He could do with them what he chose. But he "who had the power of death" and had exercised it on countless millions with full immunity now committed the most colossal blunder of all his diabolical career. In his desperate effort to break Jesus oneness with His Father he slew an innocent Man upon whom he had no legal claim. <u>In so doing he committed murder and, in the court of divine justice, he brought upon himself the sentence of death.</u> This illustrates and authenticates the meaning of Hebrews 2:14: "Forasmuch, then, as the children are partakers of flesh and blood, he also himself likewise took part of the same, that through [His own] death he might destroy [render powerless] him that had the power of death, that is the devil. "If this means anything it means that Satan is now "destroyed" (not annihilated, but destroyed); that all of his legal claims upon the earth and man are completely canceled. A person under final sentence of death has no legal rights whatever. **Therefore since Calvary, Satan has absolutely no rights or claims upon anyone or anything.** Whatever authority he carried with him on his banishment from heaven passed into the hands of the new Man along with the lost heritage of Adam which was restored by the **TRIUMPH OF THE CRUCIFIED. HALLELUJAH!**[7]

By the unique sacrifice of Christ the entire penalty of all humans from Adam until the last person born on this planet has been paid in full. He endured it all, He paid it all, He conquered it all. Since we are in Christ and He is in us, we share His full victory. **Because of this Satan is subject to us.**

These thoughts and ideas are explained and expanded in **Chapter 6.**

Billheimer writes:

Christ's victory was not only legal, it was dynamic; that is, it was won by the application of irresistible force. Justice demanded that the full penalty for every sin of all mankind be paid by someone. This meant that it was not sufficient for Christ to offer up only His physical life on the cross. His pure human spirit had to *"Descend into hell"* (Eph. 4:9 and Acts 2:27). He was an authentic man with body, soul, and spirit. His spirit must not only descended into hell, but into the lowest hell. The extreme penalty had to be paid. He must *"taste death for every man"* (Heb. 2:9). There could be no adequate substitution unless Christ actually paid, once and for all, the eternal consequences of the aggregate sin of the world. That means that He endured all that combined humanity could suffer.[8]

He continues:

In the mind of God every believer shares complete identity with Christ from the **cross** to the **throne**. According to the Word, we are crucified with Him, buried with Him, raised with Him, exalted with Him, and enthroned with Him (Rom. 6 and Eph. 2). How is this understandable? We are not surprised that He is exalted and enthroned in the heavens. What is difficult for us to comprehend is that we have been exalted with Him. Yet if "he that is joined unto the Lord is one spirit" (1 Cor. 6:17), it cannot be otherwise. The same truth is taught in the figure of the vine and the branches. While it is true that *"the branch cannot bear fruit of itself, except it abide in the vine"* (John 15:4), it is also true that the vine does not bear fruit without the branches on which the fruit appears. These are illustrations of God's voluntary limiting of Himself so that He not only needs the Church, but, due to the nature of the divine economy, He cannot accomplish His chosen goal without Her. **We are organically a part of Christ**. As a part of Him, when He conquered the forces of darkness and left them disarmed and paralyzed before He arose from the dead, we who believe were participants in that victory. **When He snatched the keys of death and hell from Satan** and burst forth from that nether abyss, <u>we were sharers in that triumph</u>. When He ascended up on high and took His seat in the heavenlies, <u>we were exalted with Him</u>. Because Satan and all the hosts of hell are beneath His feet, <u>they are likewise beneath ours</u>. When He defeated Satan it was our victory. He did not conquer Satan for Himself. **The entire substitutionary work of Christ was for His Bride elect, the Church**.

...

For although Satan knows what Christ did to him at Calvary and through the Resurrection, and realizes that as a part of Christ the believer is his master, he still carries on a guerilla warfare against the Church through the use of *subterfuge*, *deception*, and *bluff*. While guerilla warfare is illegal, it is still warfare and must be faced and overcome. God could put Satan completely away, but He has chosen to use him to give the Church "on the job" training in overcoming. Otherwise, there would be no more warfare of any kind.

Because we forget so easily that we have passed from Satan's authority, we allow him to threaten and oppress us. We forget that we are actually a part of Christ and that Satan is subject to us. We unconsciously lapse into our old life of fear and defeat, seeing ourselves as we were and not as we are. We must constantly remind ourselves and affirm that we are in Christ—and because Satan cannot touch Christ, he cannot touch us. All of this is assurance that it is God's intention that the Church militant should walk in the same life, power, and divine liberty as Jesus walked. God has given us the keys of the kingdom of heaven, but He does not compel us to use them. He waits. The rest is up to us,

His Church. In His triumph over Satan He has given us the needed weapons. How well we use them is our responsibility and may well determine our rank in the Bridehood.[9]

The mystery of prayer is that God is more interested to answer our prayers that we are interested to pray. The key factor is that **any prayer according to God's will has a grantee to be answered.**

In **Chapter 7**, Pastor Billhimer writes:

> When we ask in the will of God it is logical that, since the request has come from God in the first place, He is even more interested in our receiving the answer than we can be. The syllogism might be stated thus: "God has promised to hear and answer all prayers that are according to His will." My prayer is according to His will; therefore He has answered my prayer. (1 John 5:14–15). In the light of this and many other unequivocal promises to answer prayer, the question that arises is, "Why should there be any apparently unanswered prayers?" It must be settled once and for all that any reason for unanswered prayer is always on the human side.
> …
> **A Church without an intelligent, well-organized, and systematic prayer program is simply operating a religious treadmill.** One fears that this is an appropriate description of most church programs today. If we could see as God sees, we would behold a great forest of giant ecclesiastical treadmills operating in depth all over the United States and in many other parts of the world. Such an operation may be very exhilarating. It may employ enormous manpower, absorb almost limitless time, and demand a huge financial budget.
> …
> It may give an illusion of accomplishment and success. It may flatter the ego. But any church program, no matter how impressive, if it is not supported by an adequate prayer program, is little more than an ecclesiastical

treadmill. It is doing little or no damage to Satan's kingdom. PRAYER IS WHERE THE ACTION IS.

...

From heavens standpoint, all spiritual victories are seen not primarily in the pulpit, not primarily in the klieg light of publicity, nor yet through the ostentatious blaring of trumpets, but in the secret place of prayer. The only stranglehold is the power of the Holy Spirit, and the only power that releases the energy of the Holy Spirit is the power of believing prayer. **But the power that binds Satan and transforms men is released only by earnest, believing prayer.**

...

Many people grieve because they have been denied service on the mission field or in some other chosen endeavor. Through faithful intercession they may accomplish as much and reap as full a reward as though they had been on the field in person. This leaves no room for self-pity or envy of those more gifted, provided one is willing to fill his place as a prayer warrior. In heavens "book" the nameless saint in the most remote and secluded spot, completely lost to view, and overshadowed in the battle, is just as important, and if he is faithful, will receive just as great a reward, as the most heralded and gifted leader. Hallelujah!

...

Therefore, all apparently unanswered prayer that is according to God's will may be explained by Satan's deception, bluff, and opposition plus the believer's blindness, ignorance, timidity, personal character defects, and failure to persist in undaunted, unwavering faith. Since God is God, the responsibility for unanswered prayer cannot be laid at heaven's door. "*Let God be true, but every man a liar*" (Rom. 3:4). "*God that cannot lie*" (Titus 1:2). "*The Scripture cannot be broken*" (John 10:35). Let us no longer cast any reflection upon the integrity of the Word. Faith will never be perfected until we accept our responsibility for failure. The mystery of unanswered prayer is failure on the human side alone. Many things may hinder perfect faith, but **when faith is perfected the**

answer is received. This is an infallible divine law. The mystery of unanswered prayer is explained by human failure alone, and ultimately by the failure of an imperfect faith.[10]

I was absolutely impressed by the idea of PRAISE as the most powerful weapon of spiritual warfare. When *prayer* and *praise* go hand in hand, there is nothing that can withstand that type of spiritual practice.

The author explains this concept very well in **Chapter 8.** He writes:

> Much of the effectiveness of many well-organized prayer programs is crippled by failure to reach a triumphant faith. Since few know how to obtain and exercise this achieving faith, many prayer efforts bog down in frustration and defeat. How can this difficulty be overcome? We have had much teaching on prayer, but until recently have had little on praise. Yet there is much more emphasis in the Bible on praise than on prayer. For some reason the Church at large underestimated the importance of praise. Many have had the idea that praise is a beautiful aesthetic exercise but has little practical value. But if praise is the highest occupation of angels there must be some valid reason for it.
>
> …
>
> Here is one of the greatest values of praise. It decentralizes self. The worship and praise of God demands a shift of center from self to God. One cannot praise without relinquishing occupation with self. Praise produces forgetfulness of self—and forgetfulness of self is health.
>
> …
>
> In Psalm 22:3 we are told that God "inhabits the praises" of His people. This means that wherever there is adoration, reverence, and acceptable worship and praise, there He identifies and openly manifests His presence. And His presence always expels Satan. Satan cannot operate in the divine ambience... **The secret of**

overcoming faith, therefore, is praise. It was James who said, *"Resist the devil, and he will flee from you"* (Jas. 4:7). Thus praise assures victory in prayer because it overcomes Satan, who is the great antagonist in prayer warfare.

...

"It is continuous praise, praise that is a vocation, a way of life. *"I will bless [praise] the Lord at all times, his praise shall continually be in my mouth."* (Psa. 34:1).

...

To be most effective, then, praise must be massive, continuous, a fixed habit, a full-time occupation, a diligently pursued vocation, a total way of life. This principle is emphasized in Psalm 57:7: *"My heart is fixed, O God, my heart is fixed; I will sing and give praise."* The Apostle Paul says that one is to *"give thanks always for all things"* (Eph. 5:20). This, therefore, must include things that are painful, humiliating, and that even seem disastrous. But in the "sacrifice of praise" it is the personal ego which must be slain. One must sacrifice his own judgment, his own opinion, his own evaluation of what is right and good, and "praise God always for all things" including "good", "bad", and "indifferent." "The fruit of the lips." This means that the sacrifice of praise is incomplete until it is expressed.

...

In offering the "sacrifice of praise" one embraces faith that God is both benevolent and supreme, the faith that can "be still and know that [He is] God" (Psa.46:10). This faith knows that there is nothing at loose ends in the universe. It knows that Satan can never slip up on the "blind side" of God for He is the all-seeing One. This faith is certain that, since God is supreme, He has the skill to outwit Satan, not in some, but in all crises and dilemmas which Satan's evil genius contrives and attempts to promote. The idea that "praise always changes circumstances, but it will change the person. Since the root of all our problems is the unsanctified ego, inside change may be more important than changed circumstances.

...

The missing element in prayer that does not prevail is triumphant faith. And the missing element in faith that does not triumph is praise—perpetual, purposeful, aggressive praise. Praise is the highest form of prayer because it combines petition with faith. **Praise is the spark plug of faith.** It is the one thing needed to get faith airborne, enabling it to soar above the deadly miasma of doubt. <u>Praise is the detergent which purifies faith and purges doubt from the heart.</u> **The secret of answered prayer is faith without doubt** (Mark 11:23). And the secret of faith without doubt is praise, continuous, massive, triumphant praise, praise that is a way of life. This order of praise is the solution to the problem of living faith and successful prayer.[11]

Paul E. Billheimers did a very good job to convince us, the readers, that without PRAYER, the most sophisticated church programs are just a waste of time.

I like the way he puts it in **Chapter9.**
Billheimer writes:

Satan does not care how many people read about prayer if only he can keep them from praying. When a church is truly convinced that "prayer is where the action is," that church will so construct its corporate activities that the prayer program will have the highest priority. Unless a church is satisfied to merely operate an ecclesiastical treadmill, prayer will become her main occupation.
…
The effectiveness of the prayer program of a church will be in direct proportion to the depth of the individual prayer life of its members. Without a deep devotional life on the part of the participants, the group cannot muster great prayer power.
…
Finding time for prayer is a matter of priorities. All of us have the same amount of time in a twenty-four hour day. One's use and management of time depends upon one's system of values. Whatever one deems of greatest

importance will have priority. Even so conscientious and efficient management of time will make possible a life of daily devotion and prayer that is deeply rewarding.
...
Each church must find God's leading for its own peculiar and particular situation and circumstance. Remember, only so much as is accomplished by prayer and faith is authentic and valid. All else is frustratingly false and deceptive, mere shadow boxing and treadmill walking.
...
PRAYER IS WHERE THE ACTION IS; therefore, MOBILIZE FOR PRAYER.[12]

We are called to disciple others as well as be discipled and lead others to Christ. The need in the church today is not only to get people saved, but to take them under our wings, raise them up in spiritual truth, by discipling them. Then a natural outcome would be to send them into the world where multiplication would be a natural occurrence.

If you would be required to teach others this module, **please provide a *written plan* how you would do** it.

I would not change a thing about Module II at this point. I feel it worked wonderfully for me and my growth, and would expect the same result for others I may disciple.

3. Maturity—The Goal of Discipleship

In a few paragraphs please provide an overall evaluation of **Module III**. Please explain what you liked the most about this important module. Explain also what you disliked the most about this module. **How do you suggest we can make Module III even more helpful and appealing for future disciples/students?**

Module III dealt with spiritual growth and maturity as the goal of discipleship. Beginning with the "Ultimate Intention", by DeVern F. Fromke, who deconstructs much preconceived teachings and beliefs in the church today. That's the severely *"man centered"* thinking, the belief that redemption is God's main emphasis, and thinking little about a *"God centered life"*. As we can see, according to Fromke, there is a huge difference between the *"man centered"* thinking, and belief held by many Christians, and a *"God centered life"* and faith demonstrated by the author in the book mentioned above. The author argues that the 'Ultimate Intention' from God's prospective is, *"It was always the Father's desire and purpose to have a vast family of human-divine sons who are just like His only begotten Son, with His eternal Son included."* **This book is excellent!** It sets the disciple in the correct position for spiritual growth, transformation and maturity. This is the way Module III starts.

The remaining authors; Miles Stanford, Hannah Whitall Smith, Dr. John Best, J. Hudson Taylor, along with teachings by Dr. Juan Carlos Ortiz via DVD, bring their contributions to the overall theme of this important module, which is—*spiritual formation*. These authors and their books and video provide a rock solid foundation for the growth of any willing disciple.

Once again, I felt I came to know these authors and teachers personally! My appreciation and confidence for God's TRUTH grew a lot during this period. I also appreciate the guidance of my mentor who gave me several lesson plans to complete, as well as a few essays to write. I learned so much going through the questions and writing those essays. I wouldn't change a thing.

Please define, in your own words, **the process of *spiritual growth* and *maturity*** (or *spiritual formation*). Feel free to use Bible verses and quotes from the materials you studied during Module III.

In my opinion, 2 Corinthians 3:18, is an excellent description of the process of spiritual growth and maturity. *"But we all, with unveiled face, beholding as in a mirror the glory of the Lord, are being transformed into the same image from glory to glory, just as the Lord, the Spirit."*

In other words, the process of spiritual growth and maturity is the work of God through His grace as the inner man is empowered to die to the false-self and live to righteousness and holiness, being conformed to the image of Christ for the sake of others.

What are the main characteristics of each category of spiritual maturity: *children* in faith, *adolescents* in faith, and *mature men* (or spiritual parents) in faith. (Read: 1 John 2:12-14, Hebrews 5:11-14, 6:1-3, 1 Corinthians 3:1-3, 4:15, Galatians 4:19, etc.)

Spiritual maturity begins as children in faith.
Some of the characteristics of the newly repented Christians—
children in faith, are:

- They are *"dull in hearing"* (Hebrews 5:11).
- Tey are not yet ready for mature teaching, but
- They are still processing the elementary things of God, and
- Have a hard time discerning good and evil.
- They are still immature when it comes to faith, and
- Need to be discipled in the faith.

Adolescents in the faith are characterized by:

−They made visible progress to the point of being able to take in solid food,

−They discern the word of righteousness,

−They trained their spiritual senses (by practice), to discern good and evil (Hebrews 5:14),

−They know the Word of God, and

−Are strong to overcome the evil one (I John 2:14),

−And, because Christ is formed in them, they started to display a genuine Christian character.

Finally, ***mature men*** or spiritual parents:

− They are established in the faith without having to go back to repentance from dead works or fleshly living,

−They moved onto the place of training and discipling others in the faith,

−They are able to take in solid food,

−And they enjoy feeding others and being spiritual fathers and mothers for younger disciples in faith.

Is spiritual maturity optional? Please elaborate based on what you learned and experienced. Please feel free to use Bible verses, specific quotes from the materials you studied during **Module III**, and ideas (and quotes) from other sources to sustain your view.

Spiritual maturity should NOT be viewed or seen as optional in the life of a sincere believer. It should be the very goal in the life of any believer. According to the Great Commission, discipleship should be the biblical process and spiritual growth should be the very goal of this process.

Maturity or becoming complete in Him can be a slow process as the Lord deals with us individually. This is a tedious process: little by little, step by step, struggle by struggle, and agony by agony. We must be willing and open to embrace this process as we humble ourselves at the feet of the Savior (1 Peter 2:1-3).

What is *the ultimate intention* of God for His children? Please describe it and elaborate from your heart about this biblical concept.

(Use specific quotes and references from the book by DeVern Fromke.)

As I already wrote, the ultimate intention of God for His children is to be a part of a vast family of human-divine sons, alongside with His eternal Son—Jesus Christ. To have a glorious body and family of brothers with whom He might enjoy fellowship.

DeVern Fromke writes:

> The Father intends that in all things the Son might have pre-eminence. The Son lives to reveal the Father and bring glory and pleasure to Him. It was and still is the Fathers ultimate intention that He might have a vast family who embrace the in wrought cross which they have seen reflected from His paternal heart.[13]

Living in the glory of all that He shall someday realize in us causes to forget not only all our present suffering, but also our own private goals and ambitions.

To reflect the image of Christ is to reflect the character of Jesus Christ. Paul states: "For all who are being led by the Spirit of God, these are the sons of God" (Romans 8:14).

What does it mean to '*reflect the image of Christ*'? Please elaborate based on what you learned and experienced. Please feel free to use Bible verses, specific quotes from the materials you studied during **Module III**, and ideas (and quotes) from other sources to sustain your view.

The spiritual formation process, overseen by the Holy Spirit, deals with the transformation of the inner being of the believer. This is the only way that he or she becomes more and more like Christ. What better Scripture to illustrate the meaning of reflecting the image of Christ than 2 Corinthians 3:18 (which I quoted earlier).

In his book, "Principles of Spiritual Growth," Miles J Stanford, on the subject of faith, writes:

First of all, we must remind ourselves that *'without faith it is impossible to please Him'* (Hebrews 11:6). Moreover and this is important, **true faith must be based solely on scriptural facts,** "for faith cometh by hearing, and hearing the word of God "(Romans 10:17). Unless faith is established on facts, it is no more than conjecture, superstition, speculation or presumption.

...

Once we begin to recon (count) on facts, our Father begins to build us up in the faith.

...

Actually, we cannot trust anyone further than we know Him. So we must not only learn the facts involved but ever more intimately come to know the One who presents and upholds them! *"And this is life eternal, that they might know thee the only true God, and Jesus Christ, whom thou hast sent"* (John 17:3).[14]

In the chapter titled, *'Time'*, Stanford comments:

> It seems that most believers have difficulty in realizing and facing up to the inexorable fact that God does not hurry in His development of our Christian life. He is working from and for eternity! So many feel they are not making progress unless they are swiftly and constantly forging ahead.
>
> ...
>
> In that the Husbandman's method for true Spiritual growth involves *pain* as well as *joy*, *suffering* as well as *happiness*, *failure* as well as *success*, *inactivity* as well as *service*, *death* as well as *life*. The temptation to shortcut is especially strong unless we see the value of, and submit to, **the necessity of the time element.**
>
> ...
>
> In simple trust we must rest in His hands. *"Being confident of this very thing, that He which hath begun a good work in you will perfect it until the day of Jesus Christ"* (Philippians 1:6). And it will take that long! But since God is working for eternity, why should we be concerned about the time involved?[15]

On the subject of *'Purpose'*, Stanford writes:

> Our Heavenly Father is still carrying out His purpose of
> making man in His image. Although His original purpose
> is the same, He is not using the original man to bring it
> about. **All is now centered in the last Adam, our Lord
> Jesus.** Being born into Him through faith, we became
> *"partakers of the divine nature"* (2 Peter 1:4). And as the Lord
> Jesus is allowed to express Himself through our
> personality, this poor sin-sick world will see *'Christ in you,
> the hope of glory'* (Col. 1:27). In 1 Cor. 15:49 Paul gives us
> the heartening promise, *"As we have borne the image of the
> earthly (Adam), we shall also bear the image of the heavenly
> (Christ)."*[16]

On *'Preparation'*, Stanford writes:

> Yes, there is going to be deep, thorough and long
> preparation if there is going to be reality - if our life is to
> be Christ centered, our walk controlled by the Holy Spirit
> and our service glorifying to God. Sooner or later the
> Holy Spirit begins to make us aware of our basic problems
> as believers—*the infinite difference between self and Christ.*
> ...
> Much of His preparation in our lives consists of setting
> up this struggle-our seeing self for what it is and then
> attempting to get free from its evil power and influence...
> the value of both the struggle to free ourselves from the
> old Adam–life and the equally fruitless efforts to
> experience the new Adam-life, the Christ-life, is to finally
> realize that it is utterly futile. Our personal, heart breaking
> failure in every phase of our Christian life is our Fathers
> preparation for His success on our behalf. This negative
> processing of His finally brings us into His positive
> promise of Philippians 1:6, *"Being confidant of this very thing,
> that He which hath begun a good work in you will perfect it until
> the day of Jesus Christ."* His *"good work"* in us is begun
> through failure (and this includes our strongest points),

which continues on into His success by His performance and not ours.[17]

Finally, in his chapter *"Complete In Him,"* Stanford writes:

> There are two main aspects to this source principle. **First,** the Lord Jesus is the source of our Christian life-we were born into Him; God has made us complete in Him. This truth we are to hold by faith; it is true of each of us. *"If any man be in Christ, he is a new creature."* (2 Corinthians 5:17). **Second,** as we hold to this fact by faith, we are brought into the practical reality of it day by day in our experience. **Little by little we receive that which is already ours.** The important thing to know and be sure of is that all is ours; we are complete in Him—NOW. This fact enables us to hold still while He patiently works into our character that life of ours which is hid with Christ in God... Since we are complete in our Lord Jesus, it will not do to try and add to that finished work. **It is now a matter of walking by faith and receiving, or appropriating from the ever-abundant source within.**
>
> ...
>
> **Our part is not production but reception of our life in Christ.** This entails Bible based fact-finding, explicit faith in Him and His purpose for us in Christ and patient trust while He takes us through the necessary processing involved[18].

In her classic book, "The Christian's Secret Of A Happy Life", Hannah Whitall Smith, writes:

> And your hearts have sunk within you, as, day by day, and year after year, your early visions of triumph have seemed to grow more and more dim, and you have been forced to settle down to the conviction, that the best you can expect from your religion is a life of alternate *failure* and *victory*, one hour sinning, and the next repenting, and then beginning again, only to fail again, and again to repent.
>
> ...

But is this all the Lord Jesus (only this) had in His mind when He laid down His precious life to deliver you from your sore and cruel bondage to sin? Did He propose to Himself only this partial deliverance? Did He intend to leave you thus struggling under a weary consciousness of defeat and discouragement? Did "*delivering us out of the hand of our enemies*", mean that they should still have dominion over us? Did "*enabling us always to triumph*", mean that we were only to triumph sometimes? Did being made "*More than conquerors through Him that loved us*", mean constant defeat and failure? Does being "*saved to the uttermost*" mean the meager salvation we see manifested among us now? Can we dream that the Savior, who was wounded for our transgressions and bruised for our iniquities, could possibly see of the travail of His soul and be satisfied in such Christian lives as fill the Church today?

..

In the very outset, then, settle down on this one thing, that **Jesus came to save you now**, in this life, from the power and dominion of sin, and to make you more than conquerors through His power. If you doubt this, search your Bible, and collect together every *announcement* or *declaration* concerning the purposes and object of His death on the cross. You will be astonished to find how full they are. Everywhere and always. His work is said to be to deliver us from our sins, from our bondage, from our defilement; and not a hint is given, anywhere, that this deliverance was to be only the limited and partial one with which Christians so continually try to be satisfied.[19]

In her chapter "God's Side and Man's Side", Smith writes:

Now, there are two very decided and distinct sides to this subject, and, like all other subjects, it cannot be fully understood unless both of these are kept constantly in view. I refer of course to ***God's side*** and ***man's side***; or, in other words, to God's part in the work of sanctification, and man's part. To state it in brief, I would say, that ***man's part is to trust***, and ***God's part is to work***; and it can be seen at a glance how these two parts contrast with each other, and yet are not necessarily contradictory. I mean this: there is a certain work to be accomplished. We are to be delivered from the power of sin, and are to be made perfect in every good work to do the will of God. *"Beholding as in a glass the glory of the Lord,"* we are to be actually *"changed into the same image from glory to glory, even as by the Spirit of the Lord."* We are to *"be transformed by the renewing of our minds, that we may prove what is that good, and acceptable, and perfect will of God."* A real work is to be wrought in us and upon us. Besetting sins are to be conquered; evil habits are to be overcome; wrong dispositions and feelings are to be rooted out, and holy tempers and emotions are to be begotten. **A positive transformation is to take place**.

…

The maturity of a Christian experience cannot be reached in a moment, but is the result of the work of God's Holy Spirit, who, by His *energizing* and *transforming* power, **causes us to grow up into Christ in all things.** And we cannot hope to reach this maturity in any way other than by *yielding ourselves up*, utterly and willingly, to His mighty working. All that we claim, then, in this life of sanctification is that <u>by an act of faith we put ourselves into the hands of the Lord</u>, for Him to work in us all the good pleasure of His will, and then, <u>by a continuous exercise of faith, keep ourselves there</u>. **This is our part in the matter.** And when we do it, and while we do it, we are, in the Scripture sense, truly pleasing to God, although <u>it may require years of training and discipline</u> to mature us into a vessel that shall be in all respects to His honor, and fitted to every good work.

Our part is *the trusting*; it is **His to accomplish the results**. And when we do our part, He never fails to do His, for no one ever trusted in the Lord and was confounded.[20]

I also like what she wrote in chapter "How to Enter In":

In order, therefore, to enter into a practical experience of this interior life, the soul must be in a receptive attitude, fully recognizing the fact that <u>it is God's gift in Christ Jesus</u>, and that it cannot be gained by any efforts or works of our own. This will simplify the matter exceedingly; and the only thing left to be considered then will be to discover upon whom God bestows this gift, and how they are to receive it. To this I would answer in short, that **He can bestow it only upon the fully consecrated soul,** and that **it is to be received by faith**. To some minds perhaps the word "*abandonment*" might express this idea better than the word "*consecration*." But whatever word we use, we mean an **entire surrender** of the whole being to God, *spirit, soul, and body*, placed under His absolute control, for Him to do with us just what He pleases. We mean that the language of our hearts, under all circumstances and in view of every act, is to be "*Thy will be done*." We mean the giving up of all liberty of choice. **We mean a life of inevitable obedience**.

...

Faith is the next thing after surrender. **Faith is an absolutely necessary element in the reception of any gift;** for let our friends give a thing to us ever so fully, it is not really ours until we believe it has been given, and claim it as our own. But this faith of which I am speaking must be a present faith. No faith that is exercised in the future tense amounts to anything. A man may believe forever that his sins will be forgiven at some future time, and he will never find peace. He has to come to the <u>now belief</u>, and say by a present appropriating faith, '*my sins are now forgiven,*' before his soul can be at rest. And similarly, no faith that looks for a future deliverance from the power of sin will ever lead a soul into the life we are describing. The enemy delights in this future faith, for he knows it is powerless to accomplish any practical results. But he trembles and flees when the soul of the believer dares to claim a present deliverance, and to be free from his power. To sum up then, in order to enter into this blessed interior life of rest and triumph, you have two steps to take:

(1) First, <u>entire abandonment</u>; and
(2) Second, <u>absolute faith</u>.

No matter what may be the complications of your peculiar experience, no matter what your difficulties, or your surroundings, or your *'peculiar temperament,'* these two steps, definitely taken and unwaveringly persevered in, will certainly bring you out sooner or later into the *green pastures* and *still waters* of this life hid with Christ in God.[21]

In her chapter "Difficulties Concerning Consecration" Hannah writes:

How am I to know when I am consecrated? We cannot believe we are consecrated until we feel that we are, and because we do not feel that God has taken us in His hand, we cannot believe that He has. As usual, we put *feeling* first, and *faith* second, and the *fact* last of all. No, God's invariable rule in everything is, *fact first, faith second, and feeling last of all;* and it is striving against the inevitable when we seek to change this order.

…

The way, then, to meet this temptation in reference to consecration, is simply to take God's side in the matter, and to adopt His order, by putting *faith* before *feeling*.[22]

In chapter six "Difficulties Concerning Faith" I found this statement so profound:

Trust in the dark, trust in the light, trust at night and trust in the morning, and you will find that the faith that many begin perhaps by a mighty effort will end, sooner or later, by becoming the easy and natural habit of the soul. **It is a law of that spiritual life that every act of trust makes the next act less difficult, until at length,** if these acts are persisted in, trusting becomes, like breathing, the natural unconscious action of the redeemed soul.[23]

The chapter called, "Difficulties Concerning Temptation", was especially enlightening to me, as Hannah Whitall Smith explains:

Then, next, they make the mistake of looking upon temptation as sin, and of blaming themselves for suggestions of evil, even while they abhor them. This brings them into condemnation and discouragement; and discouragement, if continued in, always ends at last in actual sin. Sin makes an easy prey of a discouraged soul; so that we fall often from the very fear of having fallen.
...
We also make another great mistake about temptations in thinking that all time spent in combating them is lost. But it often happens that we have been serving God far more truly during these hours than in our times of comparative freedom from temptation. For we are fighting our Lord's battles when we are fighting temptation, and hours are often worth days to us under these circumstances. We read, *"Blessed is the man that endureth temptation,"* and I am sure this means enduring the continuance of it and its frequent recurrence.
...
Nothing so cultivates the grace of patience as the endurance of temptation, and nothing so drives the soul to an utter dependence upon the Lord Jesus as its continuance. And finally, nothing brings more praise and honor and glory to our Lord Himself than the trial of our faith that comes through manifold temptations. Temptation is plainly one of the instruments used by God to complete our perfection; and thus sin's own weapons are turned against itself, and we can see how it is that all things, even temptations, can work together for good to them that love God.[24]

Moreover, in "Is God Everything?", Smith writes:

Nothing else but this seeing God in everything will make us loving and patient with those who annoy and trouble us. They will be to us only the instruments for accomplishing His tender and wise purposes toward us, and we shall even find ourselves at last inwardly thanking them for the blessings they bring.[25]

In chapter Seventeen "The Joy Of Obedience", Smith writes:

> Having spoken **of some of the difficulties in this life of faith,** let me now speak of some of its joys. And foremost among these stands the *joy of obedience.* Long ago I met somewhere with this sentence, "Perfect obedience would be perfect happiness if only we had perfect confidence in the power we were obeying.
>
> ...
>
> More blessed even than to have been the earthly mother of our Lord, or to have carried Him in our arms and nourished Him in our bosoms (and who could ever measure the bliss of that?), is to hear and obey His will![26]

Furthermore, in Chapter Eighteen "Divine Union", Smith states:

> All the dealings of God with the soul of the believer are in order to bring it into oneness with Himself, that the prayer of our Lord may be fulfilled: *"That they all may be one; as thou, Father, art in Me, and I in Thee, that they also may be one in Us. I in them, and Thou in Me, that they may be made perfect in one; and that the world may know that thou hast sent Me, and hast loved them, as thou hast loved Me.*[27]

In his book, "Resolving Misunderstandings of the Exchanged Life", Dr. John E. Best writes:

1. *Are We to Be Passive?*

> Christ was not passive then, nor is He passive today. When we experience the reality of Christ being our life, we will not be passive either, for we are joined to His active life. **Jesus was active, but not independent.** Likewise, our union with Him will not lead to active or passive independence, but rather to a life of independent activity, laboring while resting in His adequacy. The child is credited as the one who builds the dog house or makes the cake, though it would not be possible without the parent. So it is with the believer. Just like the child, we are

the doers, but the Lord is the enabler. In our case, however, the point goes even further: without the Lord, we can do nothing, yet without the Lord we can do all things. We are told in Philippians 2:13, "for it is God who is at work in you, both to *will* and to *work* for His good pleasure." God works in us both to *motivate* us to *take action* and to *enable* us to do what needs to be done. Knowing that God has given us a Christ-like spirit frees us to let that Christ-likeness show forth through our unique personality.

...

Rather than eradicating our personality, embracing Christ as our life actually liberates it. We are free to be our unique selves in Christ. Believing in our shared life with Christ enables us to turn from an introspective focus on ourselves to a focus on Christ. In doing this, we get on with living, loving, serving and obeying by His sufficiency, which is wedded to our spirit (John 7:37–38; 15:1–17; Romans 8:2–4, Galatians 5:13–17, Ephesians 3:16–21; Colossians 1:27–29).[28]

2. Does Spiritual Union Mean We Become Gods?

Dr. Best writes:

Just as in Hebrews 3:14 when we are told "For we have become partakers of Christ..." it does not mean we become Christ. Never do we become a god, or a little god, nor are we becoming gods. **This is a union of distinction without separation.** For instance, Romans 8:16 states, "The Spirit Himself bears witness with our spirit that we are children of God." Paul makes the distinction between the *Spirit of God* and the *spirit of man.* Paul writes in Galatians 2:20, "I have been crucified with Christ, and it is no longer I who live, but Christ who lives in me; and the life which I now live in the flesh I live by faith in the Son of God..." **The old man was crucified and died.** As the new man, Paul now lives his life dependent upon the indwelling Christ. There is no hint that Paul's personality (soul) is merged into Christ's in such a way that he is no longer a distinct, finite person himself. Paul identifies the life he lives as his own, yet he acknowledges his union with Christ. This relationship between God and the child of God is one in which the child remains a distinct identity, yet he is one with (spiritually connected to) God, who is spirit.[29]

5. *Can Believers Be Sinless?*

Best explains it:

> The strongest biblical proof that a believer still sins is found in 1 John 1:8, "if we say we have no sin, we are deceiving ourselves, and the truth is not in us." John is writing to correct false teachings and to encourage believers in the truth. Clearly he views sin as a real issue in the life of the believer. Furthermore, the entire Scripture abounds with commands telling the believer not to sin. If the believer could not sin, no such commands would be necessary.
>
> . . .
>
> It is not that we no longer sin, but the power of sin is broken so that **we do not have to sin.** Not only was the penalty of sin paid, but the power of sin was broken on the cross of our Lord Jesus Christ. That is why Paul can write: "...our old self [old unregenerate in-Adam man] was crucified with Him, that our body of sin might be done away with, that we should no longer be slaves to sin; for he who has died is freed from sin" (Romans 6:6–7).
>
> . . .
>
> We have a new identity in Christ Jesus in which the dominance of sin's power has been broken, **but we are not sinless**.
>
> . . .
>
> Why, then, do we still sin? Because as long as we remain in our unredeemed earthly bodies we still have "flesh," which is a propensity to seek life through our own resources, apart from God. *Flesh is not who we truly are* (Romans 7:13–23), but it remains temporarily with us, and is something we must deal with. And, as the Scriptures

make clear, we are accountable to God for the choices we make: whether to walk in dependence upon God ("by the Spirit") or dependence upon ourselves ("by the flesh").

6. *Are We Responsible For Sin?*

The author writes:

> Sin entered into the world through Adam, and although the power of sin is broken, **sin continues to exist.** Just as God held Adam accountable for his sin, <u>the believer is responsible for any sin in his life.</u> We are not responsible for the temptation to sin, but we are responsible for our reaction to the temptation. **Obeying sin leads to enslavement to sin,** lawlessness results in further lawlessness, and the wages of sin is death (Romans 6:16, 19, 23).
> …
> <u>Understanding our true identity in Christ is key to avoiding sin, not engaging in more of it</u>. The believer who understands his identity, when confronted with temptation, is able to say, "That's not who I really am. That's my flesh. It may want to do that, but it does not reign over me, and through the power of the Holy Spirit, I can choose to act in accordance with who I really am and how my inner man truly wants to act.

7. *Should We Die To Our Emotions?*

Talking about emotions in Christian's circles is complicated and something confusing. Dr. John best sheds some light into this topic:

> "The *denying* or *stuffing* of the emotions is a coping device of the flesh. This is the opposite of God's purpose in arranging for our death with Christ. This was a spiritual death, not a *soulical* death. The soul (personality) is where the emotions are located. This death of who we were in Adam **leads to our emotions being liberated, healed and restored.** In our one-on-one personal ministry, we

have often seen God accomplish this in people's emotions. If we really consider ourselves crucified and risen with **Christ**, He becomes the foundation for our emotional well-being, and we can begin to enter into the most emotionally healthy state we have ever experienced. Our emotions were not crucified, but because Christ is our life and power, we no longer need to be controlled by them.

Because **emotions are a result of the way we think**, Paul's urging to "be transformed by the renewing of your minds" (Romans 12:2) is basic, practical advice.

...

So, **if our thinking is grounded in God's truth, we will be emotionally healthy**, but if we are deceived by the world, the flesh and the devil, we will be emotionally unhealthy. What we need is a reliable thought life, and only in resolutely trusting in God and seeing from His perspective can we trust our thinking and our emotions. Of vital importance is for us to see ourselves as God sees us, based upon our identity in Christ Jesus. When we come to a realization of our identity in Christ and rely upon Him, for the first time in our lives our thinking is grounded in the truth of all ages, Jesus Christ Himself. Because our old man was laid aside our emotions can be awakened to the truth of God and to real freedom of expression. **Christ's life gives us freedom to feel, a basis for truth amidst feelings**.

8. *Are We Helpless To Experience Christ's Life?*

God desires all of His children to experience Christ's life (1 John 5:12). However, not all Christians got to this level of experience.

Best writes:

> ...although all believers are "in Christ," not all come to a personal realization of their life in Christ at the same time or in the same way. For some reason, be it through *lack of knowledge*, *adherence to flesh patterns* or just *plain unbelief*, some believers are unable to appropriate what Christ has done

because they do not come to a realization of their identity in Christ. Until the Lord brings them into an understanding of these truths or "reveals" these truths, they are unable to appropriate them. <u>Just as we needed God to give revelation of our need of a Savior and bring us to Himself, we need Him to continue to reveal His truth</u>.

...

God has disclosed the truth of our identity in Christ in His written Word, but it is the indwelling Holy Spirit who gives clarity and enlightenment to this truth. We can choose to trust God and yield to Him frequently. Then God will respond to us with ever increasing illuminations of His Word and Himself. He will do this according to His will and timing, to bring about His highest good for us. It is the cooperative effort (John 15:4, 5). **We must seek Him.** However, God is the One who brings renewing to our soul (Romans 12:2), illuminates deeper truths to us through His Spirit into our spirit (Proverbs 20:27, Romans 8:16, 1 Corinthians 2:11, 1 John 2:20–21) and uses circumstances to reveal our weakness so that He will be our strength (2 Corinthians 12:9) and life.

10. *Is Positional Truth Real?*

In our culture, in the recent period the concept of truth became controversial; everybody claims to have his or her version of truth. This affects the churchgoers too.

The author explains:

It has been said you can always tell what someone truly believes by what comes after the "but"... Those who espouse view Number Two are saying, "God sees me as righteous, **but** I am really still sinful." Adherents of view Number One say, "I still sin, but God has made me righteous." **The question is which viewpoint does God want us to have?** Does He want us to base our view of ourselves on our experience, or on what He says is true of us? The Scriptures are clear: **God wants us to see ourselves based on what He says is actually true**

about us. In Romans 6:1–11, Paul says *we died to sin*, were *crucified with Christ*, were *buried with Christ*, were *raised with Christ*, are *freed from sin* and are *alive to God*. Based on these truths, Paul instructs us in the remainder of Romans 6 to **yield** our members to God, not to sin. Our experience as believers is to flow from what is true about us; what is true about us does not flow from our experience!

...

If we say we have to wait until we die to go to heaven to experience the reality of our righteous identity in Christ and our union with Him, then we are misunderstanding what is meant by the word *positional.* Using the term *positional truth* becomes a cop-out when it pushes things into future that are intended for the present. Because a believer's essential identity is his spiritual identity in Christ, this *positional truth* is the reality God intends for us to experience right now. <u>God intends the spiritual reality of who we are in Christ to be the foundation of how we live our life upon earth at this present time!</u>

12. *Can There Be Diversity Within Man's Unity?*

Not everybody agrees with the tripartite (spirit, soul and body) view of man. Many believers view man as two part: immaterial and material part.

Best writes:

> It is true that throughout Scripture God deals with the whole man, but He also addresses the distinctive areas of man. We see no conflict in accepting both perspectives. Together they describe diversity within *unity*. For instance, in the garden, God commanded Adam not to eat from the tree of knowledge of good and evil, "*for in the day that you eat from it you shall surely die*" (Genesis 2:17). We know Adam rebelled and ate from the tree. On the day Adam ate from the tree of the knowledge of good and evil, in what way did he die? **That day he died spiritually.** Many years later his physical body died. Although Adam reaped the full consequences of sin, there was a definite

distinction in the occurrence of the consequences for Adam's spirit and his body.

...

Another example of diversity within unity is revealed in passages such as Romans 6:6: "our old man was crucified with Him." We were not physically alive 2000 years ago to be crucified upon the cross with Jesus. **Yet God's Word says we were crucified.**

13. *Do All Problems Disappear?*

Problems are part of life. Both Christians and non-Christians have issues. How to deal with this dilemma? "I thought that if I become a Christian all problems disappear!"

The author explains it:

> Union with Christ is not a life of freedom from trials and suffering. It is freedom in and through the trials and suffering of life. "In all these [horrible—see Romans 8:35–36] things, we overwhelmingly conquer through Him who loved us" (Romans 8:37). We are not set free from trouble in this world. **We were never promised a trouble-free life.** In fact, Jesus told His followers that they could expect persecution (John 15:20). Paul tells us to "exult in our tribulations" (Romans 5:3). He goes on to explain that these tribulations build character and hope into our lives (5:4). He talked at length about the difficulties he experienced in this world, but he encourages believers to trust in God to see them through their present hardship (2 Corinthians 4:1–18).
>
> ...
>
> **God intends for us to experience victory in the midst of our troubles,** for our highest reality is Who He is and what He has already done, not the circumstances of the world, the flesh or the devil![30]

I like what Hannah Whitlall Smith wrote about the topic of Divine Union:

This divine union was the glorious purpose in the heart of God for His people before the foundation of the world. It was the mystery hid from ages and generations. It was accomplished in the death of Christ. It has been made known by the Scriptures; and it is realized as an actual experience by many of God's children. [31]

The concept of the exchanged life captivated me a great deal during the process of Advanced Discipleship Training. Below are some highlights that impressed me deeply from the biographical letter written by J. Hudson Taylor regarding "The Exchanged Life."

Taylor writes:

> I felt the ingratitude, the danger, the sin of not living nearer to God. I prayed, agonized, fasted, strove, made resolutions, read the Word more diligently, sought more time for retirement and meditation -- but all was without effect. **Every day, almost every hour, the consciousness of sin oppressed me.** I knew that if I could only abide in Christ all would be well, but I *could not.* I began the day with prayer, determined not to take my eye from Him for a moment; but pressure of duties, sometimes very trying, constant interruptions apt to be so wearing, often caused me to forget Him. ...
>
> Each day brought its register of sin and failure, or lack of power. To will was indeed present with me, but how to perform I found not. Then came the question, "Is there no rescue? Must it be thus to the end—constant conflict and, instead of victory, too often defeat?
>
> ...
>
> All the time I felt assured that there was in Christ all I needed, but the practical question was how to get it out. He was rich, truly, but I was poor; He strong, but I weak, I knew full well that there was in the root, the stem, abundant fatness; but how to get it into my puny little branch was the question.
>
> ...

But I had not this faith. I strove for it, but it would not come; tried to exercise it, but in vain. Seeing more and more the wondrous supply of grace laid up in Jesus, the fullness of our precious Savior--my helplessness and guilt seemed to increase.

...

Unbelief was, I felt the damning sin of the world—yet I indulged in it. I prayed for faith but it came not. What was I to do?[32]

Moreover:

When my agony of soul was at its height, a sentence in a letter from dear McCarthy (John McCarthy, in Hangchow) was used to remove the scales from my eyes, and the Spirit of God revealed the truth of our oneness with Jesus as I have never known it before McCarthy, who has been much exercised by the same sense of failure, but saw the light before I did, wrote (I quote from memory):

...

But how to get faith strengthened? Not by striving after faith, <u>but by resting on the Faithful One</u>."

As I read I saw it all! *"If we believe not, He abideth faithful."* I looked to Jesus and saw (and when I saw, oh, how joy flowed!) that He had said, "I will never leave you." "Ah, there is rest!" I thought. "I have striven in vain to rest in Him. **I'll strive no more.** For has He not promised to abide with me—never to leave me, never to fail me?" And, dearie, He never will!

...

As I thought of the vine and the branches, what light the blessed Spirit poured direct into my soul! How great seemed my mistake in having wished to get the sap, the fullness out of Him. I saw not only that Jesus would never leave me, but that I was a member of His body, of His flesh and of His bones. The vine now I see, is not the root merely, but all—root, stem, branches, twigs, leaves, flowers, fruit: and Jesus is not only that: He is soil and sunshine, air and showers, and ten thousand times more than we have ever dreamed, wished for, or needed. Oh, the joy of seeing this truth! I do pray that the eyes of your understanding may be enlightened, that you may know and enjoy the riches freely given us in Christ.

...

The sweetest part, if one may speak of one part being sweeter than another, is the rest which full identification with Christ brings. I am no longer anxious about anything, as I realize this; for He, I know, is able to carry out His will, and His will is mine. It makes no matter where He places me, or how. That is rather for Him to consider than for me.

...

So, if God place me in great perplexity, must He not give me much guidance; in positions of great difficulty, much grace; in circumstances of great pressure and trial, much strength? No fear that His resources will be unequal to the emergency! **And His resources are mine, for He is mine, and is with me and dwells in me.** All this springs from the believer's oneness with Christ, and since Christ has thus dwelt in my heart by faith, how happy I have been!

...

I am no better than before (may I say, in a sense, I do not wish to be, nor am I striving to be); but I am dead and buried with Christ--aye, and risen too and ascended; and now Christ lives in me, and "the life I now live in the flesh, I live by the faith of the Son of God, who loved me, and gave Himself for me." I now believe I am dead to sin. God reckons me so, and tells me to reckon myself so. He knows best. All my past experience may have shown that it was not so; but I dare not say it is not now, when He says it is. I feel and know that old things have passed away. I am as capable of sinning as ever, but Christ is realized as present as never before. He cannot sin; and He can keep me from sinning. I cannot say (I am sorry to have to confess it) that since I have seen this light I have not sinned; but I do feel there was no need to have done so. And further—walking more in the light, my conscience has been more tender; sin has been instantly seen, confessed, pardoned; and peace and joy (with humility) instantly restored; with one exception, when for several hours peace and joy did not return—from want, as I had to learn, of full confession, and from some attempt to justify self.

...

Faith, I now see, is "the substance of things hoped for," and not mere shadow. It is not less than sight, but more. Sight only shows the outward forms of things; **faith gives the substance.** You can rest on substance, feed on substance. Christ dwelling in the heart by faith (i.e. His Word of Promise credited), is power indeed, is life indeed. And Christ and sin will not dwell together; nor can we have His presence with love of the world, or carefulness about many things.

...

Do not continue to say in effect, "Who shall ascend into heaven, that is to bring Christ down from above." In other words, do not let us consider Him as afar off, when God has made us one with Him, members of His very body. Nor should we look upon this experience, these truths, as for the few. They are the birthright of every child of God, and no one can dispense with them without dishonor to our Lord. The only power for deliverance from sin or for true service is Christ.[33]

As part of this Module, I was required to watch a Video Seminar[34] by Dr. Juan Carlos Ortiz containing three DVDs. In the one titled, "Accepted in the Beloved," Dr. Ortiz, has a unique, non-threatening style of presenting difficult subjects, by braking them down into easy-to-understand terms. He used a lot of humor in his presentations, which made a tough seminar pleasant to my ears. His amusing style disarmed me and facilitated my understanding of deeper teachings. At the end of the seminar I felt encouraged to apply these new concepts into my spiritual life. What follows are some of the "golden nuggets" I got from his Video teaching.

Dr. Ortiz based his teaching on Colossians 2:13–14:

When you were dead in your transgressions and the uncircumcision of your flesh, He made you alive together with Him, **having forgiven us all our transgressions,**

having canceled out the certificate of debt consisting of decrees against us, which was hostile to us; and He has taken it out of the way, having nailed it to the cross.

Then he broke the text down, piece by piece. He pointed out deeper meanings that I was not familiar with them before.

I am quoting from memory:

> *"And when you were dead…"* "Total incapacity. Nothing to lean upon, **a perfect nothing**. Worse than nothing. Because nothing is nothing—but a corpse is a problem! It's minus!" And *'when you were dead'*, He gave you Life." **That is an act of God.** A sovereign act of God. *"He made you alive together with Him,* **having forgiven us all our transgressions,** *having canceled out the certificate of debt consisting of decrees against us, which was hostile to us; and He* **has taken it out of the way,** *having nailed it to the cross."*
>
> …
>
> Think about it. *"When you were dead"*. It couldn't be worse than that. A dead person not only can do nothing for himself. A dead person cannot even desire that anymore. Not even the desire is there. It's completely dependent on somebody else that has love. To take that thing, stinky thing, and bury it.

Here are other nuggets:

> "I don't understand how God could love a sinner such as I! Are you a father or mother? Do you have children? Do they behave properly? Do they revolt? Why don't you shoot them? My friends, we are His, He made us, He loves us!"

He made the point, didn't he?

> God created us with a clear purpose. He made us with the purpose of showing off His grace. An undeserving grace, and were helping Him a LOT! To all these dead people He gave us life because He loves us. If you think God's love is a mystery, stop thinking like that!

"He has *forgiven us all our trespasses.*" God not only knows all you have done, but He knows all you haven't done yet. <I AM.> He lives in a continual present. That's why He said we are seated in the heavenly. You mean we will be seated? "No! No! No! **You are!**"

With his specific humor, Ortiz added:

"I see you are in the 3rd row on the right!"

Pointing out an old Hymn, Juan Carlos wants to drive his point home:

"He Took My Sins Away," and *"At the Cross, at the Cross."* He asked a rhetorical question: "How do you know? You were not even born yet when He died? He had it in His books. He knew everything you would do! Everything. *"For those whom He foreknew, He also predestined..."* (Romans 8:29a). This is my peace, that knowing me He predestined me. I cannot commit a sin that He forgot about it. Knowing everything He called you anyhow! That's our peace!"
...
He crucified me. All of me, to the cross and made me – NO, He actually **killed me** – and **made me a whole new person in Christ!** Nothing to do with adding anything! **In Christ I'm a new creation.** He's radical! You mean He's forgiven the sins I haven't done yet? Exactly, that's what I'm trying to say! Because the Church has emphasized forever that our **past sins** are forgiven. But sometimes it seems that the Church tells us that He forgave us until we got saved, and then, from that point onward, it is up to us. Grace is not that. **Even the sins we haven't done yet have been taken care of at the cross.** Grace is killing the cause, the root, the problem and making a new creation! **Grace has many dimensions, one of it is forgiveness.**

Dr. Ortiz compares living the Christian life to that of flying the trapeze[1]. In gymnastics or in circus performances, performers play dangerous moves—called the *flying trapeze*. How this can be? It is so dangerous!

Ortiz explains, "But of course there's a net underneath! (Similarly…) God gave us a *new heart* and the *Holy Spirit*, that we may be on the trapeze, *'the life of the Spirit.'*

As these performers play dangerous moves, **so, we, too, should be a show to the world.** "But, if we fall down God will never let you break our neck! (Here is our NET.) The blood of the Lord Jesus Christ has provided forgiveness for all our trespasses and sins. The net also helps us to jump and get back on the trapeze. The net is there to help us not to cause us to fall. How? (How is this possible?) If there were not a net we'd be very self-conscious, we would be scared, nervous and most likely miss it. But, because the net is there we are relaxed. **You can try those new acts on that trapeze.**

In other words, he explained it:

> From a position of security in Christ you perform better. There is a rest for the children of God. The rest is there to help you improve. How? Well, if the net was not there we would not dare to try new things! Double jumping, triple turn over in the air. We get to perform better because the net is there. Oh, my friends, we don't dare to do greater things for God because we don't trust ourselves!

> *"He cancelled out the certificate of debt consisting of decrees against us"*, everything which was contrary to us and against us. But, be careful, Satan took copies of your past history, and uses it to fool you, to put you down, and to make you feel condemned, giving you a sense of guilt; the sad story is that he has succeeded many times. Not only that God

---

[1] https://www.collinsdictionary.com/us/dictionary/english/flying-trapeze

cancelled it out, but He took it out of the way. Our file is clean... He erased the hard disk.

Wow! He erased it? Yes He did. This is my interpretations of what Juan Carlos said in the Video Seminar.

He nailed it to His cross. (When the enemy wants to use his '*copy*'), God is saying: <Satan has to pass over My dead body to see it!!!> All my sins, even the ones I haven't done yet!" (All have been erased.)

I like the fact that Ortiz was vulnerable and made this concept personal. He said:

> When I have a self-condemning talk like this:
> "Lord, I know myself too well. I cannot accept myself as I am!" He answered me, "*I know you better than you know yourself. Actually, you are worse than you think! But, I have accepted you because of the performance of my Son, Jesus Christ. I have accepted you because I have forgiven you! And you need to learn to forgive yourself because the blood of my Son Jesus is good enough for Me.*" **Why is it not good enough for you? Who are you that the blood of my Son is not sufficient for you?**"

What are the '*main ingredients*' necessary for spiritual growth and to '*attaining*' spiritual transformation? Please feel free to use Bible verses, specific quotes from the materials you studied during **Module III**, and ideas (and quotes) from other sources to sustain your view.

The main ingredients necessary for spiritual growth and attaining spiritual transformation are:

– Need, and
– Hunger.

Without spiritual hunger we cannot feed on the Lord Jesus Christ. Therefore, no need—no growth. No hunger—no food. And as the result of not having this need (for spiritual formation), not hungering for spiritual food—no spiritual growth. (See 1 Peter 2:1-3).

Other important ingredients are:

– Time, and,
– Preparation.

Spiritual growth or transformation takes time. As I said earlier, little by little, step by step, struggle after struggle, agony after agony, the preparation brings us to this important realization—that in order to be complete in Him, we need to surrender our lives on God's altar and invite the Holy Spirit to perform the deeper work in us.

If you would be required to teach others this module, **please provide a *written plan* how you would do it.**

If I were required to teach others this module, I would use the written plan prepared by my mentor to disciple me.

4. The Flesh—The Major Obstacle Towards Spiritual Maturity

Please explain what you liked the most about this important module. Explain also what you disliked the most about this module. How do you suggest we can make Module IV even more helpful and appealing for future disciples/students?

Module IV dealt with the flesh. I feel, that this topic was one of the most important modules I studied so far. There seems to be much confusion as to exactly what the term "the flesh" really means. How it applies to the believer, and what holds it has or doesn't have in his Christian walk.

Many questions were put to rest as to what the flesh is, and how it can influence our lives in a negative way. I was required to read a few excellent materials. The authors and the questions from the Lesson Plans challenged me with various probing questions. I felt that this module clearly answered all of my questions.

I would heartily recommend this study to anyone seeking to cultivate a deeper walk with the Holy Spirit. This module can also be used as an essential tool to reach spiritual maturity in Christ.

What does the apostle Paul teach about the flesh? Please briefly and succinctly elaborate on it. From this perspective how can Christians be categorized? Please briefly elaborate. (Feel free to use insights from Romans 8:3–13, Galatians 5:16–21, Philippians 3:1–7, etc.) Use examples and quotes from Dr. Bill Gillham's book "Lifetime Guarantee."

In Romans 8:5–6, the apostle Paul states:

For those who are according to the flesh set their minds on the things of the flesh, but those who are according to the Spirit, the things of the Spirit. For the mind set on the flesh is death, but the mind set on the Spirit is life and peace.

In Galatians 5:16, we can read:

But I say, walk by the Spirit, and you will not carry out the desire of the flesh. For the flesh sets its desire against the Spirit, and the Spirit against the flesh; for these are in opposition to one another, so that you may not do the things that you please.

From the two passages quoted above it is clear that Paul, in his teaching, conveys with clarity the idea that we, as believers, have to choose a path:

(1) To follow the flesh, or
(2) To follow the Spirit.

We still live in fleshly bodies with their pre-conditioned reactions and responses to trigger buttons in our lives. However, as Spirit-filled believers, we have to exercise our free will:

(a) To refuse the influences of the flesh, or
(b) To allow the Holy Spirit to give us self-control.

Our behavior will reflect the result of our choices: *fleshly* or *spiritual.*

I really like the way Bill Gilham puts it:

The precious Holy Spirit wants to reveal to you what Christ has made available to you to liberate you from 'walking after the flesh' to get your acceptance needs met in Him.[35]

87

In chapter 3, of his book, titles, "How Anabel and I Got into Our Fix," Gillham explains, using his own and his wife experiences, struggling to understand their unique version of the flesh.

He writes:

> I dare not challenge you to come to the end of your flesh trip without first having come to the end of mine. That certainly is not to say that I never fall back and walk according to the flesh, but it certainly is to say that I experience 95 percent better victory than I did before. I held a good funeral for that way of life. As each Christian's unique version of the flesh is heavily, although not totally, shaped by his formative years. I'm going to have to talk about my relationship with my mom and dad. According to the manufacturer's instructions (the Bible), my folks' marriage was upside down. Mom was "lifting out" more of the husband's role in that she was definitely the stronger of the two personalities. When decisions were to be made, she made them. Pop meanwhile, was "lifting out" more of a wifely role in that he totally submitted to mom. When mom said, "frog," he jumped. Pop avoided decisions.

He continues sharing:

> The Holy Spirit has shown me through counseling with hundreds and hundreds of people that a boy in an environment such as I have described will respond in one of three ways, although he can combine them:
>
> (1) First, he may become a homosexual. He may be so intimidated by his environment that he will come to see the normal male role that God intended him to walk in as impossible.
> (2) Second, he may become passive. He just semi gives up on being male and begins to journey through life passively getting his need for love met by taking whatever acceptance crumbs the women and stronger males will sweep to him from their tables.

(3) Third, he can go the macho route. He "sucks it up" and says to himself, "I will be male. I can do it. I desperately need to see myself as male, I've got to make it."
…
This is the route I took. I rebelled against my mom's dominance and my dad's passivity. I tried awfully hard to "overcome" my past by proving to myself that I was male. Do you see that I was being driven by my need for love?

He added:

I am not proud of what I just told you about myself. Quite the contrary. But do you see a picture of a seventeen-year-old boy struggling for self-esteem? Do you see that's how he played Lord of the Ring in an effort to generate and maintain self-esteem? And when I got saved, all this garbage was going to become my "old ways," my flesh that I would have to struggle against.

What can I say: I appreciate Bill's transparency and honesty!

The author expands on the vision of Paul from 2 Corinthians 12.

He writes:

In 2 Corinthians 12, Paul speaks of having known a man who was lifted up into heaven. He then says that he, Paul, was given a thorn in the flesh to keep him humble. The emphasis in the passage is not on the thorn, but on its purpose. It was to make Paul's flesh trip (pride) unproductive. Take Anabel and me, for example. One of my eight-lane, green highways is that supercritical tongue. One of Anabel's is a super-sensitivity to any evaluative comments about her performance. Our omniscient God left those in there at our salvation for us to "work out our own salvation" (mature in Christ; see Philippians 2:12–13). He could have zapped them out, but He left them there for us to work on as a learning and maturing activity so Christ could be glorified through our victory the Lord gave Anabel and me to each other for keeps.

...

Our toothbrushes are in the same glass. There's no way we can run from one another. We have to stay hitched and "make no provision for the flesh" (Romans 13:14). We are learning how to let Christ live through us to overcome the flesh. And praise God. It's working! We are making progress to His glory. How about you? Are you receiving the thorns you need for dealing with your flesh, or are you murmuring at God about them? All murmuring will get you is a season pass on the wilderness merry-go-round. You've got a funeral for that kind of behavior.[36]

Having a holistic view on the human being is extremely important in order to understand the flesh.

In chapter 4, "An "Old Man" in a "New Earthsuit,'" Gillham writes:

Each individual is, of course, a whole, but the Word teaches that the whole person is composed of three integrated parts: *spirit, soul, and body* (1 Thessalonians 5:23). The soul, then, is your **personality**—*mind, will,* and *emotions*—**your unique version of them**. Your **body** is the vehicle here on planet earth that houses your soul and spirit. Second Corinthians 5:1-8 refers to it as an earthly tent. Author C. S. Lovett has called it an "earthsuit" which seems a good way to describe it. The earthsuit is simply a vehicle through which my soul interacts with the earthly environment. **The earthsuit is good. It's not an evil thing,** but it's vulnerable to being used by the devil to get or keep us in a lot of trouble.

...

The scriptures also teach that God is spirit and that humanity is made in His image. Therefore, we are **spirit-beings.** We are not physical creatures with spirits; we are spirit-creatures with bodies. God doesn't have an earthsuit, He doesn't need one. He's using ours if we're born again. **He lives in here with me**. By being born from above through receiving Christ as Savior, a redeemed person acquires a second vehicle through which he can express himself in addition to his earthsuit. He can now fellowship with people through his earthsuit and with God through his spirit.

Working with that overall model of man, let's now break the soul down into its three component parts: *mind, will, and emotions*—your *thinker*, your *chooser*, and your *feeler*. Then let's add a brain to our model. The brain must be a part of the body. Logic will dictate that **the brain** and **the mind** <u>cannot be the same</u>, because the brain is made out of meat. **Thus, your mind cannot be your brain.** Your mind uses your brain here on earth, but the brain is simply a hunk of meat like a heart or a liver. Thus, your mind cannot be your brain. Your mind uses your brain here on earth, but the brain is simply a hunk of meat like a heart or a liver. The brain does have a unique function, however. It's a computer. Your mind and your emotions are your computer analysts. Now, the will has two polarities like a light switch: You either do or you don't. You can't sit in the middle, since that would be choosing not to choose, and that's a don't. You either do or you don't.

...

Christians have a free will that can override the recommendations of both mind and emotions. You see, Christian, we're really on the hook to obey God. We now have a free will that can rule over and resist the "recommendations" of our emotions. I had always thought that eternal life was an extension or a continuation of my life. My life began in 1927, and I assumed that when I accepted Christ as my personal Savior, God attached an extension onto my life that would last forever. That's not true. **His plan was to exterminate my old life and *exchange* it for new life.** And that life is a person, Jesus Christ. A common objection the Evil One often serves up into the mind of a Christian is that this would rob us of our identity. We'd become a water pipe that Jesus flows through; we'd all be exactly the same. Let's defuse that deception. You were specifically recreated in Christ to offer your members to Him to express His life through. It's His Life that gives you your identity that enables you to experience the true eternal you. **Just think:** *You and the God of the universe cohabitating in the same earthsuit!"*

...

Since God is not time dimensional, He can see forever into the future. That's how He dictated the Revelation to John. But consider also that He can see forever into past as well. If He couldn't He'd be limited by time just as we are. The Bible states that Jesus Christ is "the Lamb slain from the foundation of the world" (Revelation 13:8). Imagine this now! God solved the "problem" before the problem ever occurred in the time-dimensional setting by "seeing" the lovely, innocent Jesus crucified before the foundation of the world.

...

Just what is the sinful nature, anyway? The term **"sin nature"** simply means a natural bent to rebel against God's authority, to view God as a party pooper, unnecessary in one's life, someone I can live quite well without, someone to whom I refuse to submit. In short, I refuse to acknowledge Him as my God. **I am my God.** I do things my way. **I am *Lord* of my Ring.** God is not real to me if I have no intention of obeying Him. We must not observe a person's behavior and, from that point of reference, infer his nature. We must use the Word of God to make that determination, and the Bible will make such a determination on the basis of the man's birth, not his performance. If he is still a spirit-son of Satan in Adam's lineage by his first birth, he has a dead-to-God spirit. If he has become a spirit-son of God by a second, spiritual birth in the second Adam, Jesus, he has a live spirit (Ephesians 2:4-6).[37]

It is vital to have a correct theological view on salvation.

In chapter 5 called "A "New Man" in an "Old Earthsuit,"" Gillham writes:

Salvation is a two-sided coin. Side A represents Jesus' coming into the believer; side B represents the believer's coming into Jesus. **He is in me, and I am in Him.** This is a package deal; you can't get one side at a time. I discovered that for every verse you can find in the New Testament stating that the believer is indwelt by Christ, you will discover ten verses stating that the believer indwells Jesus. Ten to one!

I've heard thousands of sermons on the one side of the relationship, how to get Christ to come into you and save you. But on the other hand, if the word is weighted ten to one with side B verses, do you see that many Christians are being fed on short rations? **A straight diet of salvation messages to the church won't bring us to maturity** (Hebrews 6:1).

What was accomplished by the cross of Jesus?
Gillham addressed this question in the following paragraphs:

What doe's the Bible state that God accomplished for you in Christ? How did this solve the problem of your alienation from Him? Consider Ephesians 1:4: "[God] chose us in Him before the foundation of the world." Thus, imagine yourself being in Christ as He came to planet earth to solve your problem. **God placed you in Him.** Ultimately, He went to the cross. Where were you? In Him. As the lovely, innocent Jesus died, you, too, were crucified. The difference is that you deserved it and He didn't. But it wasn't your earthsuit that died; not the physical you, but the spiritual you. You must deal with the abundance of verses which describe your death in Christ. You must deal with the question, "What died?" I have dealt with it, arrived at the conclusion that it was the old self, the old identity that died, and have appropriated this in my own life. When I did all that, I immediately began to experience a vastly more consistent victory over lifelong hang-ups.

Some results in the Christian life are done/obtained because of the Blood of the Lamb, and others because of the Body of Christ.
Gillham explains:

> All born-again people know that God solved the problem with their sins (performance) through the shed blood of Jesus Christ: "without shedding of blood there is no forgiveness" (Hebrews 9:22b). Through the body of Christ you experienced a change in your identity. You were changed from a *sinner-man* to a *saint*. It means that as new creatures in Christ, we have been made pure and holy before God through the body of Christ, not through His blood. **Finally, through the Spirit of Christ, the Holy Spirit, you have exchanged your old Adamic life for Christ's Life.** By His indwelling Spirit, He longs to express Himself through you and fellowship with you. Christ's blood, Christ's body, and Christ's Spirit, it takes all three to give you victory over the world, the flesh, and the devil.

There is a deeper meaning of being born-again.
Brother Bill explains it:

> Humanity's definition of a sinner is performance-based. If a person sins, he's a sinner. But that is not God's definition. His view is that a sinner is a sinner because he was born that way, and neither good nor bad performance can alter it. It's not sins that send a person to hell; his nature sends him to hell. All you have to do to go to hell is be born and get old enough to be accountable. Unless you submit to God's plan to get your nature changed you're sunk! When a sinner gets saved, he does not become a sinner saved by grace. He becomes a saint who sins. Fifty-six times after the cross, the Word refers to born-again to a Christian.

Eternal life, according to Gillham, is not an IT, is HIM—Jesus Christ.
He writes:

Did your old sin nature have resurrection power? Could that life walk out of a grave? No. It had no such capability. Tell me, will you obtain that life someday, or have you already got it (Him)? If you are born anew, you already have eternal life in the person of Jesus. **Eternal life is a synonym for Jesus** (see 1 John 1:1–2). Colossians 3:3, 4a says, "For you have died and your life is hidden with Christ in God. When Christ, who is our life..." Did you say that you died! Yes! Yes! When did you die? You died in Christ's body when He died. How did you get alive again? You were made new in Him, and He is now your life. Notice that your life is hidden, gang. You have to discern that Christ is your true life through your eye of faith. God's plan is that you would cooperate with Christ to let Him express His life by filtering that life through your personality and earthsuit.

...

Jesus remained on earth forty days after the resurrection, and then He ascended to the right hand of the Father. Now, if you are in Him, where are you right now? Ephesians 2:5–6 says: "Even when we were dead in our transgressions, [He] made us alive together with Christ and raised us [already] up with Him, and seated us [already] with Him in the heavenly places" In other words, we are already there, friend. You say, "I don't feel like I'm in heaven." Well, rain on how you feel. God says you are there, and if your feeler seems to tell you that you aren't, which is the liar, God or your feeler?

To be a new creature is an amazing thing!
The author writes:

God's plan was to execute the rebellious man and give birth to a new spirit-creation, one who adores Him and has His law of love written on his heart and mind. But He placed this new man into the same old earthsuit. It has the same old brain with the same old, green highways in it. Someone says, "Oh, no, Bill, you don't understand. That's just the way God sees us. It's positional truth." Listen to me: There is no such thing as "positional truth."

The term positional truth is simply Satan's deception that will block you from accepting the present reality of God's solution to your problem.[38]

Please define the flesh. What are the main characteristics (or classifications) of the flesh. Please elaborate briefly. What did these aspects affected (or still affects) you? Please be as vulnerable as the Holy Spirit leads you.

There are several definitions, but I like Gillham's definition:

The flesh refers to the old ways or patterns by which you have attempted to get all your needs supplied instead of seeking Christ first and trusting Him to meet your needs.

I feel we can explore a few more thoughts and ideas from Bill Gillham's book, especially from the chapter 1, titled, "Why You Struggle."
Gillham writes:

You have programmed your brain with earthly techniques for satisfying your needs for love and self-esteem—again, the greatest needs in life—or for believing yourself to be unworthy of either and thus living your life to keep love away because it makes you uncomfortable. Both of these techniques are do it yourself projects that God calls '*flesh*.'

When it comes to the term "flesh," there are a few meanings in the Scripture. Our interest here is about "the old patterns" by which we have the tendency to fulfill our needs apart from God.
Gillham writes:

These patterns develop as you are growing up in your parents' home. And when the Holy Spirit begins the work of tearing them down, most Christians panic at the idea of losing them.
...
"Psychologists teach that by the time a child reaches the age five, 85 percent of his personality is established and is irreversible. Unfortunately, those psychologists never

heard of 2 Corinthians 5:17, which says that any person in Christ is a new creation, that old things have passed away, and that all things are new. What psychologists are observing is that kids' feelers get programmed, and this controls the person throughout his entire life. **But praise God, we walk by faith, not by feel.** There is a way out. And the Holy Spirit is the oil who can deal with the problem I'm describing.

This means that we can choose to walk by the Spirit not by the old patterns of the flesh.

The author explains:

> The precious Holy Spirit wants to reveal to you what Christ has made available to you to liberate you from "walking after the flesh" to get your acceptance needs met in Him, Ask the Lord to reveal this truth to you from His Word as you study this book. **We are totally accepted in Christ!** It's not necessarily a feeling; it's a fact. It is to be primarily believed, not felt.

Before we can walk in the freedom provided by Christ through the Holy Spirit, there are some things that we need to know about our own version of the flesh. I like the way Bill Gillham explains what the flesh *is* and *does*. In chapter 2, "How You Got into Your Fix."

He writes:

> Have you ever pondered the question posed by Romans 7:15: *"Why do I do what I do, when I really don't want to do it?"* I know exactly why. It's because I sometimes walk after the flesh. But for a long time, I didn't know what my flesh was. And how could I know I was free unless I got a handle on just what it was I needed to be free from? You likewise need to gain insight into your unique version of the flesh. **That's the purpose of this chapter.** Next we need a biblical definition of "flesh." In Philippians 3: 3–9, we find a very clear explanation. This passage leaves no doubt that the term "flesh" in this context refers to the Christian's "old ways." Please don't misunderstand me:

The term "flesh" does not refer to the Christian's body in this context. **The body is not the "bad guy."** God made the whole man and redeems the whole man—*spirit, soul and body.* In other biblical contexts, the term "flesh" is sometimes used to refer to the body, **but here the term simply means the Christian's old ways.**

...

Our struggle is not against flesh and blood, but against {the forces of evil}" (Ephesians 6:12). I want to caution you as we begin to look at how this all may have worked out in your life that when I point out mistakes made by your parents and peers, you should direct your hostility toward the biblically identified target, Satan, not toward your folks. It isn't them you ought to be angry with; it's the Evil One who has worked through your parents to try to destroy you. Satan! He is the one who first deceived, who hates and destroys families. Direct your anger at him—that's biblical.

...

I have attempted to describe briefly some of the major mistakes that may have been made by your parents that could have resulted in your growing into an adult Christian who has a lot of difficulty making the Christian life work. But I believe we have yet to hit upon the devil's biggest weapon. His most effective technique, visible in epidemic proportions, is "performance-based love," or "performance-based-acceptance," which I'll sometimes refer to as PBA. It works like this. If you perform (act) as I want you to, I'll accept you. If you don't, I'll reject you. In other words, I realize that I possess something that you need—love. So I'm going to use my "supply" to control you.

...

Every religion from Mormonism to voodoo is based on PBA, humanity's seeking acceptance from God by earning it, Christianity, however, is relationship, not religion. God reaches out to us with grace (unmerited favor) through Jesus Christ's finished work. This relationship is not for sale. Jesus bought it with His life. It cannot be earned through PBA. You don't earn a gift, you gratefully accept it. The world system, on the other hand, is based totally on PBA, whether you're trying to get the acceptance of peers in the jungles of the Amazon or the jungles of Harlem; whether you're reared in a Mafia members home or a pastor's home. Performance is the name of the game. <u>Perform well enough and you can earn you're love supply out of your environment, even in your church.</u>

...

One of the best-kept secrets in Christianity is that God accepts us. True, He can't stand our sinful acts, but He loves us. He doesn't have us on performance-based acceptance; **He has us on Jesus-based acceptance.** If you have accepted Jesus as your Lord and Savior, the Father has accepted you completely. Performance has nothing whatsoever to do with it. You can be the greatest performer on the block at keeping God's standards, and you'll still be totally rejected by God if you are unsaved. But God accepts you perfectly in Christ already. God doesn't grade on a one-to-ten scale; He grades pass-fail. His acceptance of you and me is not contingent on our performance, but on what we have done with Jesus Christ's performance for us. He couldn't love or accept you more if you had never sinned. And He'll never love or accept you less no matter how often you do sin.[39]

Some characteristics of the flesh are:

Paul writes:

> Now the deeds of the flesh are evident, which are: immorality, impurity, sensuality, idolatry, sorcery, enmities, strife, jealousy, outbursts of anger, disputes, dissensions, factions, envying, drunkenness, carousing, and things like these, (Galatians 5:19–21)

These are some of the ways that the flesh can be exhibited in us when we fail to allow the Spirit to give us self-control, especially if we have certain trigger points in our past that may spark fleshly reactions. For me, I am especially vulnerable to become jealous if I don't allow the Holy Spirit to influence me and bring forth the spiritual fruit of self-control.

Please describe the process of "laying aside" the old-self and "putting on" the new self. In other words, what does it mean to take up the cross and follow Jesus daily?

According to 2 Corinthians 5:17, we are a "new creation in Christ." Our old man "was crucified with Christ" (Romans 6:6). However, as I said earlier, we are still living in a body of flesh. Therefore, we can easily fall into the old patterns of living trying to meet our life's needs.

"Laying aside" the old-self is an intentional process of "putting to death the deeds of the body," by the empowerment of the Holy Spirit (see Romans 8:12–13). Also, "putting on" the new self is an intentional process of letting the new-self manifesting the life of Christ hidden in us (Colossians 3:3, 8–10, Ephesians 4:20–24). Simply put, this is the process of mind-renewal.

Please elaborate on the tremendous blessings when one appropriates the cross in his or her life. Share experiences from your own life. Please be as open as you feel guided by the Spirit.

Appropriating the cross stands at the heart of genuine discipleship. In other words, when I am taking up the cross and follow Jesus in my daily walk, I find that I am successful in overcoming the flesh in my life. Moreover, this is not self-effort, or the result of the Law, this is the GRACE of God working in and through me, and by the Holy Spirit I am placed under a higher law— "the law of the Spirit of life in Christ Jesus." (Romans 8:2). This is the meaning of walking in the Spirit. The result is evident: the flesh will no longer control my life (See Galatians 2:20, 5:24—25).

In his book, Bill Gilham explains the concept of appropriating the cross this concept in simple terms:

> Sin rules the spirit, soul, and body of the unregenerate person, but sin only indwells the body of the new creation in Christ.[40]

In chapter 6, titled, "You Can Keep a Good Man Down," Gillman talks about the contributing factors to failing to live out a successful Christian life.

He writes:

> Look at Romans 7:15, the defeated Christian's verse: "For that which I am doing, I do not understand; for I am not practicing what I would like to do, but I am doing the very thing I hate." How many actors are there in that verse? One: "I." Now jump down to Romans 7:20: "But if I am doing the very thing I do not wish, I am no longer the one doing it, but sin which dwells in me [is doing it]." How many actors do you count in this verse? Two: "I" and something called "sin." What I'm saying is an entity called **sin** somehow suggested that I do it. I bought into sin's idea, <u>it became mine</u>, and I did the very thing I do not wish. Sin rules the spirit, soul, and body of the unregenerate person, but <u>sin only indwells the body of the new creature in Christ</u> (Romans 7:23).
>
> …
>
> The Word says that Satan "disguises himself as an angel of light" (2 Corinthians 11:14). What is "light" in the Word? Truth! He can come at you as "truth," as "revelation," as "insight into reality." But how? It's simple. He gives you a thought in your mind and disguises it to seem as if it is your thought. You say, "How could he do that?" By speaking to you with first-person singular pronouns (I, me, my, myself, etc.)! You grab the idea and convert it into action. <u>You sin!</u> Yes, you did the evil thing, but the genesis of it, the origin was the power of sin, not your mind. Your body isn't evil; the Holy Spirit lives in it. It's neither good nor evil, but neutral. It's sort of like an oak tree; it can be used for a pulpit or a totem pole. Satan's kingdom is here on planet earth. Satan has agents through which he works to accomplish his goals, including the *world* (system), the *flesh*, and (the power of) *sin*. Employing our definition of "flesh" as "the old ways," we will place these green highways in the brain. <u>These are the memory traces, the habit patterns</u>, the software in your computer. If you are deceived into staying locked in on this software,

your brain will play the same program over and over. Sin is in the body, not in the personality or the spirit. Your soul and spirit have been "sealed with the Spirit." **They are holy now.** The idea is for you, the *created*, to turn to Him, the *Creator*, in total dependency on Him, worshiping Him, loving Him, fellowshipping with Him, cooperating with Him and His plan for you. Part of this agreement is that He promises to "supply all your needs" (Philippians 4:19). <u>But Satan's strategy is to get you to opt to live to get your needs met.</u> He wants you to be deceived into making this your goal. Thus, he offers you "Plan B" for getting your needs supplied your "old ways." That's what **sin** is all about. **It is independence from God**.

Then Gillham gives us an example of how *temptation* and *sin* operate, and how Christians can have victory over sin and sinful behaviors.

He writes:

The curvy lady is not the temptation. She's the object of the temptation. The temptation is going to come from (the power of) sin, Satan's agent through which he seeks to control. What you believe about your identity is what is going to make a difference. You will live out whatever you believe to be your true self, your true identity. Now, for the record, **it's not a sin to be tempted**. Jesus Himself "has been tempted in all things as we are, yet without sin" (Hebrews 4:15). <u>It is very normal for a Christian to be tempted</u>. I have seen many Christians who spend a great deal of time begging God for forgiveness simply because they are tempted to do evil. That's error! Just being tempted doesn't make you guilty any more than it made Jesus guilty. It will seem as if the old man is alive and well. But if he is, God's Word is not true. Do you see it? The Evil One's strategy is to disguise himself in your thought life as your old man resurrected from the dead. But the old man has no resurrection capability. He cannot resurrect. God did not raise him up. Satan can't do it. But <u>sin surely can deceive you by impersonating the old man in your thought life</u>. And that is exactly how sin is controlling Christians. Your victory lies in appropriating your true identity as the saint you are in Christ. You must counter the temptation along these lines: "No! I'm dead to that! That is not my thought. I recognize that strategy. Then act as though you're dead to sin's thoughts coming to you. How does a dead man respond when you try to stimulate him? He doesn't! He just sits there![41]

According to Gillham, there are various "flavors" of the flesh: USDA Choice Flesh, Plain Vanilla Flesh, Yukky Flesh.

Gillham explains:

You can see from the development of this biblical perspective that <u>each Christian's flesh is essentially his self-image that he has generated while walking as a rebellious, lost person and then later as a deceived and controlled saved person</u>. If he has been successful at getting his need for self-esteem satisfied, he has generated **USDA Choice Flesh**; if moderately successful, he has an average self-image—**Plain Vanilla Flesh**. If he's been unsuccessful, he has **Yukky Flesh** with its low self-esteem.

...

No matter which general category of flesh you may fall into, it is all of this world system, not of God. If you keep on listening to those familiar thoughts that seem to be your old sin nature, you will be a pawn in the Evil One's hand. You will be neutralized in the spiritual warfare. I am going to call this "Channel #1." Stay tuned to Channel #1 and be deceived. That's the way the Evil One works, especially on a Christian who believes he has two natures. Tragically, many high-profile Christians are falling and bringing great harm to the name of Christ. They seem powerless to "life out" the victory they teach. Somehow their Christianity is not working. The reason it's not working is they do not understand their true identity and how to offer themselves as a living sacrifice to Christ to live the victorious Christian life through them.[42]

In chapter 7, called "Living Like a New Creation," Gillham, explains how to live based on the New Identity.

He writes:

> We have already seen in Romans 7:15–25 how the law of sin will control the believer to keep him captive. Sin continually condemns many Christians in their thought life. This is especially true for those with perfectionistic flesh. Sin hammers these dear people constantly, "telling" them that they are failing because they cannot achieve perfect results. "For I know that nothing good dwells in me, that is, my flesh."
>
> …
>
> Note, he doesn't say that he is no good, but that nothing good dwells in his flesh. Now, the Holy Spirit dwells in his earthsuit, and He is certainly something good. So <u>Paul must be speaking of the</u> old, green highways definition of the term **flesh**, and truly, "nothing good" dwells there. I believe I would be too charitable to say that most Bible teachers take the position that Christians are "half good and half evil" as new creatures in Christ. What most imply is that we are 90 percent evil and 10 percent good. Many are even harder on us than that. Their messages to Christians imply that we are 100 percent evil and 0 percent good, citing, "in me dwells no good thing" as "proof," failing to complete the verse, which states, "in me dwells no good thing, that is, in my flesh." Of course there is "no good thing" in my flesh (old ways), but the person in Christ is now "the one who wishes to do good." **We're the good guys!** <u>The new creature in Christ has had a heart transplant!</u> We deeply desire to do good. Evil is present in this man. This doesn't say that he is evil, but that he (the one who desires to do good) has evil present in him. That's a very real and crucial distinction. He is a good man.
>
> …
>
> Now we identify the location of the problem. Sin still resides in the body. It is not in the soul or the spirit. Those two parts are the righteous new man (see 2 Corinthians 5:14-21). But technically, the body has not been saved yet:

Later in the epistle, Paul says that we are "waiting eagerly for the redemption of our body" (Romans 8:23). **Our bodies aren't evil, but they are earthy.** I call the body the *"vehicle of vulnerability."* It is vulnerable to be used by the evil one if we submit to him. The word wretched does not mean evil; it means unhappy. This man is stating that he is terribly unhappy living like this, as will be any person who has only one nature, a godly one, and who has not claimed his true identity in Christ. When he chooses to walk in the Spirit (in his true identity), he serves the *law of love*, but when he is deceived into walking after the flesh, he is serving the *law of sin*. He doesn't have to sin. He is free to obey God through Christ's indwelling life. You are literally a brand-new person in Him, a good person who loves Jesus and deeply desires to submit to His Kingship. The kingdom of heaven has arrived. It's in us! Let's turn Him loose to reign in us by acting dead to sin and alive to God!

...

Now that the deception, the "walking according to the flesh" pattern, has been identified, let's trust the Holy Spirit together to put some practical handles on how to implement God's provision for victory. As with every spiritual principle, this victory will not be so much a matter of fighting against the power of the Evil One, but rather a matter of starting up a new method of walking, moment by moment, experiencing Christ as your very life while simultaneously you "act dead" to those thoughts that will be served up to your mind through the flesh in the brain. The Word says you are "dead to [the power of] sin" (Romans 6:11). To make this an experiential reality, you must act dead to it regardless of feelings.

...

If you have been raised up with Christ, keep seeking the things above where Christ is, because you're in Him there, too, seated at the right hand of God. Set your mind on the things above, not on the things that are on earth." What "things above" should you think about? Well, don't dwell on golden streets and mansions. That won't transform you. Rather, see yourself relaxing there in Christ. All your needs are met. Your Father has everything under control. **He is totally accepting you and loving you.** You are a son or daughter in the Father's forever family. You are holy and blameless before Him. You have become a "partaker of the divine nature." Think on these things. Pump this truth through and through your mind. It's reality! You are a new person resting in heaven, while simultaneously here on planet earth, Christ is expressing His loving life through you.

…

"Setting your mind" must be attainable or God wouldn't command you to do it. In fact, you do it every day. Friend, what if you set your mind on the reality I've described for about three or four hours each day? What would happen to you? You'd be *"transformed by the renewing of your mind."* Because, you see, this process would leave you four hours less time to set your mind on "Channel #1. And what would happen to those green highways in your brain because of that disuse? The same thing that happened to your high school algebra. They would dissipate.

…

Since God says the **Channel #2** perspective **is truth,** what does that make the Channel #1 perspective? Deception. If you are embracing and living out **Channel # 1,** you are **living a lie.** Pay attention, now. This is another one of the most powerful truths the Holy Spirit has ever shown me as a key to living victoriously. It has helped to liberate me as well as thousands of other people over the years.

Without this understanding, you'll be set up for failure:

God's Definition of a Hypocrite:
Pretending to Be What You Are Not

Satan's Definition of a Hypocrite
Acting Contrary to How You Feel

The devil's definition of a phony is based totally on the condition of our emotions. If you buy into it, you will never be able to walk in your true identity in Christ! Tragically, all world-system counseling embraces his definition and much of Christian counseling naively does as well. The majority of counselors major on how people feel, and if their techniques make the counselee feel better, they pronounce him "better." **A person is only better if he is "walking in the light,"** gang. We determine truth by what God says, not by the state of our emotions.

…

Choose with your will to force your mind to generate appropriate, biblical, productive, true thoughts while refusing to accept sin's thoughts fed through the brain to your mind. Force yourself to keep at this five minutes, ten minutes, whatever time is necessary until the "attack" of sin's thoughts begins to ease off. If he tries to crank it up again, you crank up again with thoughts contrary to his. You see, it's the setting of your mind in Channel #2 (*truth*) that will enable you to experience being dead to Channel #1 (*lie*). You're going to be "transformed by the renewing of your mind" (Romans 12:2). You'll begin to mature experientially into what you already are in Christ. Your emotions will begin to settle down into the normal Christian ballpark, and the ultimate outcome will be the emergence of godly character that will evolve out of your godly nature and godly behavior. **So, start setting your mind. Your character will take on the properties of Christ.** The fruits of the Spirit will begin to emerge from you as a natural product of your obedience. You don't see the branches on a grapevine straining and groaning to produce grapes. They simply abide, and the life of the vine produces the fruit. That is what you will see happening to you when you begin to appropriate your true identity in Christ. Praise His name![43]

In chapter 8, "Handling your Emotions," Gillman delves into our emotions and how to handle them.

He explains:

> You often arrive at "truth" by trusting in your emotions; you make them the object of your faith. (<u>Faith is a function of the mind</u>; it means believing something, and <u>it must have an object</u>. It is never a feeling, but a belief upon which you take action. And it's a fatal mistake to make feeler faith's object.) What good would your faith do you? None, because it is faith without works. **Faith without appropriate action won't do you one whit of good.** You might as well not have any faith at all (see James 2:17). Feeler's recommendation is five times stronger than mind's at this point. Will is intimidated and chooses to go along with feeler's demands in an effort to relieve the pressure. But remember who's boss. **Will can overrule feeler or mind or both simultaneously,** no matter how intensely they apply pressure to sway his choice. Will is in charge.
>
> ...
>
> This disparity between faith and feelings has a direct and important spiritual parallel. They want to feel saved. Typically, these are the "feeler folks." Unless they can feel something, they have difficulty accepting it as reality. The Word of God never says, however, that anyone will feel saved. It says things like, *"Believe in the Lord Jesus, and you shall be saved,"* not feel saved (Acts 16:31). But even if He should give you a zingy feeling to boost you off the launching pad into the Christian life it's going to dissipate. It's got to at times, because the Lord has no interest in strengthening your fleshly pattern of being controlled by your emotions. *"Without faith it is impossible to please Him"* (Hebrews 11:6). Walk in the Spirit by faith and a critical part of that training is to teach you that you cannot trust your feeler, but you can trust Him. Your job is to keep believing He has everything under control. It's just that He's allowed a testing time to come upon you. Don't be anxious about it (see Philippians 4:6). Keep operating by what you know.
>
> ...

You are bringing your behavior into line with the truth, according to your faith. The Bible calls this *"walking in the light."* You are choosing to go against feeler's recommendation because mind has gotten more information about the security of your situation you can never get complete control over your emotions. True, you can exercise some control over them, but never total control. **As a saved person, you can control your mind and your will, but not your feelings.** God's plan is for us to believe Him and choose to submit ourselves to His loving care and authority regardless of how we feel. All together now, Rain on how I feel!

...

I have great peace. But it's a peace that passes {human} understanding. The peace I have is knowing something. It's a function of the mind, not the emotions. It's knowing that My Father has everything under control. Silence is a very normal part of the victorious Christian life at times. I am to behave according to my understanding of His Word and ways, believing that He is leading me Christ would then continue to say of emotions. Human beings often cannot understand the peace of which I speak, because the only peace they typically comprehend is a feeling. They want to feel peaceful. They will tell you that they have great peace of mind, but they don't. It's just that they feel good, so they set their minds on how good they feel. It was feel peace instead of mind peace all the time.

Sharon's example:

Don't bother me with the facts. I know how I feel. Do you see how the power of sin has taken a circumstance in this lady's life and, capitalizing on her unique version of the flesh, has deceived her into arriving at "truth" through her emotions? This dear lady may be quite logical in her thinking when it comes to following a recipe's instructions, but when it comes to interacting with other people, herself, or God. She makes her emotions the object of her faith and goes by what feeler says is truth. This whole process takes perhaps two or three seconds, and then she's under sin's control. You see, mind has the capacity to change instantly. Sin is going to feed thoughts rapidly into her "sound mind" to try to take advantage of feeler's inability to respond quickly to truth. See how effective this would be, especially if it is laced through with truth and near-truth? The Evil One will serve up whatever sequence of thought patterns will best enable him to deceive the believer under the circumstances. The trick is that he must maintain a low profile to keep from being discovered, and the key is to serve up very "familiar" thoughts, thoughts that were very much a part of the "old man's" experience. Once Sharon embraces these thoughts, she is now sinning in her thought life (in that she failed to refuse the thoughts). You can never make the victorious Christian life a reality approaching it by the faith, feel, stronger faith, truth, actions sequence. God has prescribed one and only one way to consistent, moment-by-moment victory. And that way is the way of faith and obedience, never the way of the emotions. It is applying the biblical steps in proper order: *truth, faith, behavior, and feelings.* Finally, the state of your emotions is never the criterion of whether you are walking in victory or not. Lining up on the Word of God by faith and obedience is the sole criterion you can trust.[44]

In chapter 9, "Making your Behavior Match your Identity," Gillham explains how to pray in order to experience victory in the day-to-day life.

He writes:

I got on my knees in my bedroom and prayed, "Lord I don't understand this, but the Bible says that the "old me" died, the "new me" was born, and Your desire is to express your life through the new me.

Thus, I began my new walk of utter dependency. I dared not depend on my university training, my skills as a communicator, my cleverness, my ability. I had depended on all those things before, and they had let me down like the Titanic. I was going to let the Lord do it all through me. And it worked! Praise God, it worked, and it's still working! It's working just as well for multitudes of Christians who have come to the end of themselves and claimed their true identity in Christ with Christ as life. Our brother Paul said it best, "For me to live is Christ" (Philippians 1:21). You have commanded me to cast my burden upon You in Psalm 55:22. That's not an option, but an order! Okay, I'm casting this on You. You do it." And then I set about acting as though He was doing it all through me. I simply had to believe that He had taken over, that everything was now under His control and was His responsibility. The monkey was on His back to produce, not on mine. Hallelujah! This is what He meant when He said His yoke is easy. What freedom! Not freedom to goof off, but freedom to see His power through me.

…

Oh, dear friend, God's grace is (not will be) sufficient for your situation. He wants to carry it all for you. Won't you give up and let Him live through you? You don't need to wait for one single thing to be added to who already possess if you know Christ as Savior. Just celebrate a good funeral for the "old man," and then celebrate the birth of the new, victorious you who arose in Christ by beginning to act like who you are. Testing times will come, but the one who is in charge of the "obstacle course" has designed it to motivate you to claim Him as your strength. He will not allow it to destroy you. The "course" is specifically designed to conform you to the image of your lovely older Brother. Relax in it. Keep your mind on this. Our moment-by-moment battle is to fix in our minds that we are resting in Christ while simultaneously setting our minds to move through our daily tasks, believing that Christ is meeting them through us.[45]

In the previous chapter Gillham proposed a Four Step Process: Truth, Faith, Works, and Feelings. Following is the practical application of this process.

He writes:

We will now apply the **four-step sequence** of *truth, faith, works, and emotions* for walking in the Spirit rather than "according to the flesh." I have a friend, Paul Burleson, who states, "Just as it is important for every Christian to know who he is in Christ, it is also important for him to know who he was prior to salvation if he is to understand walking according to the flesh." That's true, and if you check the areas where you seem to have the most difficulty walking in the Spirit, you'll discover it's in those areas where your emotions seem to be stuck.

Step 1: Truth
The truth is:
1. The believer is identified with Christ in His death, burial, resurrection, and ascension to the Father's right hand.
2. Christ is now my life here on earth, and His will is to express His life through me.
3. I am resting in Him in His victory. The Bible states these truths in Romans 6, Colossians 3, and elsewhere. These verses are true, whether people accept them or not, because God said so. They are true of all who are born again. "What you don't know won't hurt you." That may apply in some cases, but in the Christian faith, what you don't know will destroy you.

Step 2: Faith
You don't need more faith. **You need more knowledge of the Object of your faith.** You must put your faith in Him, the beautiful object of your faith. You don't need great faith, but more understanding of the Object of your faith.

Step 3: Works, Performance, Behavior
It isn't enough just to "have faith." You have to add something to your faith if you would walk in the Spirit. You have to act as if you have faith. "Faith, if it has no works, is dead" (James 2:17). ... The flesh always "seeks for a sign" so it can hang its hat on the sign instead of on the Word of God. It wants to use the sign as the object of

its faith rather than the Word that God has spoken. You may ask, "But Bill, if I were to act like Christ is living through me but be unable to feel Him doing it, wouldn't this make me a phony?" No. Remember God's definition of a hypocrite: *pretending to be what you are not.* **When you act like Christ is expressing His life through you**, you are simply acting out reality, **acting like who you are.** You're being obedient.[46]

We must keep in mind that God's acceptance is not God's approval.

Gillham explains:

> The method by which God accepts you is never performance-based, but Jesus-based, and He grades pass-fail. You must understand that it's your works which will be judged, not you who will be judged. Failing to see this results in fearing the judgment for the wrong reason. Many feel like God is going to subject them to public humiliation for certain sins they've not overcome. Come on. Has God removed your sins as far as the east from west through Christ or not (Psalm 103:12)?

> *Step 4: Feelings*
> As I continue to walk by faith and obedience, setting my mind on the reality of how things are rather than on how I feel or on "circumstantial evidence" that belies God's Word, God will begin to bring my feeler's "stuck threshold" more into line. I'll be transformed by the renewing of my mind (Romans 12:2). God is never going to bring your feeler totally into subjection so long as you remain in your earthsuit. He has deliberately designed it to vacillate so as to force you to walk by faith, not by feel, if you would experience the "peace that passes understanding." Remember, that peace is not a feeling, but a knowing—knowing that the Father has everything under control; that you are in Christ, seated in heaven, resting; and that He is in you now, living.[47]

In chapter 10, Dr. Bill Gillham expounds on the Law vs. Grace and One Nature vs. Two Natures concepts. He sincerely states that he believes that born-again people have only one nature—*the New Nature.* According to Gillham, *salvation, baptism, security, and sanctification,* are the byproduct of God's grace, which God bestowed on us—His children, based on the finished work of Christ on the Cross.

He writes:

> The Bible can be interpreted as saying that salvation, security, sanctification, and all the rest of God's blessings must be earned through performance. But it can also be interpreted that these are bestowed upon the believer solely by grace through faith in the finished work of Christ. Discerning the correct interpretation is critical to consistent victory over your version of the flesh. I believe "rightly dividing the Word of truth" on all the attainable growth plateaus for the new creation in Christ is critical to consistent victory.
>
> ...
>
> This book interprets the Bible as teaching that no human being has two spiritual natures. Lost folks have one; saved folks have one. The Bible teaches that all people are spiritual creatures who temporarily dwell in earthsuits, not physical creatures who have spirits (2 Corinthians 5:16a). With this in mind, let's compare a Christian with an unbeliever as follows:
>
> 1. Unregenerate man has a sin nature, meaning that he has a deep-seated desire to avoid Jesus' authority over him.
> 2. Regenerate man is a "partaker of the divine nature." He has a deep-seated desire to submit to Jesus' authority over him. He is committed to submitting his life and destiny to Jesus.
>
> ...
>
> The Lord showed me that the Christian life is like a road upon which I travel and upon which I encounter a series of forks, each of which demands that I turn either to the right or to the left. A right turn on this road leads to an area I'll label "Law." <u>This stands for the concept that God</u>

114

has people on a performance-based acceptance. Taking a left turn on this road, however, leads to "Grace," *God's unmerited favor poured out upon undeserving humanity through Jesus Christ.* I believe correctly understanding the Word requires separating law from grace. Thus, a left turn is the right turn to take on this road, and hence the title of this chapter.

Salvation:

A group of people approached me with a tract containing "fifteen verses" in the Bible to "prove" I'd best turn right toward Law if I hoped to make it to God. I chose the left-turn option and much to my delight, I have discovered through the Word and my experience that I now have the Holy Spirit of Christ Himself indwelling me. **I am saved.**

Baptism:

Another group of well-meaning folks approached me to "prove" that unless I got baptized (and the message was urgently pressed upon me lest I die and miss my opportunity), I could not be saved. There came a second group. They explained that baptism was a picture of God's grace. I chose to turn left at this fork also, believing it to be the rightly divided grace rather than the law position. **I have received reinforcement from the Word,** as well as from the indwelling Holy Spirit, that this was the correct way.

Security:

Well-meaning brothers and sisters in Christ will approach with a tract that quotes "fifteen verses" "proving" that I have to keep holding onto Jesus lest I slip and fall away into hell. In other words I must perform to retain what I couldn't perform to acquire in the first place. Then another group quoting "fifteen verses" takes the position that my security lies in the fact that Jesus holds me, not vice versa. As I have walked in this position over the years, the Holy Spirit has again and again reinforced the truth of it to my inner man.

Sanctification:

Are Christians a truly holy people, or are we trying to become a holy people? As an oak sapling grows, It doesn't get "oakier." **Oak is oak.** <u>It simply matures into what it is, a full grown oak tree.</u> It's the same with us. We are the holy sons of God. We don't get holier, more accepted, more justified, or more forgiven. We simply experientially "life out" who and what we already are. It's not a "from-to" situation with us. We are a holy people. Now let's get on with acting like who we are.

I believe every word in the Bible is inspired and absolutely true. It breaks my heart to hear a Christian leader state that in his "wisdom" he has come to "understand" that Jonah wasn't a literal man swallowed by a literal fish, or something like that. What a grief to the heart of God! In giving me the opportunity to either believe or disbelieve, however, God has made Himself so vulnerable as to structure His Holy Word so that the devil can use even that to deceive me. That's the way he tempted Jesus in the wilderness. He seeks to malign God's integrity in your thoughts and deceive you. **The focal point of all eternity is Christ on the cross.** Everything prior to that blessed event points to it; everything after it points back at it. It will always be so. Our God has scars in His hands that we will see daily throughout eternity. Therefore, where Law appears to conflict with grace in biblical interpretation, <u>fix your eyes on Jesus Christ on that cross to "rightly divide" the passage.</u> Put on Son-glasses, and filter every interpretation of the Word through Him there. **The Holy Spirit will always point me toward grace, always.** The Law is intended exclusively for the unregenerate man, to motivate him to salvation (Romans 6:14; Galatians 3:19-26; 1Timothy 1:9a). The new man in Christ is motivated to righteous living by the Holy Spirit within (Ezekiel 36:26, 27).[48]

Dr. Bill Gillham doesn't shy away to state that Christians are not under the Law but under Grace. The Law is for the undegenerated people not for the born again ones. In fact, he says, "Law is the "gasoline" that fuels sin's engine." I think he is right.

He continues:

> (1 Timothy 1:9, 10) The Law is not for you if you're a new creation; it was used by the Lord to convict you of your hopeless state and thus motivate you to accept Jesus Christ as your Savior. Now that the Law has served its purpose for you, you are no longer under it. *"The power of sin is the Law"* (1 Corinthians 15:56). **Law is the "gasoline" that fuels sin's engine.** You give the power of sin a law to work with and it will eventually beat you, because God's provision for the believer is grace, not law.
> …
> Truly, any time a person takes a turn toward law, seeing himself on a performance-based acceptance with God, God will allow the individual to travel that wrong road until he hits a brick wall. That person will never go on with God until he turns around and goes back to the fork where he made the wrong turn. I care not whether the fork represents a law position on baptism, eternal security, forgiveness, acceptance, righteousness, holiness, justification, or anything else. You turn right and you'll be left. You'll wear out trying to measure up to the law, and you'll crash sooner or later. **You cannot earn God's acceptance.** You will never get good, solid victory in this battle we all experience until you see by His Word and appropriate the truth that **the old man literally died in Christ.** It's not positional, it's literal. Dead men tell no tales. Those "tales" you experience moment by moment are being offered up to your mind by the deceiver of the brethren through your flesh.[49]

In chapter 11, titled, "Is God Trying to Tell You Something?" Dr. Gillham explains the importance of walking according to the Spirit, and holding fast on Jesus—the only One Who can supply all of our needs, so we don't walk according to the flesh in order to get our needs met by the flesh.

The author writes:

117

It is my conviction that Satan's most effective tool against Christians is to deceive them into continuing to use their old, green highways to satisfy this need we all have for love and self-esteem. Jesus desires that we look to Him as the source, moment by moment, to supply this as well as all our needs.

Walking after the flesh" could range from clinging to physical beauty to striving for perfectionism in performance; from displaying Christmas cards from the "right people" to craving an invitation to the party where many of the "in" group at church will be gathering tonight. **All these things are fleshly techniques for obtaining acceptance and self-esteem from the system rather than from the Lord, your Husband.** It's infidelity! Jesus, the committed Husband, reveals His divine plan for wooing His bride away from all competition. He fixes things so that flesh trips cease to be productive. He dries up the supply so His bride will wake up and turn to the one who really loves her instead of chasing after those who are looking to her as their needs supply.

...

I will go back to my first husband, for it was better for me then than now!" (Hosea 2:7) Jesus likewise allows you to walk in your old ways, patiently wooing you and suffering through your infidelities to Him. He allows you to begin experiencing a diminishing return on your efforts.

...

Finally, the adulterous bride realizes there is something drastically wrong in her life. It's at this point that she is most receptive to "returning to her first love," Christ, her Bridegroom, to adore Him (see Revelation 2:4) and seek Him alone as her source. Can you discern with spiritual eyes how a well-meaning but unbroken, world-system-trained Christian counselor actually defeats God's purpose if he "helps" such a "self-sufficient" person by making his fleshly techniques more productive? The client might get "better," but he is working against the Holy

Spirit's goal of weakening the flesh. Why bring her into a wilderness? Did you ever consider how well your flesh will supply your needs in the wilderness? Your going to find one source and only one out there, and that's Jesus. He is your only hope in the wilderness. Everything else is unproductive. He will take you there because He loves you, not because He's mad at you. He had to take her to a point of despair before He could trust her to know who her source was. This way she got the message loud and clear that her flesh could not meet her needs. Then God further stated, "The valley of Anchor [will be her] door of hope." (Hosea 2:15). Anchor means "trouble." God has to bring a Christian to the end of the "trusted old ways" before she will turn from her "former lovers" to Him alone. This is often painful but always essential.[50]

Next, the author explains that the purpose of suffering in our lives as Christians is for developing a deeper level of oneness in our relationship with the Lord Jesus.

Gillham writes:

The only permanent , lasting song that any Christian will experience on this planet—the only one with a lifetime guarantee—is the one she learns to sing in the valley of Achor, where she comes to the end of depending on her flesh. This may happen in different ways for different Christians. There will be different degrees of suffering for different folks. It's all relative, and God is the one in control. He never causes it, but He allows it, and its purpose is love. He's taking you to a deeper level of oneness. This is not something to fear. It is simply a matter of keeping your eyes of faith on Jesus. He is totally committed to your best welfare.

Many times the trials and tribulations we experience in this life are just pointers towards a deeper oneness with our rightful Husband—Jesus Christ, Who is fully capable to meet our needs for love and significance.

He writes:

Dear, unhappy bride of Christ. If you are under the load, you are in the valley of Anchor. Stop trying to milk your needs supply out of this world by the flesh. That's the wrong spouse. You are loved. You're the beloved bride who has "no spot or wrinkle or any such thing; but [is] holy and blameless" (Ephesians 5:27). Turn from leaning on the "trustworthiness" of your talent, your attractive earthsuit, your spiritual gifts, your intelligence, your position, your popularity, your good job, your financial security, your good marriage, and your obedient kids as your primary means of generating and maintaining your inner peace and satisfaction in this life. **That's playing the whore!** It's fine that you have been blessed by your Husband (the Lord) with all the above, but don't concentrate on that. Remember who you are, and concentrate on and praise your Husband. You entered into an oneness relationship with your spiritual Husband, but you must agree with His view (the only true view) and walk with Him as His beloved if you would experience abundant life on this planet. The music and lyrics of this song are usually born in the valley of Achor. It often takes that to get us to turn loose of the old ways.[51]

In the last chapter called, "God's Ultimate Purpose for You," Gillham explains that the life here on earth is the training ground for the Bride of Christ, which he calls it "the University of Earth." for the various leadership roles she is going to hold in eternity.

The author writes:

If I'm already holy, blameless, accepted, righteous, and all those wonderful adjectives I see in God's Word, what's the purpose in God's leaving me here? Why doesn't He just take me home? That's a good question and the answer is glorious! Oh, the fantastic opportunity that lies before you between now and the time you go home! You and I have been offered the privilege of preparing ourselves for our future roles in the celestial order God has planned. Earth is very much like graduate school or an NFL training camp. We're all winners in Christ already, but we have only one opportunity to train for our eternal leadership role, and it's here on planet earth.

...

When you were born, God closed a door behind you so you could never cross back over that threshold. Let's face it, a person can never cease to exist. Let's presume that you chose to repent and accept Jesus Christ as Savior and Lord. Once you did, God slammed another door behind you. I believe that just as a person cannot cease to have been born physically, so he cannot cease to have been born spiritually. Keeping him in this position is God's business, and He is well able to do so (see Philippians 1:6). Notice that word predestined. That means God is going to do it to you. You've been placed into the loving obstacle course; I call it the University of Earth in which the Lord is hard at work conforming you. What's more, He says that He is going to finish what He started with you (Philippians 1:6). God has two plans for accomplishing His goal. Plan A is for you to see truth in the Word and respond in faith and obedience. So God has to revert to Plan B, Romans 8:28. He has to let a little "all things" come into a person's life. God hates independence. He wants you to be dependent on Him as Jesus was. So He'll let something happen to jerk the rug out from under a person's self-sufficiency, then show him the alternative of opting for Christ's sufficiency in us. Through this trauma, the person will learn how to pray without ceasing and accomplish his work simultaneously. In fact, he'll learn that this is the easier way to fly. He will have "entered into God's rest" by trusting Christ to accomplish the work through him. You will find "life" through allowing Him to express Himself through your talents, your abilities, your gifts, and your personality to a hurting world to do His will. That's the way Jesus walked. He let the Father do it through Him.

...

Once a person is born from above, his nature is already Christlike, but it's infantile in maturity. He is like an oak sapling that can mature into a fully grown oak tree, He is not half oak and half briar bush. Just as an oak sapling does not get *oakier* as it matures, neither does a new creature in Christ get holier, more forgiven, more accepted, etc. By faith and obedience, as he begins to act consistently with his new nature, he will look more and more like Jesus.

Gillham has a very interesting way to explain what <u>total commitment</u> really means.
He writes:

> One door we must pass through if we are to go on with God is total commitment. I used to think that total commitment was performance-based. Total commitment is coming to the point where you are willing to place nothing between you and the Lord. I will place nothing between me and You. "I commit it all to You." And He slams the door behind you. You are now totally committed. It's a one-time decision that you make with your will, with your teeth gritted. It then becomes His job to choreograph the circumstances of your life to make your decision experientially real to you (see Philippians 1:6, 2:13).
> …
> I believe the Lord has shown me what the last major door is. It's claiming the cross. **The cross is not an instrument of service it's an instrument of death.** When you step across this threshold on your pilgrimage, you have got to hold a funeral. Your own! And I don't exactly see Christians lining up to die. Many seem to want just one more trip to the pizza parlor. Let me reiterate, you do not attempt to crucify yourself. Nor do you attempt to "die to self." <u>You do not die to anything; you simply agree with God's Word that you already have.</u> When you do, He will slam the door behind you. **You will have entered into claiming your true identity in Christ.** Accompanying every new commitment by the believer is a time of testing. The testing time is for me to know if I am going to stay hitched. The only way I can really know that is when it gets hot in the kitchen. Testing is purposeful. So when it happens, just Praise Him and get

with the program. I have depicted these testing times from the cross toward your becoming conformed to the image of Christ as mini-crosses. These are daily choices when you will be faced with choosing either Channel #1 or Channel #2. You can either buy into the deception and blow it, or you can say, "I know where that's coming from! I'm dead to you! Buzz off!" Then you appropriate truth.

...

Only a broken person is fit for leadership in the Kingdom of God. You can bank on it. **Show me an unbroken Christian, and I'll show you a person who is leaning on the arm of his own flesh to accomplish the task.** Show me an unbroken Christian, and I'll show you a person who is milking his need for acceptance and self-acceptance out of his work. He needs the work. Take it away from him and he'll get depressed. You see, Jesus wasn't the source from whom he was drawing his esteem; it was the work.

...

It is time to move you a step "from glory to glory." The one with the nail-scarred hand inserts the key into the lock to the protective hedge and says, "You may do thus and so, but you may not do this and that." He gives the Evil One permission to attack the flesh. Don't sell out to today's popular "*prosperity gospel.*" **That is such error.** It falls so short of the true riches that God has for all who are in Christ. <u>Don't kick against your loving Father's refining process.</u> He is allowing your circumstances to chip away all your dependence on your own flesh and instead opt for your identity in Christ. You are so beautiful as the new person you truly are in Christ! See it! Get the vision of it from God's Word to you. Believe it and appropriate it as your own.[52]

The next ideas are taken from a different source that I studied during Module IV, "The Normal Christian Life," a book by Watchman Nee.

Watchman Nee begins his book with a rhetorical question, "What is the normal Christian life?"

He elaborates:

> We do well at the outset to ponder this question. The object of these studies is to show that it is something very different from the life of the average Christian. Indeed.[53]

Then Nee continues by establishing the normal Christian life using Galatians 2:21: "It is no longer I, but Christ."

Nee writes:

> He is, we believe, presenting God's normal for a Christian, which can be summarized in these words: I live no longer, but Christ lives His life in me. He works by taking us out of the way and substituting Christ in our place.
>
> He lives instead of us for our deliverance. So we can speak of two substitutions: a Substitute on the cross who secures our forgiveness and a Substitute within who secures our victory." ... "The blood disposes of our sins, while the cross strikes at the capacity for sin.[54]

Nee articulates on the blood atonement:

> We need forgiveness for the sins we have committed, lest we come under judgment; and they are forgiven, not because God overlooks what we have done, but because He sees the blood. The blood is therefore not primarily for us but for God." ... "Whenever I come before Thee, it is always to be on the ground of the precious blood. Then our conscience is really clear before God. No conscience could ever be clear apart from the blood. It is the blood that gives us boldness.
>
> The root problem is the sinner; he must be dealt with. Our sins are dealt with by the blood, but we **ourselves are dealt with by the cross.** The blood procures our pardon for what we have done; **the cross procures our deliverance from what we are.** Let me say at once, the

blood cannot take us out of Adam. There is only one way. Since we came in by birth, we must go out by death. To do away with our sinfulness, we must do away with our life. Bondage to sin by birth; <u>deliverance from sin comes by death.</u> And it is just this way of escape that God has provided. **Death is the secret of emancipation.** We died to sin (Romans 6:2).

For if we have become united with him in the likeness of his death, we shall be also in the likeness of his resurrection" (Romans 6:5). We died in Him as the last Adam; we live in Him as the second Man. **The cross is thus the mighty act of God which translates us from Adam to Christ.**[55]

In his chapter "Knowing," Nee writes:

But what is true of your forgiveness is also true of your deliverance. The work is done. There is no need to pray, but only to praise. God has put us all in Christ, so that when Christ was crucified, we were crucified also." ... "That Christ has died is a fact, that the two thieves have died is a fact, and that you have died is a fact also. Let me tell you, You have died! You are done with! You are ruled out! The self you loathe is on the cross in Christ, And "he that is dead is freed from sin" (Romans 6: 7, KJV). This is the gospel for Christians.

The normal Christian life must begin with a very definite "knowing." Which is not just knowing something about the truth, not understanding some important doctrine. It is not an intellectual knowledge at all, but an opening of the eyes of the heart to see what we have in Christ." ... "So our first step is to **seek from God a knowledge that comes by revelation**—a revelation that is to say, not of ourselves, but of the finished work of the Lord Jesus Christ on the cross.

We are the factory; our actions are the products. The blood of the Lord Jesus dealt with the question of the products, namely, our sins. Do you believe the Lord would cleanse away all our sins and then leave us to get rid of the sin producing factory? He has done away with the goods and also made a clean sweep of the factory that produces the goods. <u>The finished work of Christ really has gone to the root of our problem and dealt with it</u>. There are no half measures with God. He has made full provision for sin's rule to be utterly broken (Romans 6:6).[56]

The, in the chapter titled "Reckoning, The path of progress," the author continues:

When we know that our old man has been crucified with Christ, then the next step is to reckon it is so (Romans 6:11)." ... "If you look to yourself, you will think death is not there, but it is a question of faith not in yourself, but in Him. You look to the Lord and know what He has done. "Lord, I believe in Thee. I recon upon the fact in Thee." Stand there all the day.

How God deals with sins committed and with the principle of sin? That is a great question. The sad part is that many church goers have no idea about these concepts.

Nee explains:

We know that in dealing with sins committed, God's method is direct—to blot them out of remembrance by means of the blood—but when we come to the principle of sin and the matter of deliverance and its power, we find instead that God deals with this indirectly. **He does not remove the sin, but the sinner.** Our old man was crucified with him, and because of this the body, which before had been a vehicle of sin, is unemployed (Romans 6:6). Sin the old master, is still about, but the slave who served him has been put to death, and so is out of reach and his members are unemployed. The gamblers hand is unemployed, the swearers tongue is unemployed, and these members are now available to be used instead "as instruments of righteousness unto God" (Romans 6:13).

Sin is still there, but we are knowing deliverance from its power in increasing measure day by day.

How the theological truth that we are dead to sin is implemented in the Christian Life? This is a fundamental principle in discipleship and spiritual grotw.

The author explains:

> As soon as we have accepted our death with Christ as a fact, Satan will do his best to demonstrate convincingly by the evidence of our day to day experience that we are not dead at all, but very much alive. So we must choose: **Will we believe Satan's lie or God's truth?** Are we going to be governed by appearances or by what God says?

> God has put me in Christ, and therefore **all that is true of Him is true of me**. I will abide in Him. God's injunction is to "abide" in Christ, and that is the way of deliverance it opens the way for God to take a hand in our lives and to work the thing out in us so that the facts of Christ do <u>progressively</u> become the facts of our daily experience. Where before "sin reigned" (Romans 5:21) we make now the joyful discovery that we are truly "no longer . . . in bondage to sin" (Romans 6:6).

> Look at Christ, and see yourself in Him. Abide in Him. Rest in the fact that God has put you in His Son, and live in the expectation that He will complete His work in you. It is for Him to make good the glorious promise that "sin shall not have dominion over you" (Romans 6:14).[57]

In chapter 5, "The Divide of the Cross," Nee writes:

> The cross was the means God used to bring to an end "the old things" by setting aside altogether our "old man," and the resurrection was the means He employed to impart to us all that was necessary for our life in that new world. (Romans 6:4). It is a blessed thing to see that the cross ends all that belongs to the first regime, and that the resurrection introduces all that pertains to the second.

Everything that had its beginning before resurrection must be wiped out. **Resurrection is God's new starting point.** The cross is God's declaration that all that is of the old creation must die. Nothing of the first Adam can pass beyond the cross; it all ends there.

Baptism in Scripture is associated with salvation. "He that believeth and is baptized shall be saved" (Mark 16:16). To be saved is to make our exit from his world system into God's. What then is my answer to God's verdict on the old creation? I answer by asking for baptism. Why? In Romans 6:4 Paul explains that baptism means burial: "We were buried therefore with him through baptism." Baptism is, of course, connected with both death and resurrection, though in itself it is neither death nor resurrection: it is burial. But who qualify for burial? Only the dead! So if I ask for baptism, I proclaim myself dead and fit only for the grave. There is an old world and a new world, and between the two there is a tomb. God has already crucified me, but I must consent to be consigned to the tomb. **My baptism confirms God's sentence, passed upon me in the cross of His Son**. It affirms that I am cut off from the old world and belong now to the new.

It is not that my natural life has been changed at all; it is that another life, a life altogether new, altogether divine, has become my life. God has cut off the old creation in Christ by the resurrection. He has shut the door to that old kingdom of darkness and translated me into the kingdom of his dear Son. My glorying is in the fact that it has been done—that, through the cross of our Lord Jesus Christ, that old world has "been crucified unto me, and I unto the world" (Galatians 6:14). My baptism is my public testimony to the fact. By it, as by my oral witness, my "confession is made unto salvation" (Romans 10:10).[58]

In Chapter 6, "Presenting Ourselves to God," Watchman Nee explains how Christians may walk in their blood-bought victory. It all starts with knowing that we are no longer ourselves but we belong to Christ.

Nee writes:

> The "presenting" spoken of is the outcome of my knowing my old man to be crucified. Knowing, reckoning, presenting to God: That is the divine order. Death has cut off all that cannot be consecrated to Him, and resurrection alone has made consecration possible. Presenting myself to God means that henceforth I consider my whole life as belonging to Him." "Present yourselves . . . and your members," says Paul, and again: "Present your members" (Romans 6:13, 19). God requires of me that I now regard all my members, all my faculties, as belonging wholly to Him. **It is a great thing when I discover I am no longer my own but His.** Real Christian life begins with knowing this.
>
> I am the Lord's and now no longer reckon myself to be my own, but acknowledge in everything His ownership and authority. This is the attitude God delights in, and to maintain it is true consecration. I do not consecrate myself to be a missionary or a preacher; **I consecrate myself to God to do His will where I am**, be it in school, office, or kitchen or wherever He may, in His wisdom, send me. Whatever He ordains for me is sure to be the very best, for nothing but good can come to those who are wholly His. May we always be possessed by the consciousness that we are not our own.[59]

What is the purpose of creation? What is the purpose of redemption? These are hard question to address. In Chapter 7, "The Eternal Purpose," Nee give the answers to these important inquires. He writes:

> What is God's purpose in creation, and what is His purpose in redemption? God's purpose for man was glory, but sin thwarted that purpose by causing man to miss God's glory. The result of sin is that we forfeit God's glory; the result of redemption is that we are qualified

again for glory. God's purpose in redemption is glory, glory, glory.

What was God's objective? It was that His Son Jesus Christ might be the firstborn among many brethren, all of whom should be conformed to His image. How did God realize that objective? "Whom He justified, them He also glorified." **Thus God's purpose in creation and redemption was to make Christ the firstborn Son among many glorified sons.**

The Lord Jesus was the only begotten Son, and as the only begotten He has no brothers. But the Father sent the Son in order that the only begotten might also be the first begotten, and the beloved Son have many brethren. There you have the whole story of the Incarnation and the cross; and there you have, at the last, the purpose of God fulfilled in His "bringing many sons unto glory" (Hebrews 2:10).

We must all go to the cross, because what is in us by nature is a **self-life**, subject to the law of sin. Adam chose a self-life rather than a divine life; so God had to gather up all that was in Adam and do away with it. Our "old man" has to be crucified. God has put us all in Christ and crucified Him as the last Adam and thus all that is of Adam has passed away. Then Christ arose in new form; with a body still, but in the Spirit, no longer in the flesh. "The last Adam became a life-giving spirit" (1 Cor. 15:45).

Do you notice that, in this consideration of the eternal purpose, the whole question of sin ultimately goes out? It no longer has a place. Sin came in with Adam, and even when it has been dealt with as it has to be, we are only brought back to the point where Adam was. But in relating us again to the divine purpose—in, as it were, restoring to us access to the tree of life—redemption has given us far more than Adam ever had. It has made us partakers of the very life of God Himself.[60]

Nee continues with another important subject—The Holy Spirit.

In Chapter 8 the author writes:

> We must consider something which lies at the heart of all our experience as the vitalizing power of effective life and service. I refer to the personal presence and ministry of the Holy Spirit of God. And here too let us take as our starting point two verses from Romans. "The love of God hath been shed abroad in our hearts through the Holy Spirit which was given unto us" (Romans 5:5). "If any man hath not the Spirit of Christ, he is none of His" (Romans 8:9).
>
> Now the principle on which we receive the endowment of the Holy Spirit is the very same as that which we receive forgiveness of sins. The Lord has been crucified, therefore our sins have been forgiven; The Lord has been glorified, therefore the Spirit has been poured out upon us. Is it possible that the Son of God shed His blood and that your sins, dear child of God, have not been forgiven? Never! Then is it possible that the Son of God has been glorified and you have not received the Spirit? Never!
>
> The basis upon which we receive the endowment of the Holy Spirit is not our praying and fasting and waiting, but the exaltation of Christ. Those who emphasize tarrying and hold "tarrying meetings" only mislead us, for the gift is not for the "favored few," but for all, because it is not given on the ground of what we are at all, but of what Christ is.
>
> Do you know, my friends, that the Spirit within you is very God? Oh that our eyes were opened to see the greatness of God's gift! Oh that we might realize the vastness of the resources secreted in our own hearts! I could shout with joy as I think. "The Spirit who dwells within me is no mere influence, but a living Person; He is very God. The infinite God is within my heart!" I am at a loss to convey to you the blessedness of this discovery,

that the Holy Spirit is dwelling within my heart is a Person. I can only repeat, and repeat again, "He is a Person!" Oh, my friends, I would fain repeat it to you a hundred times: **The Spirit of God within me is a Person!** I am only an earthen vessel, but in that earthen vessel I carry a treasure of unspeakable worth, even the Lord of glory.

Our complete surrender of ourselves to the Lord generally hinges upon some one particular thing, and God waits for that one thing. He must have it, for He must have our all. If we yield wholly to Him and claim the power of His indwelling Spirit, we need wait for no special feelings or supernatural manifestations, but can simply look up and praise Him that something has already happened. We can confidently thank Him that the glory of God has already filled His temple. "Know ye not that your body is a temple of the Holy Spirit which is in you, which ye have from God?[61]

How God delivered us from under the Law? This is yet another topic of vast importance that seem to be unknown by many believers. Nee provides answers in Chapter 9, "The meaning and Value of Romans 7."
He writes:

Romans 6 deals with freedom from sin. Romans 7 deals with freedom from the Law. But what is the difference between *deliverance from sin* and *deliverance from the Law*? We all see the value of the former, but where, we wonder, is the need for the latter? For answer, we must first of all ask ourselves what the Law is, and what is its special value, for us.

The trouble in Romans 7 is that man in the flesh tried to do something for God. As soon as you try to please God in that way, then you place yourself under Law, and the experience of Romans 7 begins to be yours.

So, what the disciple of Christ supposed to do?

Nee continues,

> So we can say, reverently, that God never gave us the Law
> to keep; He gave us the Law to break! He knew that we
> could not keep it. We are so bad that He asks no favor
> and makes no demands. **Never has any man succeeded
> in making himself acceptable to God by means of the
> Law.**"
>
> ...
>
> "No, the Law was not given in the expectation that we
> would keep it. It was given in the full knowledge that we
> would break it. And when we have broken it so
> completely as to be convinced of our utter need, then the
> Law has served its purpose. It has been our schoolmaster
> to bring us to Christ, that in us He may Himself fulfill it
> (Gal. 3:24).

More about the role of the Law:

> When I have died, my old master, Sin, still continues to
> live; but his power over his slave extends as far as the
> grave and no further. So it is with regard to the Law. While
> the woman lives, she is bound to her husband; but with
> her death the marriage bond is dissolved, and she is
> discharged from the law of her husband. "The Law may
> still make demands, but for me its power to enforce them
> is ended. How do I die? "**Ye also were made dead to
> the law through the body of Christ**" (Romans 7:4).
> When Christ died, His body was broken; and since God
> placed me in Him (1 Cor. 1:30), I have been broken too.
> When He was crucified, I was crucified with Him. In the
> sight of God, His death included mine, On the hill of
> Calvary, it was forever done" "On the third day He rose
> again. And since we are still in Him, we too are risen. The
> body of the Lord Jesus speaks not only of His death, but
> of His resurrection; for His resurrection was a bodily
> resurrection. Thus, "through the body of Christ," we are
> not only "dead to the Law," but alive unto God.

Human weakness works in our favor...

Nee writes:

> I do not know why I am so weak. "The trouble with you"
> I said, "is that you are weak enough not to do the will of
> God, but you are not weak enough to keep out of things
> altogether. You are still not weak enough. When you are
> reduced to utter weakness and are persuaded that you can
> do nothing whatever, then God will do everything." We
> all need to come to the point where we say, "*Lord, I am
> unable to do anything for Thee, but I trust Thee to do everything in
> me.*"

> *Justification vs. sanctification:*

> We know that justification is ours through the Lord Jesus
> and requires no work on our part, but we think
> sanctification is dependent on our own efforts: We know
> we can receive forgiveness only by entire reliance on the
> Lord; yet we believe we can obtain deliverance by doing
> something ourselves. We fear that if we do nothing,
> nothing will happen "it is finished" (John 19:30). He has
> done everything on the cross for our forgiveness, and He
> will do everything in us for our deliverance. In both cases
> He is the doer. "It is God that worketh in you." God
> wants to do all the work, for He must have all the glory.
> If we did some of it, then we could claim some of the
> glory ourselves. But God must have it all. He does all the
> work from the beginning to end.[62]

What does it mean to be led by the Holy Spirit and to walk
according to the Spirit? The author clarifies these aspects in Chapter
10, "Walking In the Spirit."
Nee writes:

> We think it enough to be "in Christ," but we learn now
> that we must also walk "in the Spirit" (Rom. 8:9).

> Living in the Spirit means that I trust the Holy Spirit to
> do in me what I cannot do myself. This life is completely
> different from the life I would naturally live of myself.

Each time I am faced with a new demand from the Lord, I look to Him to do in me what He requires of me. It is not a case of trying, but of trusting; I shall look to the Spirit of God to produce in me the needed purity of humility or meekness, confident that He will do so. This is what it means to "stand still and see the salvation of Jehovah, which he will work for you" (Exodus 14:13).

Where is our Victory?

Our victory lies in hiding in Christ, and in counting in simple trust upon His Holy Spirit within us to overcome our fleshly lusts with His own new desires. The cross has been given to procure salvation for us; the Spirit has been given to procure salvation in us. Christ has risen and ascended is the basis of our salvation; **Christ in our hearts by the Spirit is its power.**

The greatest gift—Jesus Christ:

God will not give me humility, or patience, or holiness, or love as separate gifts of His grace. He is not a retailer dispensing grace to us in packets, measuring out some patience to the impatient, some love to the unloving, some meekness to the proud, in quantities that we take and work on as a kind of capital. He has given only one gift to meet all our need: His Son Christ Jesus. As I look to Him to live out His life in me, He will be humble and patient and loving and everything else I need—in my stead.

Growing in grace is the key to the spiritual life:

Growth in grace is the only sense in which we can grow, and grace, we have said, is God doing something for us. Another letting go, a fresh trusting in Christ, and another stretch of land conquered. "Christ my life" is the secret of enlargement. "Lord, I cannot do it, therefore I will no longer try to do it." This is the point most of us fall short of. "Lord, I cannot; therefore I will take my hands off;

from now on I trust Thee for that." "I have no time to feel condemned, but only to praise Him who leads me on from one fresh victory to another. (Rom. 8:6)

If we will let go of our own wills and trust Him, we shall not fall to the ground and break, but we shall fall into a different law of the Spirit of life. For God has given us not only life, but a law of life. If we will let ourselves live in the new law, we shall be less conscious of the old. It is still there, but it is no longer governing and we are no longer in its grip.

Walking after the Spirit:

What does it mean to walk after the Spirit? It means two things.

(1) First, it is not a work; it is a walk. Praise God, the burdensome and fruitless effort I involved myself in when I sought "in the flesh" to please God gives place to a quiet and restful dependence on "His working in me mightily" (Col. 1:29).

(2) Then second, to "walk after" implies subjection. Walking after the flesh means that I yield to the dictates of the flesh, and the following verses in Romans 8:5–8 make clear where that leads me. It only brings me into conflict with God. **To walk after the Spirit is to be subject to the Spirit.** What the Father has devised concerning us, the Son accomplished for us, and now the Holy Spirit communicates it to us. That is His ministry, He has come for that very purpose—that He may make real in us all that is ours through the finished work of Christ.[63]

In Chapter 11, "One Body in Christ," Nee, presents various aspects accomplished by the cross of Christ. These aspects are fulfilled in the body of Christ—the church.

The author writes:

Getting more than Adam got:

We have spoken already of the purpose of God in creation and have said that it embraced far more than Adam ever came to enjoy. What was that purpose? God wanted to have a race of men whose members were gifted with a spirit whereby communion would be possible with Himself, who is Spirit. That race, possessing God's own life, was to cooperate in securing His purposed end by defeating every possible uprising of the Enemy and undoing his evil works. That was the great plan.

All too often we have thought of the church as being merely so many "saved sinners." "Saved sinners—with that thought you have the whole background of sin and the Fall; but **in God's sight the church is a divine creation in His Son**. The one is largely individual, the other corporate. With the one the view is negative, belonging to the past; with the other it is positive, looking forward.

God has a Son, His only begotten, and He seeks that the Son should have brethren, from the position of only begotten, He will become the first begotten; and instead of the Son alone; God will have many sons. One grain of wheat has died, and many grains will spring up. The first grain was once the only grain; now it has become the first of many.

It requires an entire Body to reflect God's glory:

But now in chapter (Romans) 12:1 the emphasis is a little different: "I beseech you therefore, brethren, by the mercies of God, to present your bodies a living sacrifice, holy, acceptable to God, which is your reasonable service." This new appeal for consecration is made to us as "brethren," linking us in thought to the "many brethren" of chapter (Romans) 8:29 alone in isolation man can never fulfill God's purpose; It requires a complete body of Christ to attain to the stature of Christ and to display His glory. Oh, that we might really see this!

The body of Christ is not an illustration, but a fact. The Bible does not just say that the church is like a body of Christ, but that it is the body of Christ.

This is where we are now. The age is closing, and Satan's power is greater than ever. Our warfare is with angels and principalities and powers (Rom. 8:38, Eph. 6:12) who are set to withstand and destroy the work of God in us by laying many things to the charge of God's elect. Alone we could never be their match, but what we alone cannot do, the church can. Sin, self-reliance and individualism were Satan's master-strokes at the heart of God's purpose in man, and in the cross God has undone them... We, His church, are "more than conquerors though him that loved us" (Rom. 8:37).[64]

Chapter 12, "The Cross and the Soul Life," is such an amazing chapter. It reveals that God has provided all the resources for the church in the cross of Christ.
Nee writes:

We have said that the work of the cross have two results which bear directly upon the realizing of that purpose in us. On the one hand, it has issued in the release of His life that it may find expression in us through the indwelling Spirit. On the other hand, it has made possible what we speak of as "bearing the cross"—that is, our **cooperation in the daily in-working of His death** whereby way is made in us for the manifestation of that new life through the bringing of the "natural man" progressively into his right place of subjection to the Holy Spirit.

Man a living soul living by the soul:

The whole fruit ministered to the expansion and full development of the soul, so that not only was the man a living soul, but from henceforth man will live by the soul.

It is not merely that man has a soul, but that from that day on, the soul, with its independent powers of free choice, usurps the place of the spirit as the animating power of man. There is something in man today which is not just the fact of having and exercising a soul, but which constitutes a living by the soul.

Living by the life of Another:

By taking the fruit, Adam became possessed of an inherent power to act, but a power which, by its independence of God, played right into Satan's hands. You lose that power to act when you come to know the Lord. The Lord cuts it off, and you find you can no longer act on your own initiative. **You have to live by the life of Another;** you have to draw everything from Him.

What energizes us?

We forget that, in the matter of our resource for handling the things of God, it is a question not of comparative value, but of origin—of where the resource springs from. It is not so much a matter of what we are doing, but of what powers we are employing to do it, and who is controlling those powers. We think too little of the source of our energy and too much of the end to which it is directed.

So anything for which we are sufficient in ourselves is "nothing" in God's estimate, and we have to accept His estimate and write it down as nothing. "The flesh profiteth nothing." It is only what comes from above that will abide. The word "purity" is a blessed word. I always associate it with the Spirit. Purity means something altogether of the Spirit. Impurity means mixture.

Seeing reality through the Light of God:

(Hebrews 4:12-13) Yes, the Word of God, the penetrating Scripture of truth, that settles our questions. It is that which discerns our motives and defines for us their true source in soul or spirit. Then it is we see something which we have never seen before. We are convicted. We know where we are wrong, and we look up and confess, "Lord, I see it. There is impurity there. There is mixture..." Light comes in and we see light.

We know fear and trembling as we recognize the corruption of our nature, the hatefulness of self, and the real threat to the work of God of our soul-life and energy, untamed and uncontrolled by His Holy Spirit." "But here the cross, in its widest meaning, will come to our help again, and we shall seek now to examine an aspect of its work which meets and deals with our problem of the human soul. For only a thorough understanding of the cross can bring us to that place of dependence which the Lord Jesus Himself voluntarily took when He said, "I can of myself do nothing; as I hear, I judge; and my judgment is righteous; because I seek not mine own will, but the will of him that sent me" (John 5:30).[65]

In chapter 13, called, "The Path of Progress—Bearing the Cross," we discover a few important concepts.
Nee writes:

The whole subtle object of Satan was to get the Lord to act for Himself—that is, from the soul. By the stand He took, Jesus absolutely repudiated such action. "The Son can do nothing out from Himself" (John 5:19). So we can safely say that all the work which the Lord Jesus did on earth, prior to His actual death on the cross, was done with the principle of death and resurrection as its basis, even though as an actual event Calvary still lay in the future can we do otherwise?

The budding almond rod speaks of resurrection. It is death and resurrection that marks God's recognized ministry. Without that you have nothing.

A living personal holiness:

Then another phase is presented to us in Romans 7 where the question of holiness of life is in view—a living personal holiness. There you find a true man of God trying to please God in righteousness, and he comes under the Law and the Law finds him out. He is trying to please God by using his own carnal power, and the cross has to bring him to the place where he says, "I cannot do it, I cannot satisfy God with my powers; I can only trust the Holy Spirit to do that in me... We are used in a sense, but at the same time we destroy our own work, and sometimes that of others also, because of there being something undealt with by the cross.

The cross and its purifying work:

Some of us know well what is meant to lose our soul. We can no longer lightly fulfill its desire; we cannot just give in to it and gratify it. That is the "loss" of the soul. We are going through a painful process to discourage what the soul is asking for... We are held up because of some secret love somewhere, some perfectly innocent natural affection diverting our course, the cross has to come in there and do its purifying work (Mark 8:34–35).

The secret to fruitfulness:

He let go His life that we might receive it. It is in this aspect of His death that we are called to die. It is here that He makes clear the value of conformity to His death, whereby we lose our own natural life in order that, in the power of His resurrection, we may become life-imparters, sharing thereafter with others the new life of God which is in us. This is the secret of ministry, the path of real fruitfulness to God.

Yet here too there may be a crisis that, once reached and passed, can transform our whole life and service for God. It is a wicket gate by which we may enter upon an entirely new pathway... God must bring us to a point—I cannot tell you how it will be, but He will do it—where, through a deep and dark experience, our natural power is touched and fundamentally weakened, so that we no longer dare trust ourselves through difficult and painful ways, in order to get us there. At length there comes a time when we no longer "like" to do Christian work—indeed we almost dread to do things in the Lord's name. But it is then, at last, that He can begin to use us.

But when this is really established in you, you have come to a new place which we speak of as "resurrection ground." Death, in principle, may have had to be wrought out in a crisis in your natural life, but when it has, then you find God releases you into resurrection. You discover that what you have lost is being given back, though not quite as before.[66]

In Chapter 14, titled, "The Goal of the Gospel," we learn about the true meaning of the Good News.
Nee writes:

To my professor it seemed a total waste to serve the Lord; but that is what the gospel is for—to bring each one of us to a true estimate of his worth. That is always the way the world reasons. "Can you not find a better employment for your life? Can you not do something better with yourself than this? It is going a bit too far to give yourself altogether to the Lord!

Pouring out the "alabaster box's" content:

We could labor and be used to the full; but the Lord is not so concerned about our ceaseless occupation in work for Him. That is not His first object. The service of the Lord is not to be measured by tangible results. No, my friends, **the Lord's first concern is with our position at His feet and our anointing of His head.** Whatever we have as an "alabaster box," the most precious thing, the thing dearest in the world to us—yes, let me say it, the outflow from us of a life that is produced by the very cross itself—we give that all up to the Lord.

Put Himself highest than the work for Him:

The more you think you can do, and the more you employ your gifts up to the very limit, (and some even go over the limit!), in order to do it, the more you find that you are applying the principle of the world and not of the Lord, God's ways with us are all designed to establish in us this other principle, namely, that our work for Him springs out of our ministering to Him. I do not mean that we are going to do nothing; **but the first thing for us must be the Lord Himself, not His work.**

Giving Him a costly gift—our entire being:

And the Lord will not be satisfied with anything less from us than that we too should have done what we could. What the Lord Jesus looks for in us is a life laid at His feet, and that in view of His death and burial and of a future day. Yes, then we shall pour out our all upon Him! But it is a precious thing—indeed it is a far more precious thing to Him—that we should anoint Him now, not with any material oil, but with something costly, something from our hearts.

There must be something—a willingness to yield, a breaking and pouring out of everything to Him—which gives release to that fragrance of Christ and produces in other lives an awareness of need, drawing them out and on to know the Lord. This is what I feel to be the heart of everything... The Lord grant us grace that we may learn how to please Him. When, like Paul, we make this our supreme aim (2 Cor. 5:9), the gospel will have achieved its end.[67]

The tremendous blessings when one appropriates the cross in his or her life are many.

Scripture makes it very plain that the soul of man can be dealt with in one way and in one way only, by our bearing the cross daily and following Him, as Nee explained it in his book: **the cross has borne me, now I must bear it.** This bearing of the cross is an inward thing. It is this that we mean when we speak of the subjective working of the cross. Moreover, it is a continuous process. A step by step following after Him.

There is more about the cross that I would like to share with you. In his book, "The Cross of Christ: The Center of Scripture your Life and Ministry," Dr. John Best, offers a lot of teaching about this important topic.

In the Introduction, Best, shares about his own discoveries about the cross, which he calls it—"the magnificent work of Christ." He writes:

> Why is the Christianity of our day so superficial? I wonder how I could have been a Christian for 37 years and had such a shallow concept of the magnificent work of Christ for and with me at Calvary!
>
> My superficial view of the cross was that it was only the instrument of execution where Christ died for me. I had no working concept that I had personally died with Him there. As a result my Christian life lacked depth. I had no apprehension of either **my union with Him** or **my unlimited resources in Him**. Not embracing my death with Christ, my union with Him and my resources in Him, I floundered for almost four decades. I was often soundly defeated by the power of sin and discouraged. I was desperately afraid of losing the love and acceptance of other people. I was controlled by my fear of their rejection.
>
> I had no power in my life. I was seeking for any method I could find to make me successful. Although I did not grasp this truth at the time, <u>I was not miserable because of the cross of Christ, but because I had never known it!</u>[68]

Dr. John Best, continues:

As we continue to appropriate His life rather than relying on ourselves, Christ meets our inner needs and gives us His joy, peace, power and a deeper walk with Him (friends of the Spirit) in the midst of life's difficulties and problems. Experiencing the cross allows us to depend upon Christ alone for life and service. We choose to behave more consistently with who we truly are, responsively dependent on Christ to live His life through us... **the end result of the cross is to bring us to resurrection life.** Life after the cross.[69]

The cross indeed is the "is the central axis of the entire Bible," Best, writes:

In Chapter 1, titled, "The Cross of Christ: The Center of Scripture," the author writes:

Even before the establishing of sacrifices, Christ's death on the cross was illustrated in God clothing the fallen Adam and Eve in the skins of sacrificed animals (Genesis 3:21) and by God receiving Abel's offering of bloody animals while his brother's vegetable offering was rejected (Genesis 4:15). The command of God came to Abraham to offer his son Isaac on Mount Moriah. At the last moment the surprising gracious substitution of the ram God provided became a perfect picture of the coming vicarious death of Christ (Genesis 22). The fact is, the cross is the central axis of the entire Bible.

Then, he quotes other important authors who wrote on the subject of the cross before.

Dorman Followwill asserts that "The cross was witnessed by the Law and Prophets. In fact, the cross of Christ is what the entire Hebrew Bible points toward. Without the cross of Christ, the Hebrew Scriptures is a book of empty promises.

Best gives plenty of Bible verses, considered by the author as being important for this subject.

In Galatians 6:14 Paul personally took up his pen and made clear what the message of the early church was. He proposed, "But may it never be that I should boast except in the cross of our Lord Jesus Christ, through which the world has been crucified to me and I to the world." This message is repeated throughout the New Testament.

In his book, "The Cross," Martyn Lloyd-Jones relates that many people today would insist that the cross is not really important. According to many, all we need to do is follow Christ's teaching and His example. But as Lloyd-Jones says, "Without the cross, Jesus' teaching and His example only lead to condemnation. If you only preach the teaching of the Lord Jesus Christ, not only do you not solve the problem of mankind, in a sense you even aggravate it. You are preaching nothing but utter condemnation because nobody can ever carry it out.

Because of an incomplete understanding about the cross, many believers lack real victory in their lives.

Best explains:

Because our death with Christ is not viewed as essential, God's people in general only hear that they must live for Him. Just as my Christian life lacked depth because of this limited view, many times theirs also does.

Because our burial with Christ most often is neglected or not understood, Christians flounder with a perceived inner civil war, when the battle really is to be waged as Galatians 5:16–18 says it should be fought.[70]

There is no real change unless Christians experience the exchange, I mean the exchanged life.

The author explains:

Jesus did not die and rise again to enhance a life we already had but to give us a new life, exchanging our old man (Romans 6:6) for a new creation man (2 Corinthians 5:17).

All our vapid, empty efforts to change or enhance ourselves apart from union with Christ at the cross takes the focus off of Christ and onto our efforts. When people only hear that Christ was raised for them and not that He was raised with them, and they are tragically deceived, as I was trying to change what God already has exchanged!

As in the Old Testament prophecies, the Gospels, Acts, and the Epistles, the chief thing on the mind of God is Jesus and His wonderful saving acts on the cross and in the resurrection. He is forever worthy to be praised because of Who He is and what He has done through the cross!

The key to victorious Christian living is linked to our death with Christ, and to our resurrection with Him. Without a correct understanding of these truths, Christians are deceived and live defeated lives.

When I saw the full work of the cross in sharp focus, God used it's power to overcome those long-standing sin problems. I also saw in the cross my new identity in Christ and was able to accept myself on the same basis that God accepts me. What a change this was! My life also began to "work" because God taught me that Christ is my life and can live His life in me based on my death and resurrection with Him.

Jesus Christ's sacrifice on the cross is the crux of our faith, the axis of the Scriptures, the pivot point of human history, and the defining moment of God's redemption history. The main thing God wants for us is not swelling wisdom and seeking after signs, but to know more and more about His Son, His cross and the work He did there. (1Corinthians 1:18) "The word of the cross is to those who are perishing foolishness, but to us who are being saved it is the power of God." Paul knew that there was great power in proclaiming the full work of the cross. To experience God's power we must seek nothing but the cross of Christ. It is not a focus on what God might do some time. It is a steady gaze at the wonder of what God has already accomplished in the full work of the cross.

Best is cementing his thoughts and ideas regarding the wonderful effects and benefits of the Cross on Romans chapter six. The key point here is that Christians are not half evil half good; the main point is that a genuine child of God is a new creature altogether. He argues that, *"Both the death and life sides of the cross are foundational."* This truth here is the key to Christian victory.

The author explains:

> In Romans 6, he placed our union with Christ in His death and resurrection first in his teaching on Christian living. In this grandest of all epistles, he focused on the central place of the cross in the life of every believer...
>
> The cross of Christ is also the foundation of our lives as believers, for God's plan was that through the cross our old nature would be crucified, and the power of the Holy Spirit would be unleased to change our hearts and lives. If we do not know this, if we think we are half evil, all our efforts to stop sinning are doomed to failure. Temptation is not a roadblock anymore. He learned that what is impossible to do in imitation of Jesus is possible in union with Jesus! It's all because of the cross. **We are now alive to God**: "Even so consider yourselves to be dead to sin, but alive to God in Christ Jesus." (6:11). We are commanded to count on who we are. It is a call to believe our identity is what God says it is! Both the *death* and *life* sides of the cross are foundational. If believers are shaky here, everything else will be shaky in their lives. They can try many formulas for Christian living, but if they do not understand this, they will not have consistent victory. Other parallel truths may be embraced, but without this foundational truth, victory will elude them.

The Christian life is not Christ-PLUS, but Christ-ONLY.

The author explains:

Legalism was not being presented to the Galatians as a substitute for Christ. It was an add-on. Christ-only had been perverted into Christ-plus. But what began as an addition to Christ became a substitute for the Savior. Legalism always has such an effect, because anything added onto Christ implies that Christ is somehow insufficient. The legalists promoted Christ-plus because Christ-plus is not an offense, whereas Christ-only is! That exclusive emphasis would result in persecution. For them, it was better to distort the gospel than to suffer for Christ by preaching the full message of Calvary.

Christ brings us with Him out of the grave to walk as new creations in newness of life (Romans 6:4)! The truth of our death and resurrection with Christ brings us to the point where we have to believe it and walk in it to do anything of lasting value.[71]

The new creation in Christ is a miracle. Let's never diminish its value.

Best writes:

It is not ritualistic obedience or the lack of it that is important. What is important is that people become new creations through the full work of the cross. That happens as we place our trust in Christ and are united with Him in His death and resurrection. We are new creations, containers of Christ Himself, who lives through us (2 Corinthians 4:10, 5:17; Galatians 2:20; Romans 6:2-11; 15:18). The inner man, produced by our union at the cross, is what matters, not the outer man. Seeing ourselves as the new creations we are eliminates the need to argue about which religious practice is better, which cultural norm is better, ad infinitum. So what if some are too legalistic or too loose for our taste? Compared to Calvary, Paul said, these things mean nothing. What is important is glorying in the cross and remembering that we are new creations! God has chosen to wrap up everything. He has for us in His Son, especially His Son's work at the cross.

149

Let us make central in our lives what God has made central the full work of Christ at the cross.[72]

People are sinners not because they sin; people are born sinners therefore they act according to their nature. Christ, at the CROSS, dealt with the SIN problem.

In Chapter 2, "The Center of Your Life," Best explains:

> Before you reached the point where you knew you were sinning and were responsible for it, you had sinned many times. This became a habitual way of coping with life to get your own way, to get your needs met first and to protect yourself. These habitual independent attitudes and actions are often called "flesh" in the Bible. So you have two initial problems from your early life:
>
> – You were born a sinner in Adam and without the life of God in your spirit
> – As a sinner, you did what comes naturally, you sinned
>
> Both of these problems were taken care of in love by God through the finished work of the cross. Here is what you could experience if you were to appropriate what God has provided for you:
>
> – Your dead, unrighteous, identity as a sinner in Adam can be exchanged at the cross for a new identity.
> – Your second problem that separates you from God is the sin that you have committed (Romans 3:1–23).
>
> Never take your eyes off the cross as the solution to your sins. It is the singular satisfaction that will satisfy God's righteous anger at your sins.

On the CROSS, Jesus took care not only of the SIN problem, but also of the sinner. The CROSS is the single point in the universe where the identity of a Christian is changed, or better yet— EXCHANGED.

Best, writes:

> If you have already or have just trusted Christ's work on the cross to remove all separation between you and God, you now have the fantastic opportunity to experience daily what I will call "the exchanged life." It is also centered in the finished work of the cross. It speaks of an experience based upon the exchange of our old essential personhood (identity) in Adam for a new basic spiritual personhood in Christ... This was accomplished through our union with Christ in His *death, burial, resurrection and ascension* (Romans 6:1-7; Ephesians 2:4-6; Galatians 2:20). So we could say:

> "The exchanged life is the exchange [with Christ at the cross] of a
>   Self-centered life
>   Lived out of the Christian's own resources
>   As if he were still in Adam,
>   For a Christ-centered life
>   Lived out of Christ's resources
>   Because he is in Christ."

The transformation which took place at the cross is absolutely radical: from the old man in Adam to the new man in Christ; from sinner to saint. And all of this was possible because of the *death, burial, resurrection, and ascension,* of Christ and *baptism* with the Holy Spirit.

Best writes:

> At the moment of our salvation, God took us out of spiritual death in Adam and *transformingly* put us into union with Christ. He exchanged at the cross our old identity as sinners in Adam for a radically new identity in Christ. We are now not just sinners saved by grace, our essential nature and identity is that of new creation saints in Christ. Our union with Christ in the full work of the cross is so real, so vital, so complete so trans-historical that the "*old us*" (our spirit) in Adam died, and was buried. The "*new us*" (our spiritual identity) is now raised up in union with

Him. We have been set free to live as ones who have been recreated in Christ's resurrection (Romans 6). This is God's doing. He traded our old identity in Adam for a new identity in Christ.

This is the FOUNDATION of the exchanged life. God's uniting us with Christ, whose life is eternal. This results in a shared life, a life of union with Christ: our spirit in union with Christ's spirit (Romans 8:9–13).

The victorious life is available to all Christians, but it is experienced only by the few—those who agree and embrace the truth spelled out by Paul in Galatians 2:20.

To EXPERIENCE what God has provided us in the exchanged life, and to walk in victory over the power of indwelling sin (Romans 6:1–14) we must resolutely trust in what the Bible says about our union with Christ in His death, burial, resurrection and ascension. "You have already been crucified in Christ, but it will do you no practical, earthly good until you agree with and embrace this truth with all of its ramifications."

Sally Rackets describes further results:

Because we believe we are new creations, united with Christ, we choose to behave more consistently with who we truly are, responsively dependent on Christ to live His life through us. Life is lived by faith, established on fact not feeling. Failure does not disprove nor destroy our faith, but can further serve as a catalyst to deeper dependence because there is no condemnation—only love and acceptance. If the Holy Spirit is urging you inwardly to embrace your accomplished union with Christ in the entire work of the cross, hesitate no longer. Trust Christ alone to be your functional source of life. Then you will be no longer living in the delusion of yourself as a being separate from God. You will be living in the truth of your union with Christ (John 14:20; Romans 6:1–11; 1 Corinthians 6:17; 2 Corinthians 5:17).[73]

Our relationship with the "*old man*" ended, once and for all, at the cross. If we forget this important truth (Romans 6:6a) we are deceived into believing that we have two natures (the old man and the new man) living simultaneously in us. This misconception causes a lot of Christians to get out of focus on the cross.

In Chapter 3, "*Keeping It Central In Your Life and Ministry,*" Best writes:

> An important safeguard is to be warned how the cross of Christ can slip out of central place in our personal lives and public ministries. Such forewarning is necessary because the history of the world and the church is strewn with the wreckage of those who have made shipwreck of the faith. They may have started their personal or public Christian journey with the cross central but have over the years departed from it slightly or entirely. You cannot maintain the cause of Christ without centering on the cross of Christ. This lesson from history is a somber one! Therefore this chapter will present causes of such *slippage* from the centrality of Calvary.

> If we get preoccupied with things other than our union with Christ, we are out of focus on the cross. There are so many things available for us to depend upon to make our lives easier that are not wrong in themselves. But when we depend upon them more than clinging to Christ, we have departed from fellowshipping with, abiding in, and drawing life from Him (John 15:5).

> If we lapse back into thinking we have two spiritual identities, we have forgotten that our union with Christ at the cross ended that first identity: "Knowing this, that our old self [man] was crucified with Him" (Romans 6:6a). In such a state of forgetfulness about our lack of relationship with the old man, we are demeaning the full work of the cross. We are living on a pittance, a small portion of what God has provided through our union with Christ![74]

Departing from the CROSS is costly. We still battling with the sins of the past instead of enjoying present and future victories.

Best explains:

> The Bible predicted that Jesus, as the suffering Lamb of Calvary, would "bear our griefs" and "carry our sorrows" (Isaiah 53:4). The iniquities that inflict the pain of guilt and other consequences were borne by Jesus at the cross (Isaiah 53:6). When we refuse the completed work of the cross ("It is finished—*paid in full*") by continually beating ourselves up for sins of our past, we are departing from the cross.

> Some teach that God only wants to relieve this pain and always wants to heal us. While it is attractive to try this approach if we are in sustained pain, in doing so we may be avoiding what God wants to do in us, to develop agape love, to measure our faith and hope and prepare us for reigning with Him. Let God use pain however He wishes in your life. If you do not do so, you will slip away from the sufficiency of Christ as seen in your union with Him in the full work of the cross.[75]

The cross offers the solution not only for salvation but for victory over sinful behaviors, like addiction to alcohol or pornography. But in order to experience this kind of victories Christians have to believe that, on the cross, they died to sin also. Failure to appropriate the full work of the cross leads to a defeated life.

The author explains:

> Many evangelicals point only to the cross for justification and even some areas of sanctification, but when they attempt to help believers with especially enslaving sins they resort to *law* and *works*. For instance, addiction to alcohol, drugs and sexual sins are dealt with in ways that are strikingly similar to the world, except that Bible verses and principles are used to shore up the sagging methods of men to handle bullying bondages. "How do I die to sin, including the sexual sins which have me bound?" The

answer is, "You can't do it!" Why not? **Because you have already died to sin at salvation**. "We died to sin" is past tense, it has already been done. This is something you <u>must believe</u>, not something you <u>must do</u>.[76]

I am amazed daily as I walk in the way of the cross. The changes I have experienced within myself toward those I am confronting on a regular basis at home and work. I see changes in me, in my own walk, as well as in the lives of people that I know: my ex-wife, my children, and fellow workers.

If you would be required to teach others this module, please provide a written plan for how you would do it.

I thought this module to be an important one. One that completely covered all areas of the cross, it's importance and effect in our spiritual lives. I felt the written plan was most appropriate and would not have any problems using it.

5. The Cross—The Mystery of Suffering that Only a Few Embrace It

In a few paragraphs please provide an overall evaluation of Module V. Please explain what you liked the most about this important module. Explain also what you disliked the most about this module. How do you suggest we can make Module V even more helpful and appealing for future disciples/students?

Once again, **Module V, the Cross** – *The mystery of suffering that only a few embrace*, is another module of pivotal importance in this Advance Discipleship Training. It is spiritually eye opening if one is generally accustomed to only hearing about the work of the cross as it pertains to its provision of our way to salvation. In this module one learns through the teachings of excellent authors and teachers the **deep workings of the cross in the believer's life**. What it really means as Paul said to *"take up our cross daily"*. How we as believers suffer in various ways, and as we learn to yield to it, taking up our cross, we will grow in Christ. I enjoyed, or rather found it a relief to experience the various teachings and rich experiences that the authors provided and went through personally in their lives. The lessons learned that I could relate to and spiritual, bible based truths presented when it comes to *suffering* and the *cross*.

I found this module complete, not leaving any unanswered questions to the subject matter. The questions and various essays and assignments were excellent, it were causing me to think and grow spiritually. I can't think of anything that would be helpful to add to what is found in this module.

Please provide the biblical definition of the cross. Please feel free to use Bible verses, specific quotes from the materials you studied during **Module V**, and ideas (quotes) from other sources to sustain your view.

John 1:29 states, "Behold the Lamb of God who takes away the sin of the world." Philippians 2:8, 9, "Being found in appearance as a man, He humbled Himself by becoming obedient to the point of death, even death on a cross. For this reason also God highly exalted Him, and bestowed on Him the name which is above every name." **These verses define what most Christians believe about the cross and it's purpose.** God's act of love on Calvary, and of course Jesus victory over sin and death. Through His death and resurrection He conquered death itself. **This, according to Watchman Nee, represents a deeper and more accurate definition of the CROSS.**

But the cross and it's work does not end there. Romans 6:4 (NASB) states:

> Therefore we have been buried with Him through baptism into death, so that as Christ was raised from the dead through the glory of the Father, so we too might walk in newness of life.

Commenting on this verse, Watchman Nee, writes:

> There are tremendous spiritual benefits that the cross provides to the disciple of Christ! *"The cross is thus the power of God which translates us from Adam to Christ.* [77]

In his book: *"Handbook to Happiness,"* chapter 1, titled: *"Experiencing the Cross of Christ,"*

Dr. Charles R. Solomon writes about his own experiences with the power of the Cross of Christ:

> Late that night I was reading Galatians 2:20: "I am crucified with Christ." I had given up hope of finding help from God or anyone else. But God graciously and sovereignly moved in my life that night and released me

from all the anxiety, depression, and pain in the back of
my head, and inferiority feelings of a lifetime.
This feeling of total freedom lasted a day or two. Then
some of the old feelings settled back in, and I had to learn
a process the Bible calls "walking in the Spirit." Beyond
the first step of being "filled with the Spirit," I had to learn
to continue the process of allowing the Holy Spirit to have
control of my life.[78]

The way of the cross is not pleasant and attractive to the majority
of Christians. But when the message of the cross hidden in Galatians
2:20 is properly understood, the light bulb comes on—*life must come
out of death and victory out of defeat.*
Dr. Solomon continues:

The cross of Christ, however, has never been a place
where many people gather for fellowship, nor will ever be.
Those who have embraced the Cross and it's teachings
don't think of themselves as having "arrived," except at
the bottom. The Cross in the life of the believer involves
brokenness and suffering, just as it did for our Lord.
There is no such thing as an "end run" around the Cross.
None of us is greater than his Master, and all must go the
way of the Cross if we are to have victory in our Christian
experience. Until believers understand this, they will
continue to resist the message that life must come out of
death and victory out of defeat, whether in counseling or
in any other kind of ministry. What I learned during those
days in 1965 was **that the experience of the Cross is an
ongoing process.** God allowed many things to come
into my life, during those days and since, to contribute to
my spiritual growth. I learned that we are all in the process
of becoming *in experience* who we already are in Christ *by
position.* Until we are one day with Him, we will have to
continue dealing with sin, in the world and in ourselves.

Everything has been accomplished by Christ on the cross once
and for all. This means that, both *salvation* and *victory* depend on us
appropriating the *death* and the *resurrected life* of Christ. Both sides of

the cross are important: *death for reconciliation,* and *life for our ongoing salvation,* as stated by Paul in Romans 5:10.

The author continues:

> The same power God used in raising Jesus from the dead is operative in us as we place our faith in what was accomplished through Christ's resurrection. Paul wrote, "if, when we were enemies, we were reconciled to God by the death of His Son, much more, being reconciled, we shall be saved by His life" (Rom. 5:10). Our identity is based on who we are in Christ, and it is to be claimed by faith, not by works—ours or any other's. We shed the trappings of the past by exchanging our fleshly identity for the Christ-life, by exchanging a life of defeat for a life of victory. Jesus told his followers, "If any man will come after me, let him deny himself, and take up his cross daily, and follow me" (Luke 9:23).[79]

The New Testament teaching places a heavy weigh on our identity in Christ. As believers, this new identity is not earned but learned by experience through the revelation of the Holy Spirit. The CROSS is the only place in the universe where we can receive our new identity. As Watchman Nee very well said: "The cross of Christ is the power of God which translated us from Adam into Christ." The life after experiencing the cross is not just a changed life but an *exchanged life.*

In the chapter, titled, "The Great Exchange," Dr. Solomon writes teaches us about the greatest work accomplished by the Cross of Christ.

He writes:

> The identity delineated in the Scriptures has nothing to do with the way we see ourselves in relation to others or what our behavior is or has been; it is an identity based on being in Christ and finding our life in Him. Any performance involved is His performance at Calvary; on our part, it is *being* instead of *doing.* In other words, as we identify ourselves with the Lord Jesus Christ, we begin to live out of our new and true identity in Him. Such an identity is

not earned—it is learned as it is taught by the Holy Spirit; it is not attained by work—it is obtained by faith.

While the identity assigned by the world is based on doing, the identity delineated in the Scriptures is based on dying and being resurrected with the Lord Jesus. As we have seen in the forgoing chapters, we must lose our life or identity, assigned or developed in the world, at the Cross if we are to find our life or identity based on our being in Christ in heavenly places and living the resurrection life (Matt. 16:24).

Walking in victory requires more than believing that Christ died on the cross; it requires experiencing our own death with Him and our own resurrection in Christ to newness of life. In Romans 6:4, Paul puts this fundamental truth this way:

> Therefore we have been buried with Him through baptism into death, so that as Christ was raised from the dead through the glory of the Father, so we too might walk in newness of life.

The author continues:

> The way to victory is to exchange the fleshly identity for the spiritual identity at the Cross. As we stated before, as soon as a person placed his faith in the Lord Jesus Christ for salvation, the Cross for the Lord Jesus became the Cross for the believer. However, most believers understand only the first aspect of the Cross, that the Lord Jesus died for our sins, and may never experience the liberating truth that they also died and rose with Him.

Dr. Solomon explains a fundamental aspect about living the Christian life.

He writes:

> Attempting to live the Christian life in one own strength is bound to fail since the flesh is in conflict with the Spirit (Gal. 5:17). The end result of this life is one that produces the works of the flesh (Gal. 5:19–21).

So what is the solution? The solution is walking according to the Spirit. How do we get there? Through the process called brokenness. But in order to accept the process of brokenness in our lives we must first realize the bankruptcy of our flesh. This is done only by the Spirit of God.

The author writes:

> The Holy Spirit brings the sinner to a place of conviction about his sinful condition; the *selfer* (one living after the flesh), must realize the destitute condition of his flesh or of living in his own strength.

Then the brokenness process can start in us.

The author explains that:

> Brokenness is a vital part of such realization, and suffering is usually a vital ingredient (Phil. 1:29–30). As the Cross becomes a revealed reality, it is absolutely amazing the things that death will cure! At the time of the exchange, there is generally a prayer of appropriation or relinquishment, at which time the Holy Spirit takes control of the life. At other times, the Holy Spirit does a **sovereign work**, and prayer takes the form of exaltation and exultation afterward.[80]

I wanted to apply what I just learned. So, here is my Prayer sample of *appropriation* or *relinquishment*:

> *Lord, the circumstances leading to my crucifixion were yours. They came not from men, as first I had thought. Father, I accept it all. All... as coming from you.*
>
> *It is from you, my Lord! For my good! This thing is wholly between You and me. There are no others involved in this bloody hour. I do not like this; it is the most difficult thing ever to enter my life. But it is You. I now call You Lord, sovereign Lord. Others meant it to me for evil; Lord you meant it to me for good! I accept this crucifixion! From You!*

Lord, my life ended with Yours on Golgotha. My life began that day
for the same reason. Nothing less could have saved me, nor worked
so much good and so much life into me.
Sincerely Yours,
— Mark

In the book "Exquisite Agony—Healing for Christians who
have been hurt by other Christians," by Gene Edwards, the author
attempts to answer the question: *"Who caused ALL of these things in the*
life of Jesus?", and *"Was the Crucifixion from the hand of God? Or*
mistreatment?"

Edwards, writes masterfully, using the crucifixion of Christ and
His Golgotha, as the frame of reference for our own suffering, many
times at the hands of other Christians.
Edwards writes:

> When you were crucified at the hands of men, in reality
> you but entered into His crucifixion. Consider the
> circumstance which led to His crucifixion. Who caused
> His cross, His crucifixion? Who was it that plotted His
> Golgotha? **It was exactly the same person who plotted**
> **yours.** That person actually desired that you enter into
> your Lord's sufferings. In recent days you have but
> partaken of His loathsome experience. After all, you—the
> believer—are in Him. Who crucified you? The same one
> who crucified your Lord. Inquire of Him as to who
> authored His crucifixion.
>
> Do you hear His response?
> Who crucified Me?
> Who planned My crucifixion?
> My Father.
> It was My Father.

In Edwards opinion, the way we consider our suffering,
determines if IT is *crucifixion* (from the hand of God), or *mistreatment*
(at the hands of other people, including Christians.)
He writes:

162

The Father willed His own Son's crucifixion. And yours. The plan and the executing of that plan was His. He even made sure it would be at the hands of Christians, just as it was the Lord's very own people who crucified Him. A double pain! Hear my words. Refusal to accept your crucifixion as wholly from the hand of God only means you were not *crucified*, you were *mistreated*. Only when you accept that it came from God... only then is it a true crucifixion. **The crucifixion of a Christian comes from the hand of God, and God alone.**[81]

When we willingly accept the crucifixion as coming from God and Him alone, IT, (no matter how painful it is), becomes a holy work of God in our lives: *transformation, destruction of the dark side of us, even resurrection.* Edwards reveals his thoughts about the purpose of Crucifixion.

Edwards writes:

Crucifixions do two things. They *reveal*—and—they *destroy*. The purpose of a crucifixion is to lay naked before the world, men, God, and angels your reaction to being crucified. A crucifixion <u>reveals one's reaction</u> to being crucified. If you become angry, fight back, argue, shout or scream, if you accuse and blame, that is where things will stay. Be sure, that is not a crucifixion. That is simply people being vicious to one another. If you accept that nightmarish ordeal as a sovereign work of God, if you acquiesce to His will. Suddenly it becomes not only a crucifixion but a holy work of God. Things needing destruction begin to be destroyed. Things He desires live on, live on in victory. Receive it as being from Him for your good. For your transformation. For the destruction of the dark side of your person. For resurrection.

Finally we will look at some of Gene Edwards writings regarding our personal Gethsemane.

He writes:

Gethsemane is not a place, nor is it a specific time. For most believers Gethsemane must come after crucifixion.

After all, <u>Gethsemane is simply that hour when you finally align your will with the will of God.</u> It is when you agree, accept, embrace your crucifixion. Some, like the second thief, have to do that after the fact! The thief had to have his Gethsemane while nailed to a cross and breathing his last breath. So might you. Gethsemane is not a when or a where, but **Gethsemane is a must.** Without facing your Gethsemane, the crucifixion you have known will destroy you with no hope of resurrection. Allowing a Gethsemane to come into your life changes all that. **Gethsemane is still a necessity!** The *cross* and *Gethsemane* are inseparably linked. Difficult to grasp, is it not, that such things as Calvary and Gethsemane are still a necessity in your day! Yet, the first time you ever heard the fundamental facts of your faith, you surely noticed the words, "We enter into the sufferings of Christ."

…

When is your time for Gethsemane? <u>The time for your Gethsemane is now!</u> Your Lord had His Gethsemane before He was crucified. The believer, of more frail material, almost inevitably must have his Gethsemane of surrender during or after. Whether it be before or after, it is always agony.[82]

Is the **CROSS** supposed to be central to Christianity and biblical spirituality? Yes or No? Please explain theologically this concept. Please elaborate from your own heart and personal experiences.

The cross is central to Christianity and biblical spirituality. The CROSS had always been God's PLAN. It was predicted, foreshadowed and foretold since the beginning of time. It is the centerpiece of God's redemptive plan for God's creation. Jesus death on the cross, His burial and resurrection provided the means for and continues to bring salvation and transformation to those who accept and follow Christ – *pick up their cross and follow Him.* Paul writes in Philippians 3:10,11, "that I may know Him and the power of His resurrection and the fellowship of His sufferings, being conformed to His death, in order that I may attain to the resurrection from the dead."

Please elaborate why the CROSS and suffering are part of the normal Christian life. Please feel free to use Bible verses, specific quotes from the materials you studied during **Module V**. You can also use ideas and quotes from other sources to sustain your view.

The cross and suffering are part of the normal Christian life. Suffering from the Christian's perspective, referred to in 1 Peter 2:13-21, and Hebrews 2:10-18 pertains to the spiritual formation in the life of Christ's disciples as we come to the cross seeking a metamorphosis to take place inside of us. This is part of the normal Christians life. This suffering is to be expected, and not a surprise as we seek to be remade into the image of Christ, while denying the demands of the flesh.

I like the way Dr. Solomon wrote about suffering: *None of us is greater than his Master, and all must go the way of the cross if we are to have victory in our Christian experience... life must come out of death and victory out of defeat.*"[83]

I like the way Bilheimer puts it: "There is simply no way to explain the biblical teaching on the glory of suffering and tribulation except as an *apprenticeship for the throne*. **No love without suffering, No rulership without love.** Therefore, ONLY if we suffer shall we reign with him."[84]

I would like to introduce to you another resource: "The Blessing of Brokenness," by Charles Stanley. Let's begin by defining Brokenness and what it consists of, and why it is necessary.
Dr. Stanley explains:

> We all know what it means to be broken—to be shattered, to feel as if our entire world has fallen apart, or perhaps been blown apart. We all have times in our lives when we don't want to raise our heads off the pillow, and when we feel certain the tears will never stop flowing. Brokenness is often accompanied by emptiness—a void that cannot be filled, a sorrow that cannot be comforted, a wound for which there is no balm. Nothing feels blessed about being broken. One of the things I have discovered through

being broken, however, is that after brokenness we can experience God's greatest blessings. <u>After brokenness our lives can be the most fruitful and have the most purpose.</u> But this blessing comes only if we experience brokenness fully and confront why it is that God has allowed us to be broken. If we allow God to do His complete work in us, blessing will follow brokenness.[85]

A lot of people in the church are confused about *Chastisement* and *Punishment*. So what's the difference between the two, and how do they apply to the believer?

The author explains:

> **Punishment** is often confused with brokenness. We must be very clear on this point: *Chastisement* and *punishment* are two different things. **Punishment is for unbelievers only.** It is an expression of God's wrath against those who have rejected the only Sin-bearer who can separate a sinful person from God's wrath. God's holiness and purity compel him to move swiftly against sin wherever and in whomever God finds it—just as bright light rushes in to overcome a dark room. God cannot tolerate sin. He must eradicate it from his presence.
>
> <u>**Chastisement** is God's method of disciplining the believer.</u> God's purpose is to lead a believer to confront, remove, or change those habits, attitudes, and beliefs that keep the believer from growing into the full stature of Christ's likeness. <u>Chastisement is a training tool that God uses in making us whole and spiritually mature.</u> It is God's method for preparing us for a supernatural ministry of service under the direction of the Holy Spirit. **Punishment flows from God's wrath**. The end result is eradication, elimination, and total estrangement from God. **Chastisement flows from God's love.** The end result is change, growth, and development.[86]

Next, Stanley, tackles the subject of what it means to be made whole.

He writes:

> When many people think of wholeness, they automatically turn to matters of health, sickness, injury, or death. **Wholeness, however, is a matter of harmony—** *body, soul, and spirit.* It is living in such a way that all facets and aspects of our lives are interrelated in a health—giving, sound, and resilient way. When God breaks us, He does so with the purpose of putting us back together again—better than before, and ultimately, so that we might be whole.
>
> *Wholeness involves all of our being:*
> Let me share several key principles with you about wholeness.
> –First, we must recognize that we have three aspects to our being—*spirit, soul, and body.*
> –The body is the way in which we relate to our environment.
> –We have a soul—a mind, will, emotions, conscience, and consciousness.
> –We also have a spirit—the inner person. With the spirit we relate to almighty God.
> …
> *Wholness is more than Skin Deep:*
> The trouble many people have is that they don't see the spiritual principles involved in the various situations and circumstances they encounter on a daily basis. Even though they have been born again in their spirits, they continue to live—by force of habit and also by force of will—according to old patterns. They see things only on the surface, and they respond to life superficially.
>
> Wholeness may not come quickly or easily, but it is worth the wait!
>
> *Wholeness takes time:*
> When we find ourselves broken, we must be very careful not to attempt to predetermine either the methodology or

the timetable for our own recovery. God will reveal His plan and purpose to us step by step.

Wholeness glorifies God:
In eternity, you and I will be God's trophies. **We are the trophies of His grace**; the trophies of Christ's death, burial, and resurrection; the trophies of the Holy Spirit's work in our lives. Our purpose is to bring Him glory. We often lose sight of the fact that this life is preparation for the life to come. In this life we are going to school. The process is one of learning and growing and developing. It is a process of becoming. And when we yield to God's purposes, the process is one of becoming whole.[87]

In chapter 7, "The Process of Breaking," Dr. Stanley describes it and provide the key aspects involved in this process.
He explains:

Being broken is a very systematic process, from God's point of view. We see only the chaos of brokenness—we feel the pain, confusion, and disorientation. God, however, doesn't react to life's circumstances. He is fully aware of what is happening to us even before it happens, and He works within and through circumstances to accomplish His purposes, God never loses control of the breaking process. The life of the apostle Peter gives us a clear illustration of the principles God uses in breaking a person. Jesus chose Peter for the same reason God chooses you and me—He sees all we can be. He chooses us for our potential to become like Christ. Jesus chose Peter because He believed he had found a man through whom he could work.

The following four key aspects in God's breaking process are applicable not only to Peter's life, but to your life and mine.

1. GOD TARGETS THE AREA.
God targets the area in each one of our lives that needs to be broken. Each of us has strengths and weaknesses. And

very often, God targets what we see as a strength in our lives. Why? Because we are much less prone to submit our strengths to Him. When we become aware of our weaknesses, we turn to God and say, "I'm weak in this area, please be my strength." But for those areas in which we are strong, we say, "Well, I can handle this on my own," We fail to turn to God and seek His help or His control. He will do no less in our lives. God will target the areas that keep us from trusting Him completely and yielding to Him fully.

2. GOD ARRANGES THE CIRCUMSTANCES.

Just as the target area for brokenness is subject to God's will, so are the circumstances that lead to our being broken. God brings about the circumstances of our breaking in two ways. (A) At times, He engineers the situation that will cause us to confront what he desires to change in our lives. (B) At other times, God will simply allow us to follow the pathway of sin that we have chosen. He will give us enough leeway and enough rope so we can entangle ourselves. Whether God brings about the breaking circumstances in our lives or simply allows us to continue to engineer our own breaking circumstances, we eventually come to the place where we are forced to say, "Okay, God. I'll do it your way."

3. GOD CHOOSES THE TOOLS.

God targets the area that needs to be broken. He arranges the circumstances that lead to our breaking. And God chooses the tools with which to break us. We don't like those tools any more than we like the circumstances with which God chooses to break us. We don't choose the tools God uses. He chooses. Just as we can't tell God when to break us, we can't tell Him how to break us. The selection of methods is his business—it's totally beyond our control. I can tell you this with a fair degree of certainty—the tool will be sharp, painful, and unavoidable. You will not be able to escape it. You will be forced to confront the area in your life that needs to be changed. There's simply no way to avoid facing the barrier that stands between you and your total reliance upon God.

4. GOD CONTROLS THE PRESSURE.

Just as God chooses the target, sets up the circumstances, and selects the tools for our brokenness, so He controls the amount of pressure we are under. He knows exactly how much pressure is enough to break us—an amount that varies from person to person. God sets limits on our brokenness. These limits cover both <u>how long</u> the brokenness continues and the <u>amount of pain and suffering</u> we experience. God limits the amount of hurting he will allow you to do. God causes brokenness to come to an end when one of two points is reached.

ONE, brokenness ends when our will is broken and we yield to God in submission.

TWO, brokenness ends when it reaches an intensity when it will damage God's purpose for your life. God will not allow you to be broken or shattered to the point where you cannot engage in the supernatural ministry He has prepared for you. That would be utterly counterproductive. **His purpose is to train you, mold you, refashion you**—*not to destroy you.*[88]

Now we will take a look at the "Preparation To Bear Much Fruit." Much of his teaching is based on John 15:2-5, 8.

The author explains:

God prunes us, and he does so for a very specific purpose—that we might come to the place in our lives where we bear fruit. Fruit in the Scriptures is of two types: (1) inner fruit—qualities of character, and (2) outer fruit—the works that we do that bring glory to God and extend His kingdom.

In the sections called: "Inner Fruit of the Holy Spirit," and "His Work in Us," Dr. Stanley explains how spiritual fruitfulness works in Christians.

He writes:

The inner fruit we are to bear is not fruit that we grow. It is fruit produced in us as we remain fruitful to the Lord Jesus, or, as Jesus said, <u>as we abide in the vine</u>. The closer we walk with the Lord, moment by moment relying upon the power of the Holy Spirit to work in and through our lives, the more we develop this fruit. We can't acquire it in any other way than to walk closely with the Lord, obeying His guidance and direction on a daily basis. **Brokenness is the pruning process that God uses in order to produce inner fruit**—his very likeness. The proper relationship with God is one in which we put ourselves into a position to do His bidding. When we look to God in any other way, we are into idolatry. When we do not seek the presence of God *in us* as much as we desire the things that we want God to do *for us*, we are not worshiping God nearly as much as we are worshiping the provision of God. We are worshipping material things.[89]

Idols? What are you talking about? Are there any idols today? In the section called, "Giving Up Idols," Stanley describes *what* they are and *how* to defuse them.

Charles Stanley writes:

Idolatry can take subtle forms. The last thing we may want to be is idolatrous—only to discover as God breaks us that we have placed too much value on certain possessions or relationships.

When we give up something to which we are clinging and counting as more valuable than our obedience to God, He often gives us something in return that is even far more valuable or beneficial to us. A person can give up the thing he knows God has asked him to give up and still not "give up" that person or thing in his heart. If God has asked you to give up something, give it up! Give it up literally, and give it up in your heart.[90]

Brokenness develops Christlike character. In the section titled: *"God is our all in all,"* Stanley describes Christlike character and the fruit of the Spirit that is developed in us.

The author writes:

> Brokenness brings us to the place where we say, *"All that matters is God and his presence in my life."* At that point we are in submission. We are desiring from God the production of inner fruit in us, not outer fruit that we can show our friends, brag about, or display as status symbols. God's greatest blessings to us are inner blessings, and foremost among them is the blessing of Christlike character, God's breaking us is aimed at bringing us to the point where we awaken with God's purposes in mind. Our prayer must become, *"What is it that you want me to do, say, and be today in order to bring you glory?"*

The fruit of the Spirit described by the apostle Paul (in the book of Galatians) is a description of the character of Jesus Christ. He is the One we are becoming like. His character is marked by:

LOVE. Sacrificial love is the hallmark of Christ's character.

JOY. A person who has not had the death grip of sin broken in his or her life cannot experience true joy each time we are broken by God, sin is defeated in our lives, and joy is the outcome. People who are genuinely broken by God know great joy.

PEACE. Brokenness produces the peace of Christ—a peace pervasive in one's personality. We are trusting him solely and fully. The result is peace. We don't have to strive anymore.

PATIENCE. When we compete with others—seeking to achieve our own glory and doing so at the expense of others—then we are not patient with them. Rather, we are "making it happen," the sooner the better. When God breaks us, we realize anew that our timetable and our definition of success are not His timetable or His definition.

KINDNESS. When we are in bondage to the desires of the flesh, rather than the desires of the Spirit, we insist on having our own way. <u>Brokenness brings us to the place</u>

where we realize we have no rights. All of our rights are turned over to God. Competitiveness is stripped away from us. When we know with certainty that our battle is not with people, but with the enemy of their souls the evil one who is the motivator and instigator of their evil toward us, we find it much easier to be kind to other people.

GOODNESS. Brokenness brings us to the place where we know that the only goodness we have in us is because the Holy Spirit lives in us. God alone is good... and God is in us and with us. His presence in us gives us the desire to do good works, make good decisions, and come up with good solutions because His very nature is good.

FAITHFULNESS. Brokenness brings us to the place where we say, "I am truly yours, Lord, and nobody else has a claim on my eternal spirit. You alone are God." That is a position of genuine unwavering faithfulness.

GENTLENESS. Brokenness brings us to the place where we are able to be gracious and gentle with others because we recognize that God has been gracious and gentle with us. We can trust others to have their needs met by God, and we can enter into a healthy relationship with other people that builds up rather than drains dry.

SELF-CONTROL. When we turn total control over to God, he gives us back self-control---that is, his ability to say no to Satan's temptations. We have the capacity to resist evil, a capacity that an unsaved person does not have.[91]

Finally, in the section called, "The Outer Fruit Of God's Inner Presence," Stanley explains how brokenness helps us redefines the concept of fruitfulness.

He writes:

Brokenness brings us to the place where we redefine the fruitfulness of our witness. The outer fruit that God calls us to produce is to declare his truth and to meet the needs of those who come across our path. We are to be ready witnesses to his love and power:

Let them do good, that that they be rich in good works, ready to give, willing to share. (1 Timothy 6:18)
Always be prepared to give an answer to everyone who asks you to give the reason for the hope that you have. (1 Peter 3:15)

The main purpose of the activities that we call "Christian disciplines"—praying, reading and studying the Bible, attending church regularly—is so that we might know what to say when a need arises and be motivated immediately to take action when we see someone who requires our assistance. Again, the reason for brokenness is so that we might realize that the life we live is no longer our life. It is Jesus' life. We must surrender on a daily basis to the life that he desires to live through us. We must be willing to be broken so that we might bear much fruit. The way to the blessing of a new character---that of the Lord Jesus Christ himself---and of a new power in your personal ministry and service to others is going to be a path that involves brokenness. God has no other plan for us. Brokenness is his way to blessing.[92]

What is the correlation between the work of the *cross* and *spiritual formation* in the life of the disciples of Christ. Please elaborate based on what Charles Stanley and Charles Solomon suggested. Please use Bible verses and quotes from the materials you studied or from other materials.

Since the cross and suffering are part of the normal Christian life, we can declare that there is a tight correlation <u>between the work of the cross</u> and <u>the spiritual formation</u> in the life of Christ's disciples. **In fact, spiritually speaking, there is no such thing as a genuine disciple without the cross.** Those disciples who willingly embrace the cross in his or her life, experience the deepest meanings and blessings. Dr. Solomon, writes: "Assuming that we remain yielded to God's processing and shaping, the length of time depends on the way He plans to use our lives **for/to** His glory. We cannot effectively share with those who suffer if we ourselves have never suffered (2 Corinthians 1:3-4). Our suffering is a time of learning and training for future usefulness."[93]

174

Once we realize that suffering is part of the normal Christian life, then we yield to the work of the Father in our lives. Dr. Stanley writes: "In choosing to be fashioned by God, we inevitably must choose to yield to brokenness and to allow God to remake us and renew us as He desires – even if that means suffering pain, hardship, and trials.[94]

How are we–*the disciples of Christ*, supposed to embrace the **CROSS** in our lives? Please elaborate on, the *meanings*, the *depths*, and the *blessings* of embracing the cross in our lives.

The great apostle Paul, is such a good example for all of us. He freely invites the work of the cross into his life.
He writes:

> That I may know Him and the power of His resurrection and the fellowship of His sufferings, being conformed to His death, in order that I may attain to the resurrection from the dead. (Philippians 3:10-11)

May the Holy Spirit compels us to follow in his footsteps.

As we willingly and freely embrace the cross in our lives, the life of Christ is made available to indwell, re-create and empower the disciple of Christ. As we willingly allow the death of the natural man or flesh, the indwelling life may be progressively manifest in us.

In his book, "Don't Waste Your Sorrows," Paul E. Billheimer, answers the question, "**why does a saint suffer?**"
He explains:

> But why should the righteous suffer? Why isn't every believer healed, and healed immediately? Why isn't he "carried to the skies on flowery beds of ease"? Why must he "fight to win the prize and sail through bloody seas"? It is difficult for most people to understand why sorrow comes to a saint. That is one of the mysteries of the ages. However, regardless of the mystery involved, we know that God is love and that, according to 2 Corinthians

4:17–18, He permits suffering to the saint only to work (create) for him an "eternal weight of glory." No one ever becomes a saint without suffering because <u>suffering, properly accepted, is the pathway to glory.</u>[95]

In chapter 5, "The Mystery Of Suffering," Billheimer explains more fully about the suffering in the life of God's saints.
He writes:

> God is calling and preparing an Eternal Companion called the Bride, who is to sit with His Son on His throne as His co-regent in the ages to come (Rev. 3:21). In order to qualify for this exalted position the members of the Bridehood must be as nearly like the Son as it is possible for the finite to be like the infinite. But as we have seen, <u>that quality of character cannot be developed in fallen humanity without suffering</u>. This explains Paul's inspired revelation: "If we suffer, we shall also reign with Him" (2 Tim.2:12). According to Romans 5:3–5 suffering issues in character (agape love), and character is a prerequisite to rulership. **Because there is no character development without suffering, suffering is a necessary preparation for rulership.**
>
> …
>
> Progress in sanctification, in the development of Godlike character and agape love, is impossible without tribulation and chastisement. "Not only so, but we also rejoice in our sufferings, because we know that suffering produces perseverance; perseverance, character; and character, hope. And hope does not disappoint us, because God has poured out His love into our hearts by the Holy Spirit, whom He has given us" (Rom. 5:3–5). "My son, don't be angry when the Lord punishes you. Don't be discouraged when he has to show you where you are wrong. For when he punishes you, it proves that he loves you.

Chastisement and Child Training

It is clear from the foregoing and other similar passages of Scripture that *sorrow, suffering, tribulation,* and *pain* which come to the believer are not primarily for punishment but for child training.They are not purposeless. Earthly parents may make mistakes in their chastisement—and often do. But not God. He is preparing the believer for rulership in a universe so vast that it appears infinite. It seems that God cannot fully decentralize fallen man, even though born again, sanctified or filled with the Holy Spirit, without suffering. Watchman Nee says that *we never learn anything new about God except through adversity.*

...

The fact that Christ's human experience had to be perfected by suffering proves that no suffering is purposeless, but that is endemic in God's economy.

The importance of Brokenness and Character

There is no way that Christlike character can be formed in man without suffering because he cannot be decentralized otherwise. If he will not suffer, if he determines to evade it, if he refuses to allow the life of nature and of self to go to the cross, to that extent he will remain hard, self-centered, unbroken, and therefore unChristlike. "Whole, unbruised, unbroken men are of little use to God" (J.R. Miller).

...

There can be no spiritual progress, therefore, except through the progressive death of the self-life. Maclaren has said that every step on the pathway of spiritual progress will be marked by the bloody footprints of wounded self-love. To make the moral choices that develop Godlike character always causes pain because even after one has been sanctified, filled with the Holy Spirit, one is still fallen. **The work of sanctification is both *instantaneous* and *progressive.*** It will continue until glorification. Suffering triumphantly accepted, slays the self-life, delivers one from self-centeredness, and frees one to love. Those who have thus suffered will form the elite, the aristocracy, the ruling nobility of the future. They will constitute the princes of the ethereal realm. In order to grow in character it is necessary to understand that nothing that God permits to come to His child, whether "good" or "ill," is accidental or without design. Everything is intended to drive him out of himself into God. "All life is intended to be a pathway to God" (Maclaren). All is for the purpose of character training. There are no exceptions.[96]

Then, in Chapter 7 "The Great Business Of Life—Learning Agape Love," Billheimer describes how God uses our life to teach us agape love.
He explains:

> Maybe God cannot get some of the rare saints He needs for certain exclusive and highly specialized vocations in His eternal kingdom any other way than by permitting them to suffer catastrophic losses, sorrow, and pain. **Those who are not healed may not need to accept second class citizenship after all**, <u>but may be nominated for enhanced rank and eternal glory</u>.
> …
> God Himself specifically chooses the tools and instruments which He knows are needed to fashion and qualify His Bride for the unique sphere of her operation and service in the eternal kingdom. Someone has said that the turning lathe that has the sharpest knives produces the finest work. When God makes a saint, He uses the sharpest knives on His turning lathe as well. He cannot shape one without pain, but He never uses needless pain.[97]

In "Preparing the kingdom—God's Full-time Occupation," Billheimer teaches us that God is intentional about getting us ready for His eternal Kingdom.
The author continues:

> There is no sense to sentiments like these unless God is working in us for eternity. Except for the preparation of her many-mansion home (John 14:2–3), training the Bride for the throne is His sole occupation. No other cosmology makes sense or harmonizes with the Word

(Rom. 8:28). Preparing the kingdom for her and her for the kingdom is His full-time occupation. All that He does until the Marriage Supper of the Lamb is concentrated upon this. Thus, when sorrow or suffering come, one may know that it is not accidental or uncontrolled. It is meant to be that way and is intended for one's eternal welfare, promotion, and glory. When a born-again person understands who he is and what God's purpose for him is, then he can better comprehend why God takes such infinite pains with him. He is God's very own beloved child (1 John 3:2).

...

But only redeemed humanity are members of God's own household and family (Eph. 2:19). This is the reason why His care is so minute that the very hairs of one's head are numbered. This, and this alone, explains the universe. It is the only cosmology that makes sense. All of the vast physical universe with its countless rolling orbs is not intrinsically important. All derive their value from their relationship to God's plan and purpose for His genetic family. Whatever God does, anywhere in His infinite universe, is not done merely as a manifestation of His power, nor for the sake of the inhabitants of outer space, nor for the angelic hosts, <u>but for the sake of His very own generic family</u>, members of His own household.[98]

Then it comes a very intriguing chapter, called, "A Mind-boggling Cosmology."
Billhimer writes:

This cosmology boggles the human mind—but unless the words of Scripture are meaningless, it is the only valid explanation of the universe. "Eye hath not seen, nor ear heard, neither have entered into the heart of man, the things which God hath prepared for them that love him" (1 Cor. 2:9).

...

It was this kind of faith that inspired J. R. Miller to write: **"Whole, unbruised, unbroken men are of little use to God."** They are of little use because they are deficient in

agape love. Miller says that agape love has to be learned—
and that is the great business of life because the law of
love is the supreme law of eternity. All the circumstances
of this life are arranged for this one purpose: *to enable one
to learn agape love in order to be qualified to administer the law of
love in eternity.*[99]

Then, in "The Great Business of life," the author explains
quoting George D. Watson, that "The Lame Take the Pray."
He writes:

> God uses for His glory those people and things which are
> most perfectly broken . . . . Those who are broken in
> wealth, broken in self-will, broken in their ambitions,
> broken in their beautiful ideals, broken in worldly
> reputation, broken in their affections, broken oft-times in
> health, those who are despised and seem utterly forlorn
> and helpless, these are the ones the Holy Ghost is seizing
> upon and using for God's glory. *"The lame take the prey"*
> (Isa. 33:23).
> ...
> This is utterly contrary to modern psychology. It makes
> no sense apart from the Apostle Paul's cosmology which
> understands that the unseen is the real and that time is
> only the vestibule of eternity. To function in that social
> order one must be decentralized. <u>This requires
> brokenness, which, properly accepted, secures utter
> deliverance from self-regard and is the basis of agape love.</u>
> Calvary love, the love that took Christ to the cross, is the
> supreme qualification for rulership in the new order of
> things to come.[100]

Brokenness, and its applications are further explained by
Billheimer.
He writes:

> One is not broken until all resentment and rebellion
> against God and man is removed. One who resents, takes
> offense, or retaliates against criticism and opposition or
> lack of appreciation is unbroken... Genuine brokenness

usually requires years of crushing, heartache, and sorrow. Thus are self-will surrendered and deep degrees of yieldedness and submission developed, without which there is little agape love.

…

Therefore before God can release His own power to meet one's crisis need, He must bring that person to the end of himself. Until one is broken, he is full of himself, his plans, his ambitions, his value judgments.

…

There are a multitude of things which are not sinful; nevertheless our attachment to them prevents our greatest fullness of the Holy Spirit and our amplest co-operation with God.

…

In contradistinction to heart cleansing, this finer crucifixion of self is gradual; it extends through months and years; the interior spirit is mortified over and over on the same points, till it reaches a state of divine indifference to it. A great host of believers have obtained heart purity, and yet for a long time have gone through all sorts of "dying daily" to self, before they found that calm, fixed union with the Holy Ghost which is the deep longing of the child of God. Again in contradistinction to heart cleansing, which is by faith, **this deeper death to self is by suffering**, this is abundantly taught in Scripture, and confirmed by the furnace experiences of thousands.[101]

I appreciate the fact that Billheimer explains the mystery of suffering.
He writes:

But God is not interested in brokenness primarily for its temporal value, great as that may be. His Bride elect is in training for the throne. She is in the school of suffering to learn agape love to qualify her for rulership in an economy where the law of love is supreme. This is why God is willing to take a lifetime to teach her love. There is simply no way to explain the Biblical teaching on the glory of suffering and tribulation, except as an apprenticeship for the throne. **No love without suffering. No rulership without love. Therefore, ONLY if we suffer shall we reign with Him.**

Believers are living stones (A.N. Hodgkin), in Christ in All the Scriptures, says, "All true believers in all ages are the living stones in that heavenly Temple, and God is preparing them in His quarry down here, amid the noise and tumult of earth, each for his place in His Temple above. Hodgkin points out that when they are removed from the quarry, the stones are rugged and shapeless. Quarry stones are insensitive but the "living stones" with which God is working are not. **This means that God cannot shape without pain.** Where there is no pain, no shaping is achieved. The tools He must use are sharp and abrasive Quarry stones cannot resist but the "living stones" may. When they do, their sorrow and pain is wasted.[102]

In Chapter 10, "Learning Agape Love Through Wrongful Suffering," Billheimer shows us why this is necessary.

He begins with these thoughts:

> If all born-again believers are in apprenticeship for rulership, and if a lofty dimension of agape love is the supreme qualification for high rank and authority in that eternal social order toward which the universe is moving, and if a high dimension of agape love cannot be achieved without suffering, could this explain why God permits many who seek healing to suffer on, even for a lifetime? If, because of the apparent evil that has come, one allows himself to fall into an attitude of self-pity, frustration, and rebellion toward people and God, his character deteriorates and he is wasting his sorrow.
>
> …
>
> But when one accepts the advice of the Apostle James, everything is different. "Consider it pure joy, my brothers, whenever you face trials of many kinds, because you know that the testing of your faith develops perseverance. Perseverance must finish its work so that you may be

mature and complete, not lacking anything" (James 1:2-
4).[103]

What are the benefits and correct thinking when it comes to
suffering?

Paul Billhimer explains:

> Rank in heaven will be determined not by magnetic
> personality, glittering talents, towering intellect, or other
> coveted endowments, but by the depth and quality of
> one's love. Earth, with its sorrow, heartbreak,
> disappointments and pain, is the only place, and this life
> is the only time, when this love can be developed. This
> love is the coin, currency, and legal tender of heaven. This
> is why God has to take many of us through refining fires,
> why many must be "battered with the shocks of doom"
> until they are bruised, broken, and made utterly empty of
> themselves. To accept criticism sweetly, without
> retaliation or resentment, is an evidence of growth in love.
> This is one reason why Jesus said to "love your
> enemies"—because they afford one the opportunity to
> grow in **agape love**, the insignia of rank in eternity (Matt.
> 5:44–48).

Billheimer describes how "on the job" training perfects and
increases one's love.

He writes:

> God is using one's temporal circumstances, personality
> clashes, personal hostilities, unjust criticism, financial
> reverses, poverty, physical affliction, frailty, pain, and
> even old age as "on-the-job" training for the exercise and
> development of agape love. None of the things, not even
> the worst things, that come to a child are ever accidental.
> They are controlled experiments intended to give him
> opportunity to exercise and learn agape love. No one in
> his right mind would count it a privilege to suffer
> wrongfully unless he sees it as an opportunity to increase
> his rank in the eternal kingdom.

This is not the devil's world as Billheimer continues:

> This is not a world of chance—there is no chance anywhere. This is not the devil's world. All the universe is under the Father's personal sway. Our adversary is a created being under God's control.
>
> The divine hand is active in all the affairs of the earth. God is using Satan for His own purposes to teach the Bride-elect the technique of overcoming (Rev. 3:21) and a deeper dimension of agape love.

Then, in Chapter 11, "Learning Agape Love Through Life's Failures," the author explains:

> God will go to any length to mold and mature one in agape love. He considers no price too great because He knows the glory that is ahead.
>
> …
>
> In one of his books, J.R.Miller has expressed this faith beautifully thus: "We do not know how much we owe to suffering. Many of the richest blessings that have come down to us from the past are the fruit of sorrow and pain." In another place Dr. Miller has said, "The world's greatest blessings have come out of its greatest sorrows.[104]

Billheimer clarifies the eternal role of the Bride-elect. He writes:

> Because God plans to use the Church, the Bride-elect, in eternity to express His love-nature to the principalities and powers, to all the intelligences of the universe, this is doubtless a principal reason He takes such pains to teach her individual members deep dimensions of agape love. The church is so close to the seat of supreme authority that she is a part of it as His body and is to be enthroned with Him. Therefore, God will go to any length necessary to prepare the individual members for their exalted positions.

How can failure be a success? Only in God's economy, as explained by Billhimer, it can be.

He writes:

> Sometimes, to suffer failure is the only way one can be decentralized. If failure works better than success to prepare a man for rulership, you can be sure that God loves him too well to shield him at the expense of his "eternal weight of glory." God seems to endorse the theme, "The worker rather than the work," because God has eternal values in view. Oswald Chambers says: "Why shouldn't we go through heartbreaks? . . . If through a broken heart God can bring His purposes to pass in the world, then thank Him for breaking your hearts. How many of us have mixed motives of which we are totally unaware until God permits purifying adversity. That "demon within us" is vain ambition, human energy, and uncrucified flesh. God will go to any length to exercise it, even to the extent of allowing failure to an apparently spiritual work. (1 Cor. 3:10–15). Only after a mighty breaking may some of us see our fault. It may take a lifetime for God to disillusion us with success, purify our motives, and mature us in agape love. He may feel that, for him, life has been a monumental failure. But from God's standpoint, if one has learned love, there would be no point in living life over again because the real purpose of life has been achieved. When one has learned love, he has succeeded in life no matter how he has failed otherwise. If all the failures in learning love in the past have at last produced this brokenness of spirit, that life has been no failure in God's sight because it was for this He was working. This is what God was after from the beginning, because agape love is essential for rulership in God's eternal social order. **Success at the cost of love is failure.** Winning at the cost of love is losing, LOVE NEVER FAILS.[105]

If you would be required to teach others this module, **please provide a *written plan* how you would do it.**

I would not change anything in the way this module was taught. I feel it is complete the way it is taught and the content is complete.

6. Identity—Knowing Who we are in Christ— The Key to Spiritual Victory

In a few paragraphs please provide an overall evaluation of **Module VI.** Please explain what you liked the most about this important module. Explain also what you disliked the most about this module. **How do you suggest we can make Module VI even more helpful and appealing for future disciples/students?**

Module VI took the time to have the student or disciple take as from a distance, a birds eye view of man in relation to God from His creation to the present. **Who we are in Christ?** This began with what man is; The fall and it's effects; born again, what it means, and it's benefits; <u>and finally</u> **who you are in Christ** – your spiritual identity.

We can't move forward until we know where we came from and who we are. Once again this module is a bedrock of importance. The way it is presented, extracted and set apart from all the other modules lead you to realize the importance of it in this series of modules.

Again the authors used; Needham and Anderson especially, were top notch picks in clearly explaining **who man is** from creation and the fall to being born again. All backed and supported with Scripture, I could not think of a better or more effective way for this segment of teaching.

What happened, spiritually speaking, in the Garden of Eden with our ancestors—*Adam and Eve*? Please explain (as Neil T. Anderson suggested) the effects of the Fall.

What happened, spiritually speaking, in the Garden of Eden with our ancestors Adam and Eve? What had been an intimate, meaningful, **innocent communion with God** and each other ended there at the eating of the tree of knowledge. They were now alienated from the life of God. "God warned Adam and Eve that if they ate of the tree of knowledge they would surely die" (Genesis 2:17).

Anderson writes:

> **They died.** Their union with God was severed and they were separated from God they ate and they died they died spiritually, they were separated from God's presence. Just as we inherited physical life from our first parents, *so we have inherited spiritual death from them.*" (Romans 5:12, I Corinthians 15:21-22)[106]

The Fall of Adam and Eve introduced a series of effects which continues to influence the entire humanity. Dr. Anderson explains that, according to the Bible (1 Corinthians 2:14–3:3), there are three types of beings or persons:

– *The Natural Person*
– *The Spiritual Person,* and
– *The Fleshly Person*

Each of these persons have their unique characteristics. Anderson writes:

Characteristics of the Natural Person:

Flesh—Romans 8:8
Inferiority, Insecurity, Inadequacy, Guilt, Worry, Doubts
Mind:
Obsessive thoughts, Fantasy, etc.
Will—Galatians 5:16–21—Walk after the flesh
Immorality, Jealousy, Impurity, Disputes, Sensuality, Dissensions, Idolatry, Factions, Sorcery, Envying, Enmities, Drunkenness, Strife, Carousing, Outbursts of anger

Body:
Tension or migraine headaches, Nervous stomach,
Hives, Skin rashes, Allergies, Asthma, Some arthritis,
Spastic colon, Heart palpitations, Respiratory ailments,
etc.

Emotions:
Bitterness, Anxiety, Depression, etc.

Spirit—Ephesians 2:1–3)—Dead to God
Unable to fulfill the purpose for which he was created,
Lacking life from God, sin is inevitable.

Then he goes on explaining various aspects from epistles
(Ephesians, Galatians, etc.).
He writes:

Ephesians 2:1–3 contains a concise description of the
natural person Paul identified in 1 Corinthians 2:14. This
person is spiritually dead, separated from God. Living
completely independent from God, the natural person
sins as a matter of course. The natural man has a soul, in
that he can think, feel and choose. However, his mind,
and subsequently his emotions and his will, are directed
by his flesh, which acts completely apart from the God
who created him. The natural man may think he is free to
choose his behavior. Because he lives in the flesh,
however, he invariably walks according to the flesh and
his choices reflect the "deeds of the flesh" listed in
Galatians 5:19–21. Living in a stressful age and having no
spiritual base for coping with life or making positive
choices, the natural person may fall victim to one or more
of the physical ailments. Medical doctors tell us that more
than 50 percent of the population is physically sick for
psychosomatic reasons. Possessing peace of mind and the
calm assurance of God's presence in our lives positively
affects our physical health. "He who raised Christ Jesus
from the dead will also give life to your mortal bodies
through His Spirit who indwells you" (Rom. 8:11). The
natural person's actions, reactions, habits, memories and

responses are all governed by the flesh. "Whatever is not from faith is sin" (Rom. 14:23). The natural person cannot help but struggle with feelings of inferiority, insecurity, inadequacy, guilt, worry and doubt.[107]

THE SPIRITUAL PERSON and the effects

FLESH (Romans 8:8)
The crucifying of the flesh is the believer's responsibility on day by day basis as he considers himself dead to sin.
MIND
Transformed (Rom. 12:2), Single-minded, Girded for action.
WILL (Gal. 5:22, 23)
Walk after the Spirit, love, joy, peace, patience, kindness, goodness, faithfulness, gentleness, and self-control.
BODY (1 Cor. 6:19, 20)
Temple of God, Present as a living and holy sacrifice (Rom. 12:1)
EMOTIONS
Peace (Col. 3:15), Joy (Phil. 4:4).
SPIRIT (Rom. 8:9)
Salvation (John 3:3; 1 John 3:9), Forgiveness (Acts 2:38; Heb. 8:12), Assurance (Rom. 8:16)
Security (Eph. 1:13,14), Acceptance (1 John 3:1), Worth

Then the author explains more about the spiritual person.
He writes:

The spiritual man also has a body, soul and spirit. Yet this individual has been remarkably transformed from the natural person he was before spiritual birth. At conversion, his spirit became united with God's Spirit. The spiritual life that resulted from this union is characterized by forgiveness of sin, acceptance in God's family and a positive sense of worth.
The soul of the spiritual man also reflects a change generated by spiritual birth. He now receives his impetus from the Spirit, not from the flesh. His mind has been

190

renewed and transformed. His emotions are characterized by peace and joy instead of turmoil. He is also free to choose not to walk according to the flesh, but to walk according to the Spirit. As the spiritual man exercises his choice to live in the Spirit, his life exhibits the fruit of the Spirit (Gal. 5:22–23).

The body of the spiritual person has also been transformed. It is now the dwelling place for the Holy Spirit and is being offered as a living sacrifice of worship and service to God.

The flesh, conditioned to live independently from God under the old self, is still present in the spiritual man, but he responsibly crucifies the flesh and its desires daily as he considers himself alive in Christ and dead to sin. "That all looks and sounds great," you may say. "But I'm a Christian and I still have some problems. I know I'm spiritually alive, but sometimes my mind dwells on the wrong kinds of thoughts. Sometimes I give in to behavior from the wrong list: the deeds of the flesh instead of the fruit of the Spirit. Sometimes I entertain the desires of the flesh instead of crucifying them." The description of the spiritual person is the ideal. It is the model of maturity toward which we are all growing. God has made every provision for us to experience personally the description of the spiritual person in His Word (2 Peter 1:3). However, most of us live somewhere on the slope between this mountaintop of spiritual maturity and the depths of fleshly behavior. As you walk according to the Spirit, be assured that your growth, maturity and sanctification toward the ideal model are in process.[108]

THE FLESHLY PERSON and its effects

FLESH (Rom. 8:8)
The ingrained habit patterns still appeal to the mind to live independently of God.
MIND
Double-minded
WILL (Gal. 5:16-23)

Immorality, impurity, sensuality, idolatry, sorcery, enmities, strife, jealousy, outbursts of anger, disputes, dissensions, factions, envying, drunkenness, carousing.
BODY
Tension or migraine headaches, Hives, Skin rashes, Allergies, Asthma, Some arthritis, Spastic colon, Heart palpitations, Respiratory ailments, etc.
EMOTIONS
Unstable
SPIRIT (Rom. 8:9)
Alive but Quenched (1 Thess. 5:19), Walk after the Spirit (seldom). Love, joy, peace, patience, kindness, goodness, faithfulness, gentleness, self-control.

Then Dr. Anderson, goes on explaining more aspects about the fleshly person.
He writes:

... the spirit of the fleshly person is identical to that of the spiritual person. The fleshly person is a Christian, spiritually alive in Christ and declared righteous by God; but that is where the similarity ends. **Instead of being directed by the Spirit, this believing man chooses to follow the impulses of his flesh.** As a result, his mind is occupied by carnal thoughts and his emotions are plagued by negative feelings. Though he is free to choose to walk after the Spirit and produce the fruit of the Spirit, he continues to involve himself in sinful activity by willfully walking after the flesh. The fleshly man's physical body is a temple of God, but it is being defiled. He often exhibits the same troubling physical symptoms experienced by the natural person because he is not operating in the manner God created him to operate. **He is not presenting his body to God as a living sacrifice, but indulging his physical appetites at the whim of his sin-trained flesh.** Because he is yielding to the flesh instead of crucifying it, the fleshly man is also subject to feelings of inferiority, insecurity, inadequacy, guilt, worry and doubt. It is evident to me that a staggering number of believers don't know how to live their lives by faith in the power of

the Holy Spirit. Are you struggling with feelings of
inferiority? To whom or to what are you inferior? You are
a child of God seated with Christ in the heavenlies (Eph.
2:6). Do you feel insecure? Your God will never leave you
nor forsake you (Heb.13:5). Inadequate? You can do all
things through Christ who strengthens you (Phil. 4:13).
Guilty? There is no condemnation for those who are in
Christ (Rom. 8:1). Worried? You can have the peace of
God and learn to cast your anxiety upon Christ (John
14:27; Phil. 4:6; 1 Peter 5:7). Doubt? God provides
wisdom for the asking (Jas. 1:5).[109]

In Chapter 6, *"The Power of Believing the Truth,"* the topic of faith
is discussed. The importance of faith in the Christian life, and it's
connection to it's object. Anderson writes:

Believing who God is, what He says and what He does is
the key to the kingdom of God. Consider how important
the concept of faith is. You are saved by faith (Eph. 2:8,
9), and you "walk by faith, not by sight" (2 Cor. 5:7). **In
other words, faith is the basis for our salvation and
the means by which we live.** If we are going to continue
living free in Christ, we need to keep in mind three simple
faith concepts. The truth is, everyone lives by faith. The
only difference between Christian faith and non-Christian
faith is the object of our faith. The critical issue is what
you believe or who you believe in.
…
Telling people to live by faith is invalid if they have no
understanding of the object of their faith. You can't have
faith in faith. Faith has no validity without an object. The
truth is, we live every moment of every day by faith.
However, some of our faith objects are valid but others
aren't. We trust people or things that have proven to be
reliable over a long time period. What happens when the
object of your faith proves unreliable? Once faith is lost,
it is very difficult to regain. Your ability to believe isn't the
problem; it is the object of your faith that has proven to
be untrustworthy. One act of unfaithfulness can all but
destroy a marriage. You can forgive your spouse and

commit yourself to make the marriage work, but it will take months and years to gain back the trust that was lost. You would be foolish to trust someone or something that has proven to be unreliable. The most accepted faith object by the world's population is the fixed order of the universe, primarily the solar system.

...

So far the laws governing the physical universe have been among the most trustworthy faith objects we have. The ultimate faith object, of course, is not the sun, but the Son, because "Jesus Christ is the same yesterday and today, yes and forever" (Heb. 13:8). The fact that God is immutable is what makes Him eminently trustworthy (Num. 23:19; Mal. 3:6). God cannot change, nor can His Word. "The grass withers, the flower fades, but the word of our God stands forever" (Isa. 40:8). This eternal consistency is why God is faithful and why we can put our trust in Him.

How well you know the object of Your faith is directly related to how much faith you have.
Anderson continues:

When people struggle with their faith in God, it is not because their faith object has failed or is insufficient. It is because they don't have a true knowledge of God and His ways. They expect Him to respond in a certain way or answer prayer a certain way—their way, not His—and when He doesn't comply they say, "Forget you, God." The problem is not with God. He is the perfect faith object. **Faith in God fails only when people have a faulty understanding of Him.** If you want your faith in God to increase, you must increase your knowledge of God. If you have little knowledge about God and His Word, you will have little faith. You can believe because belief is a choice we all have to make. Any attempt to push yourself beyond what you know to be true about God and His ways is to move from faith to presumption. You choose to believe God according to what you know to be true from His Word (Rom. 10:17). **The only limit to your faith is your knowledge and understanding of**

God, which grows every time you read your Bible, memorize a Scripture verse, participate in a Bible study or meditate on His Word. It is important to know that God is under no obligation to humankind. We can't maneuver or manipulate God through prayer. He is under obligation to Himself and to remain faithful to His covenant promises and His Word. We have a covenant relationship with God that we can count on being true. Believing doesn't make God's Word true. His Word is true; therefore we believe it.

Let me illustrate how our faith grows. When my son, Karl, was a toddler, I would stand him up on the table and encourage him to jump from the table into my arms. He would waver in unbelief for a moment and then fall into my arms. He would waver in unbelief for a moment and then fall into my arms. Then I would stand back a little bit farther, which made the step of faith a little bit bigger. Then one day I took him outside and put him on the limb of a tree and encouraged him to jump. This was a greater leap of faith, but he did it. As he continues to climb the tree of life, however, can I always be the ultimate object of his faith? The ultimate object of their faith changes when they become children of God. I can't go everywhere my children go, but God can and He does.

Faith and action. Anderson explains and makes the connection between faith and our action.

He writes:

> When I was encouraging Karl to take a step of faith, did he believe I would catch him? Yes. How did I know he believed? Because he jumped. Suppose he wouldn't jump. Suppose I asked Karl, "Do you believe I will catch you, Karl?" and he answered, "Yes," but never jumped. Does Karl really believe I will catch him if he doesn't jump? According to James, that is just wishful thinking. He says, "Faith, if it has no works, is dead, being by itself. But someone may well say, "you have faith, and I have works; show me your faith without the works, and I will show you my faith by my works"" (Jas. 2:17, 18). In other

words, really believing will affect one's walk and one's talk. If we believe God and His Word, we will live accordingly. Everything we do is essentially a product of what we have chosen to believe.

It is important for us—believers, to know the object of our faith—God. The next step is to put action to our faith; this is the only proof that we indeed believe. Just saying that we believe *this* or *that* from the Bible and do nothing about is not real faith. Equally important is to pay close attention to various movements out there which are borderline to the Christian faith, like Positive Confession, or even opposite to it, like, New Age movement. In the section called: *"Distortions of Faith,"*
Neil Anderson explains:

> Faith without action is one distortion, but the New Age and Positive Confession movements offer two other distortions of what it means to biblically believe. The New Age belief says, "If you believe hard enough, it will become true." Christianity says, *"It is true; therefore we believe it."* **Believing something doesn't make it true and not believing something doesn't make it false.** The Positive Confession movement has another interpretation of faith that is partially true. Consider the words of Jesus in Matthew 17:20: "Because of the littleness of your faith; for truly I say to you, if you have faith as a mustard seed, you shall say to this mountain, "move from here to there," and it shall move; and nothing shall be impossible to you." The Positive Confession movement correctly points out that the mountain doesn't move until you say it. But the Positive Confession reaching becomes distorted when one thinks the mountain has to move simply because one says it. Taking the Positive Confession idea too far borders on New Age thinking, which says we can create reality with our minds. To do that, we would have to be gods, and that is exactly what the New Agers are teaching. The New Agers want us to believe we are God, and the *"name it and claim it"* proponents want us to act as though we are God. **God wants His children to believe Him and live accordingly.** Those distortions often arise when

the church is not living up to its potential. Consequently, many people think the church is an infirmary where sick people go. The church is not an infirmary; it is a military outpost under orders to storm the gates of hell. Thankfully, the church has an infirmary that ministers to the weak and the wounded, but the infirmary exists only for the purpose of the military outpost. Our real calling is to be change agents in the world, taking a stand, living by faith and fulfilling our purpose for being here. The world understands the problem of unbelief. It stresses the power of positive thinking, which is illustrated in the following poem:

If You Believe You Can, You Can

If you think you are beaten—you are
If you think you dare not—you don't.
If you want to win but think you can't,
It is almost a cinch you won't.
If you think you'll lose—you've lost.
For out of the world we find
That success begins with a fellow's will;
It's all in the state of mind.
Life's battles don't always go
To the stronger or the faster man;
But sooner or later the man that wins
Is the one who thinks he can.

There is power in the truth coming from God. If we believe the truth and act upon it we can live victorious lives. Anderson writes:

Consider what the world has accomplished just by believing in itself. How much could we accomplish if we really believed in God? We are not called to just think positive thoughts. **We are called to think the truth.** Without God as the object of our faith, thinking is merely a function of the mind that cannot exceed it's input and attributes. Belief incorporates the mind, but is not limited by it. Faith actually transcends the limitations of the mind

197

and incorporates the real but unseen world. The believer's faith is as valid as it's object, which is the living (Christ) and written (Bible) Word of God. Believing you **can** live a victorious Christian life takes no more effort than believing you cannot. So why not believe that you can walk by faith in the power of the Holy Spirit, that you can resist the temptations of the world, the flesh and the devil, and that you can grow as a Christian. It's your choice.

Nobody can walk consistently in his or her faith. As believers, no matter how mature we consider ourselves, eventually we may fail here or there. If this happen, then what? In the section titled, *"What Happens When I Stumble in My Walk of Faith?"*
Anderson writes:

> Have you ever thought God is ready to give up on you because, instead of walking confidently in faith, you sometimes stumble and fall? Many Christians believe God is upset with them, that He is ready to dump them or that He has already given up on them because their daily performance is less than perfect. We will probably give up if we think God has. We stop talking faith in God, slump dejectedly by the side of the road and wonder, What's the use? We feel defeated, our purpose for being here is suspended and Satan is elated. The primary truth you need to know about God for your faith to remain strong is that **His love and acceptance are unconditional**. God's love for you is the great eternal constant in the midst of all the inconsistencies of your daily walk.

In God's economy, which we call grace, there is one constant— love. The reality is that God love us not our superb performance; God loves us because He is love.
In the section called, *"God Loves You No Matter What You Do,"* the author tells us:

> God wants us to do good, of course. The apostle John wrote: "I write this to you so that you will not sin." John continues by reminding us that God has already made provision for our failures so that His love continues

constant in spite of what we do: "But if anybody does sin, we have one who speaks to the Father in our defense-- Jesus Christ, the Righteous One. He is the atoning sacrifice for our sins, and not only for ours but also for the sins of the whole world" (1 John2:1, 2). <u>One reason we doubt God's love is that we have an adversary who uses every little offense to accuse us of being good-for-nothings.</u> Your advocate, Jesus Christ, however, is more powerful than your adversary. He has canceled the debt of your past, present and future sins. No matter what you do or how you fail, God will still love you because the love of God is not dependent upon its object; it is dependent upon His character. Because He loves you, He will discipline you in order that you "may share in His holiness" (Heb.12:10).[110]

What happened at the Cross (on our behalf) through the last Adam—*Jesus Christ*? Please explain and elaborate.

Christ—*the last Adam* born both physically and spiritually alive, **unlike the first Adam was tempted without sin.** <u>He kept His spiritual life all the way to the cross.</u> He bled and died there taking all the sins of the world on Himself. "God's divine Son willingly became a human being fulfilling a perfectly righteous human life. At the cross, having now taken into himself the sins of the entire world, the Father crushed Him with the weight of His wrath. **It was an act of perfect justice.** (Isaiah 53:4-10, 2 Corinthians 5:21) (*Alive for the First Time*, David Needham, pg. 55) **Because of this perfect justice the spiritual life of Adam and Eve lost in the fall have been reinstated to us.** (John 10:10;11:25)

In his unique book: "*Alive For the First Time*," in chapter 3—*More than Justified*, David Needham explains what it means to be a Christian and who we are (the real identity of a born again believer). He writes:

It's time we focused on what it means to be a Christian. By the time you finish this chapter, I hope that it will be clear that the answer to the problem of sin and the despair of meaninglessness is found in discovering the vast scope of the miracle God performed when he saved you—a miracle that actually changed you. I believe God has given to us this unique ability of self-consciousness, of thinking about who we are and why we are alive, for a very important reason. Without it, no one would ever respond to Jesus. With many non-Christians, it was this very questioning that broke down the barrier of resistance to the conviction of the Holy Spirit. This ability of self-awareness can also serve as a special means of grace to lead a believer deeper and deeper into the real meaning of life. In this chapter, my hope is that you will come to grips with who you are in a way you perhaps never have before. Just who are you?[111]

Needham relates his own experience of who he is in Christ. He writes:

As a Christian, I often struggled to live up to "the expected" level, whatever that was. But always close to the surface lurked a surging supply of feelings and desires vividly supporting my biblical conclusion "that nothing good dwells in me." How could it be that my desire to please God could fit inside the same person who was so captivated by desires that were just the opposite of what pleased him? What was I anyway? A spiritual failure, that was for sure. I had reckoned myself "dead unto sin" dozens of times. I "claimed by faith" that sin's power had been broken. I pled with God with all my heart for victory and joy. I confessed and received forgiveness countless times. I wore out my little packet of memory verses. I sincerely tried to lay hold of the fullness of the Holy Spirit in earnest faith. It was real faith. And it did not work! Why? Wasn't I right in what I believed, in what I was taught? The answer is both yeas and no. The yeas has to do with one of the greatest words in the Bible, a big word that in itself might tempt you to stop reading because it sounds so theological. Please don't! it's too important. **It's the word justification.**[112]

Justification, its life changing importance, and how it affects our identity is explained to us in the following paragraphs:

> Yes, I knew that I had been "justified by faith." Eventually I even found out what it meant. Because its biblical meaning has little to do with the way the word is commonly used today, let's take some time to be sure we're clear about it. Could God in any way receive me? Of course not! In my sin I was the opposite of everything He is. But wasn't I just a wee bit lovable? No, not a bit. On my own I was at heart a rebel, "a child of wrath," trapped in the power of my own sin (Isaiah 64:7). **The greatest proof of this fact is the cross.** Because of the evil of our essential natures, no matter how much God might have wished to forgive us, the eternal punishment we deserved still had to be administered. Could there be a substitute? Yes. But that substitute had to be a perfect substitute. But He did love me, didn't He? Yes He did, with agape love. "God is love." He simply chose to give Himself to me— and to you, whether or not we would respond. So what did He do? God's divine Son willingly became a human being, fulfilling a perfectly righteous human life. At the cross, having now taken into Himself the sins of the entire world, the Father crushed Him with the weight of His wrath.
>
> It was an act of perfect justice. (Read Isaiah 53:4-10; 2 Corinthians 5:21.) In the midst of my lostness, God brought me under his convicting grace and I received Christ as my Savior. In that moment God installed a marvelous "screen" between himself and me, the sinner. That screen is Jesus and everything about him—His perfect life, his substitutionary death. At the cross the Father took the entire condemning record against me— the sum total of all of my lawlessness—and placed it on Jesus, "nailing it to the cross" (Colossians 2:13-14). But God did more than that. He next replaced my old record in his judicial record book with the perfect record of Jesus' own righteous life. Because of what he saw, he declared me to be as righteous as his Son. What a fabulous screen! Simply amazing! In other words, because of that screen,

when God looks my way, what He sees is not my sin, but Jesus' righteousness. Before the infinite Judge of the universe, according to His own flawless reckoning, I now possess total forgiveness and acceptance. **I am justified!** I am judicially righteous, positionally righteous. This is the way God sees me. On that screen he sees His Son.

This then, is the yes answer regarding what I believed. But it is critically important to understand that "justification takes place outside the believer." This act of God changed nothing whatsoever inside of me. It is certainly good to know what God sees when He looks my way (the screen idea again). But what a terrible dilemma I now face! Mine is the impossible task to try fulfilling the destiny for which I was originally intended: I am to be holy. Yet at the same time, I must somehow stop being myself! "Oh," someone will say, "don't worry, you will become a different kind of person when you die. You will be holy then." True, our behavior will be perfect then. But nowhere does the Bible tell us that after we die God changes our essential nature. There is no heavenly "car wash" at the pearly gates. The Bible says only one thing about what happens to Christians when they die: They leave their bodies behind (Romans 8:18-23; 2 Corinthians 5:8; Philippians 3:21; 2 Peter 1:13–15).

There is an answer, God's answer. He does have a wonderful plan, a plan that involves more than justification. No matter how wonderful one side of God's truth—justification—was, my failure to see the other side became a major hindrance in discovering the fullness of joy that God intends for each of his children. It is to that side we now turn.

In the section, "More than justified," the author goes into more detail of the two changes God has made in us.

David Needham continues:

This side involves two changes God has made inside of us. Though the second change will be our major emphasis, we will need to catch something of the wonder of the first change, because it forms a most important bridge to the second one. Listen to Paul:

But God proves his love for us in that while we still were sinners Christ died for us. Much more surely then, now that we have been justified by His blood, will we be saved through Him from the wrath of God. For if while we were enemies, we were reconciled to God through the death of his Son, much more surely, having been reconciled, will we be saved by His life (Romans 5:8–10).

In that moment when you received Christ as your Savior, not only were you justified and delivered from God's wrath (the screen idea), but God made a very special change inside of you—He changed your attitude about Him. You see the compassionate face of a loving God with open arms reaching out to you. What do you do? You run into those open arms. You are no longer hostile! You have been reconciled to God. To your surprise, you discover that you love Him. Not only do you love him because "He first loved you," but you love everything about Him. Deep within, you "delight in the law of God" (Romans 7:22). You truly want to please God. How often David in the Psalms expressed this same attitude, for he too knew what it meant to be reconciled to God. This would seem to take care of everything—justified and reconciled. But it doesn't. It is to that second change inside of us we now turn. Jesus answered, "No one can see the kingdom of God unless he is born again... You must be born again" (John 3:3, 7). He was talking about a radical new kind of life. **He was talking about regeneration (new birth).** Leon Morris states:

"Jesus is referring to the miracle which takes place when the divine activity re-makes a man. He is born all over by the very Spirit of God." Jesus did not say being born again equals getting the Holy Spirit. He said it equaled becoming spirit. It is not getting something, it is actually becoming a different kind of person. Perhaps this "new personhood" idea seems far away from the daily reality of your life. That still doesn't change the basic fact. If you have received the Savior, you simply are not the same person you were before.

You may weigh the same,
look the same,
feel the same,
but you are not the same.

That's radical. We dare not water it down! And how could we do that? By saying: "Yes, I know I have a new nature," Or "God has clothed me with righteousness!" But what you have isn't the point. It's who you are that's the issue. By saying, "Oh, I'm just a sinner saved by grace, indwelt by the Holy Spirit," you're watering it down. You're casting an undeserved shadow on the greatest miracle God has ever performed concerning you. Don 't do it! God has not only justified you and reconciled you, He has also birthed you. The Apostle Peter shared this same sense of wonder when he wrote that we are "partakers [sharers] of the divine nature." Paul adds, "We are [Gods] workmanship, created in Christ Jesus" (2 Peter1:4; Ephesians 2:10). "So if anyone is in Christ, there is a new creation: everything old has passed away; see, everything has become new!" (2 Corinthians 5:17).

Mental programming and how it affects our perception of biblical truth is clarified by Needham.
He writes:

One of the most powerful forces any of us must deal with is the power of our own mental programming. <u>Ways of thinking have cut very deep ruts across the fields of our minds.</u> Even when we know a different way of thinking is right, it is difficult to break out of those smooth, well-worn paths. I am convinced that the major reason this revolutionary truth was so hard for me to grasp was because I had been programmed to assume that all biblical truth falls into two big bins. **The first bin is called** *positional truth*. Into it falls the most wonderful, foundational doctrine called *"justification by faith."* The other bin, experiential truth, includes all that becomes part of our conscious experience either at salvation or progressively as we grow spiritually. Most discussions place sanctification in this second bin. <u>What about regeneration?</u> I am convinced there is a third classification that deserves the title actual truth. It involves facts that certainly are not positional and may or may not be experiential. As we already have seen, those crucial miracles of reconciliation and (especially) regeneration fit in here. What does Scripture say? If you have received Jesus Christ as Savior, God says that in the deepest sense of personhood, you are not a sinner—no matter what you have been told, no matter how much you feel the pull of sin, You Are Righteous! But what "you" are we talking about? Not the "justified" you, the image seen because of the screen, but that most fundamental you. The you that most deeply and eternally gives you authentic personhood. The you that goes to heaven when you die. The you that is already qualified "to share in the inheritance of the saints in the light" (Colossians 1:12). Remember, we're talking about reconciliation and especially regeneration, not justification. **Being born again involves a radical change of being.** It is not simply a change in citizenship papers; it is a change in me! I was "by nature a child of wrath." No more. By nature I am now someone else: a "by birth" child of God.

Finding true victory is extremely important.
Needham illustrates it this way:

> Just a physical being, with a mind, will, and emotions, connected to glands and senses that cause you to respond one way or the other to what's on the television set? Is that what you most deeply are? No, it isn't! I'm born again! I am a 'partaker of the divine nature.' As such, my essential nature is 'dead to sin and alive to God.' Even though my fleshly feelings are saying one thing, I, as his divine workmanship, am saying the opposite. Sin is not my friend but my hated enemy." Well then, David, in view of

who you most deeply are—and God cannot lie—do you want to watch that?

At that moment something most wonderful happens as I hear myself say, "No!" For the first time, I'm free. Free to be what I most deeply am. Instead of feeling as though I am making a great sacrifice for Jesus, I am experiencing life. **Dear reader, this is what regeneration is all about.** This is New Covenant Christianity. After so many years of merely existing as a Christian, I felt free to live as I had never felt free before. What is life? Two things: to fulfill the destiny for which you were made while at the same time being who you are! Indeed, it is true there are no's to be said to fleshly desires. I believe this is what Jesus meant when he talked about denying yourself. But God has called us to lives of yeses far more than to no's. Yes to Life. Yes to freedom of being who we are. **Regeneration is that big of a miracle!** Becoming a Christian is more than having something taken away (sins forgiven), or having something added to you (a new nature plus the assistance of the Holy Spirit); it is becoming someone you had never been before. It is justification + reconciliation and regeneration. *Justification* is salvation as viewed from above, where God sits as a righteous judge issuing His judicial declaration. *Reconciliation* touches both "above" and "down here" as it affirms that since the wrath of God has been satisfied through Jesus' blood, we who were once enemies are now friends. *Regeneration* is salvation viewed from below, where we experience God's internal miracle of being alive with the life of Jesus by the Spirit. These together not only remove us from God's wrath, but qualify us to fit—to actually fit—in His righteous kingdom through the possession of Jesus' risen, eternal life in a restored relationship. [113]

In the same book, "Alive for the First Time", in chapter 4—*The People of the New Age,* David Needham describes the counterfeit New Age in contrast to God's glorious ***real new age***.

He writes:

Recently an ancient Eastern view of man has experienced a remarkable renewal through what is commonly called the New Age Movement, described by B.J. Wlliams in *The Oregonian* (a newsmagazine published in Oregon), as "a sort of intellectual Velcro dragged across history, picking up odd bits of philosophical lint from unlikely and often contradictory sources." It would appear that those in darkness will grasp at anything by which they can trash the humbling, biblical "flesh" evaluation of humanness. In its place they will exchange some type of elevated "spirit" level of being... Solomon was right: "Man in himself is destined to futility."

...

The book of Hebrews announced that the new covenant promise had been realized. "The completion of the ages"—"the consummation"—had arrived (Hebrews 8:8–13; 9:26). The new age had dawned. Paul declared that the law, once written on "tablets of stone," was now written on "tablets of human hearts." Life was now "resurrection life." The persons they used to be, persons who knew only life in the flesh, had been crucified with Christ. They were "risen with Christ," "alive to God" as they had never been alive (2 Corinthians 3:3; Romans 6:2–11; Colossians 3:1–4).

Some may question: *Who are the citizens of God's New Age?* Needham provides the answers:

What does this all mean? It means that by the new birth, you and I are now participants in the ultimate new age of God's eternal purposes. We are living within the fulfillment of the prophets' aching dreams and God's promised miracle. We are now, actually, the internally transformed citizens in God's kingdom of righteousness—where Jesus reigns, within the kingdom of our hearts. (2 Corinthians 4:6–7). Christ, the "life-giving Spirit," is now reproducing Himself progressively in the lives of the saints. We are "predestined to be conformed to the image of his Son" (Romans 8:29).

Remember, "The first Adam became a living being [soul]." As such, he imaged God within the confines of his flesh. Now "the last Adam [Christ]" having become "a life-giving spirit" is reproducing His very life—His image—in us! (1Corinthians 15:45) The new "image" concept is now more glorious than Adam, even in his innocence. **This is the new age**. The consummation of all the ages has begun. We are now by birth, by the Spirit, "the children of God," pulsating with the risen life of Jesus. Someday, perhaps soon, it will reach its apex when at last our "physical [soulish] bodies" will be transformed into "spiritual bodies"—at "the redemption of our bodies." Perhaps you are saying, "Oh, I know it's different. Expressions such as 'risen with Christ' prove that. It's just that my own spiritual failure proves that whatever those words are supposed to mean haven't touched me. I don't feel risen at all. I have begun to wonder if they were ever meant to be understood. Not just those words, but others too, such as:
Our old self was crucified with Him
Consider yourself dead to sin and alive to God
Those who belong to Christ Jesus have crucified the flesh
Those who are born of God do not sin
(Romans 6:6,11; Galatians 5:24; 1 John 5:18).

Those words! They sound so powerful, so radical, yet so out of reach. Did God really intend them to be beyond our reach?

The transformation that the Bible talks about is a radical change (transformation). The author uses a vivid illustration from the field of horticulture—Crab Apples vs. Golden Delicious. In this section, David Needham drills deeper into the meaning of transformation. He writes:

Our first step will be to assume that you and I agree that being a Christian is both an *external fact*—the screen idea (**justification**)—and an *internal fact*. Your relationship to and attitude toward God has been changed (**reconciliation**). And you are alive as you have never before been alive (**regeneration**). God has actually changed you. *"Crab apple"* is your essential nature (Ephesians 2:3). Then one day a momentous, momentarily terrifying thing happens to you. Someone takes a razor-sharp knife and makes a long diagonal cut and slices part of you off a few inches or so above the soil. The entire top of you is gone. Quickly this same someone takes a fresh green section of stem, cut with a matching diagonal slice from a different tree, and splices it onto what's left of you. Carefully, the splice is wrapped and sealed. Then a tag is attached to you that reads *"golden delicious."* In the days that follow, the buds above that splice burst with life. Eventually they blossom and produce. What will they produce? That's right—golden delicious apples. Why? Because this is who you now are. No one who knew what had taken place would ever think of calling you a *"crab apple."* You are not even a crab apple + a golden delicious. **You are a "golden delicious."** But what about below the graft? What if sprouts were allowed to flourish there? What would they produce? That's right—crab apples. Yet if that happened, they would be considered usurpers, aliens, deserving of only one thing: *removal.* The moment you were born again, the unregenerate person you used to be—your old self (crab apple)—was slice off, crucified. What you had been by nature, *"a child of wrath"* you are no more. There it lies on the ground, dead. At this same moment (the scion grafting moment) you became a genuine new self, a golden delicious. The name tag that is now yours is not there simply because this is the way God sees you on that screen (**justification**). No! It now truly represents who you are (**regeneration**). Yes, the root and stock below the graft remains. Nothing has changed there at all. But that part is no longer the determiner of your identity. It is true the Paul called your body a "body of sin." But I am sure he was not saying that our bodies in themselves are sinful. Yes, our energies, if expressed below the graft, would burst out with suckers. That innate mental bent toward sin is still there. But those energies, when rising above the graft, infused with risen life by the Spirit, are wonderfully transformed. This is a marvelous thing! When joined to life from God, they enable holiness to become a physical, visible reality. <u>Where does sin operate and where do the suckers grow?</u> Only in that independently functioning flesh level of our total personhood—below the graft. Romans 7:23 expresses this so well: "the law of sin that dwells in my members." Paul's final command, "present your members," is so important because, as noted above, God's intent in the new birth is more than changing your nature (to qualify you for heaven). He also had in mind changing your behavior now—in your mortal body—to golden delicious behavior. It is so important to note that even though this crucifixion and resurrection (crab apple severing + God's golden delicious grafting) took place so that our bodies of sin might be rendered powerless, it is still possible for sin to reign in our mortal bodies (Romans 6:12).

Those who have been born of God [you are now golden delicious] <u>do not sin</u> [produce crab apples], because God's seed [the essential nature of the scion, hence the tree] abides in them; they cannot sin, <u>because they have been born of God</u>. Sinning (crab apple producing) is so utterly irrational—<u>so stupid</u>—no one in their right mind would ever consider sinning a reasonable behavior. **In other words, it is as unthinkable for a Christian to sin** as it is for a golden delicious to produce crab apples (even though that is still possible below the graft, a possibility John allowed for, as seen in 2:1, "if anyone does sin").

When people are born again they experience (inside, in their spirit) a radical transformation, the author calls it—*Radically righteous through Regeneration*.

In this section, Needham writes:

John considered the miracle of being born of God so radical, it produced a person who was truly righteous. By observing 1 John 3:3, 7–8; 5:18, it is obvious that John was not thinking of *justification* (being declared righteous), but of *regeneration*, (being made righteous by the infusion of Jesus' life). John certainly allowed for the possibility that Christians might <u>occasionally sin</u> (1 John 2:1); but his assumption for himself and for his brothers and sisters was that such times would be totally out of character. To draw any other conclusion from 1 John is to be out of step not only with John, but God Himself.

Next, Needham looks into the letter to Galatians and applies Pauls's teaching to his analogy—<u>crab apple</u> vs. <u>golden delicious apple</u>.
He writes:

> And those who belong to Christ Jesus have crucified the flesh [everything below the graft is now dead to me in regard to who I now am] with its passions and desires [crab apple making]. May I never boast in anything except the cross of our Lord Jesus Christ, by which the world [everything that might encourage crab apple sucker growth] has been crucified to me [golden delicious], and I to the world (Galatians 5:24; 6:14).

> "As a tree, are you aware of the insistent urgings below the graft? Of course you are. Not only are you aware of them, but it is easy to imagine that if those budding suckers were allowed to flourish, you might falsely assume they were your true identity. Of course, those crab apple buds are there; they will be there until you die. But they are no longer where life is for you. They are really dead to you as being your life (Galatians 5:24). Not only that, but anything that might encourage them to grow—the world—is also dead to you (Galatians 6:14). **You are a golden delicious**.

> I [the crab apple tree I was] have been crucified with Christ [severing of the tree]; and it is no longer I [as I was] who live, but it is Christ [the parent tree, the source of the grafted scion] who lives in me. And the life I now live [I, the golden delicious tree producing golden delicious [fruit] in the flesh [still joined to the root and stock] I live by faith in the Son of God [total confidence in the

authenticity of the life source of the scion], who loved me and gave himself for me. (2:19–20)

The life that I live in the flesh"—is there any value in the root stock? Our present mortal, physical state is very important. Apart from it, the scion would have nothing to be attached to, no way for it to fulfill its physical golden delicious destiny.

David Needham, talking about the New Age; he asks the question: "Has it arrived?"
Then he explains:

Has the new age arrived? God's answer is an enthusiastic. Yes! In the New Covenant, the consummation of the ages began (Hebrews 9:26). Resurrection life is the new age. From the moment of regeneration, each child of God possesses "the mind of Christ" (1 Corinthians 2:16). "There is a new creation: everything old has passed away; see, everything has become new! (2 Corinthians 5:17). From that initial bursting of golden delicious life, the process continues of actually producing the fruit of that life—"the image of Christ," "from glory to glory." The zenith of that new age awaits the arrival of the King, when what we most deeply are will be joined eternally to a golden delicious body—"like unto His glorious body. [114]

Please explain why the spiritual birth is a radical thing? Please elaborate (as David Needham suggested) why this spiritual truth influences not only what happens with us after we die, but affects our identity and how we live here and now on earth. Please feel free to use Bible verses, specific quotes from the materials you studied during **Module VI** or from other materials.

Jesus said to Nicodemus (John 3:3, 7) "No one can see the kingdom of God unless he is born again you must be born again." *"Flesh gives birth to flesh, but Spirit to Spirit."*

I like the way Dr. Anderson explains what happened when I got born-again:

He was talking about a radical new kind of life. **He was talking regeneration** (new birth). He is born again all over by the Spirit of God. It's not getting something, it is actually becoming a different kind of person." (*Alive for the First Time*, David Needham, pg. 62-63) "It's a matter of being someone. A Christian is not simply a person who is forgiven and goes to heaven. **Being born again transformed you into someone who didn't exist before**. . . . What you receive isn't the point it's who you are.[115]

John 6:48 states, "I am the bread of life, I am the resurrection and the life, he who believes in Me shall live even if he dies." Even when we die physically, we continue to live spiritually for eternity. As Anderson puts it, "As believers we are not trying to become saints, **we are saints who are becoming like Christ**." (*Victory over Darkness*, Neil T. Anderson, p. 50). Since we have been born from above (John 3:3AMP), we are more than "just forgiven sinners," **we have the Holy Spirit living in us**. We are regenerated, alive, with the very life of Jesus as part of our DNA. We have been reconciled with God and are now are His friends.

I like the way David Needham explains this radical transformation.

He writes:

When you were in the flesh (Romans 8:9), life and meaning for you had to be found right there-and there alone. Your brain, your emotions, your senses, your creativity, your glands, your environment, your relationships – this was life. It could be found nowhere else. But if you have been born again, this is not so anymore, whether you know it or not!
You may weigh the same,
look the same,
feel the same,
but, you are not the same.
. . .
That's radical. We dare not water it down.[116]

In chapter 6, titled "God's Expectations for His Miracle Children," David Needham argues that all born again believers possess a new kind of life designed to express the nature and character of our heavenly Father.

The author writes:

> We who are born again know that we are a different kind of people with a new kind of life to live. A life that expresses the invisible God being made visible in human lives—in us. Our lives are the expression of His perfection, His purity in love. Certainly you are not suggesting that God expects our Christian lives to be marked by consistent holiness, are you?
>
> But let's face the real world. Not only do Christians blow it, but the Bible says right there in 1 John, "if we say that we have no sin, we deceive ourselves." That's the way it is. You know what I mean.
>
> It's one thing to be challenged to live a holy life, but come on now. God knows we won't. He never really expected us to, did he? (See Matt; 5:48, 1 Peter 1:15; 1 John 1:8)[117]

In the section titled "*Is Sinning Normal For the Child of God?*" Needham clearly makes the case that the answer is **no**!

He writes:

> To be sure we are clear, there are an ample supply of Christian speakers and writers who appear eager to soothe our consciences by asserting that sinning is quite normal for all of us. Of course they will use 1 John 1:8—"If we say that we have no sin, we deceive ourselves"—to prove their point. If that were not enough, they will throw in a few choice Old Covenant Bible biographies of sinning believers to eliminate any doubts we might have. Just like the bumper sticker says, "*Christians aren't perfect, just forgiven.*" As if this were not enough, we are reminded that the epistles are loaded with evidence that sinning was common enough in the early church. Why should we, two thousand years removed from the time of Christ, expect anything better? Well then, is the case closed? No, not until we take a second look at these passages to see if they

mean what we've been told. Since the focus of this book is on the radical nature of the new birth miracle, let's begin by checking out the message of the man who used new birth terminology more than any other writer, the Apostle John.

Now we will examine what the apostle John believes about sin in the life of a Christian.

Needham writes:

> ... I doubt if there is any other section of Scripture in which normal meanings of passages have been so skewed to make them fit typical Christian behavior. How you understand 1 John will have a major impact on how you view sin and the Christian. Let's begin by looking at a few of John's most radical statements:

> –No one who abides in Him sins; no one who sins has either seen Him or known Him...Those who have been born of God do not sin, because God's seed abides in them; **they cannot sin,** <u>because they have been born of God.</u>
> –We know that those who are born of God do not sin, but the one [Jesus] who was born of God protects them, and the evil one does not touch them (1 John 3:6, 9; 5:18).
> –Could it be that John had in mind our status rather than our actual behavior? (Once again, the screen illustration— the way God sees us in Christ.) But no, that won't work here because throughout this little epistle his focus is on very practical matters related to how we are to live. Well then, there must be other things John said that will protect us from this unrealistic—and some would say, dangerous—belief that Christians should not expect to sin. With haste they remind us that John already has stated, *"if we say that we have no sin, we deceive ourselves, and the truth is not in us,"* and *"if we say that we have not sinned, we make him a liar, and his word is not in us"* (1 John 1:8,10)...
> There. Problem solved! Sin is normal for a Christian. Still, with this type of logic, we haven't cleared up the meaning of those verses quoted earlier; at least we may rest assured

they do not mean what they appear to mean. That's good! Or is it? For many of us who have grown up in a Christian context where we were told numerous times that 1 John 1:8–10 is a passage written to remind us that sinning will be a normal characteristic of believers until they die, it takes a concerted effort even to consider the possibility that John had another purpose in mind. This purpose is well stated in Daniel J, Harrington's summary of an article by Sakae Kubo:

In 1 John 1:8 the author is answering the Gnostics who claim they have no sin, while all the time they live a life of sin. They could make this claim because their own definition of sin allowed them to do so. Because their understanding of sin is different from that of orthodox Christians, the Gnostics have claimed to be sinless (1:8) and to be born of God (3:9) but their actions have belied their claims.

Think about it. What is one of the first things non-Christians must do if they are to be saved? That's right, they must confess that they are sinners. In other words, they must express a "1 John 1:9" kind of response. Apart from this, it is meaningless for them to believe Christ died for their sins! How constructive it would be if Christians, once and for all, stopped using these verses to defend the idea that sinning is normal Christian behavior! Not only is that not the intent of 1 John 1:8, 10, but it also contradicts 1 John 2:1. Yes, we Christians do possess in our flesh a propensity toward sin (Galatians 5:17). But to admit that as true is a far cry from assuming John's intent was to support the idea that succumbing to the desires of the flesh should be thought of as characteristic of Christians. I wish I knew some way to underline the importance of recognizing this fact. Even if one holds the view that this passage represents false claims made by true Christians, it still does not support the belief that Christians are always in need of confessing sins because sinning is unavoidable. It is true that Christians have in their flesh a disposition to sin (1:8). It is also a dishonest expression of arrogance for anyone to say "I have not sinned," But neither of these facts opposes the joyous expectation of a life in which sinful behavior is an unnecessary aberration as is emphasized throughout 1 John).

Why the halfway solution is not a viable solution?
Needham explains:

Earlier I mentioned that many Bible teachers believe the claims of these verses (1 John 3:6, 9:5:18) are not as bold as they might first appear. They conclude that when John said *"Christians do not sin,"* he had in mind habitual sinning. They support this on the basis of John's use of present tense verbs. One writer goes so far as to say that John has in mind *"continuous"* sinning. Of course, this is only a halfway solution, because all of us know someone— probably ourselves—who went through times where a habitual pattern of sinning—pride, envy, self-centeredness—seemed almost unshakable. Yet most of us are hesitant to assume perhaps we were not saved at all. Well then, **a halfway solution is no solution at all.** Not only that, but a variety of recognized scholars warn that this *"habitual"* idea requires stretching the limits of Greek grammar too far. What, then, was John expressing? Could it possibly be he actually meant to say born again people do not sin? As stated earlier, John did not deny the possibility of sin in the Christian's life. Yet we may be sure John assumed his commands regarding righteous behavior would be obeyed (2:3–6, 9–11, 15; 4:7–8). From his perspective, why would anyone who possessed eternal life, who is a child of the light, a citizen in the New Covenant age, be insane enough to live as though they were, to use John's words "in the darkness"? Is it possible for a Christian to practice temporary insanity? Yes. Is sin ever a rational behavior for a Christian? Never. Might a Christian remain in an extended state of temporary insanity? I imagine so. (I know of no other explanation for such times in my own life.) It should be noted that most sins Christians commit are the products of spiritual weakness overwhelmed by the power of temptation rather than expressions of rebellion. Even if willingness is present, often the Christian hears him (her) self-saying, "*I know this is wrong, but I simply can't help it.*" I believe one of the evidences of the regenerating work of the Spirit is the degree to which we Christians will try to avoid a mindset that might suggest we are in open defiance against our Savior. I wonder—how would you respond to some particular temptation to sin if you paused long enough to acknowledge (1) that your thoughts (sin always begins with thoughts) were not motivated by the Spirit, but by your own self-centered flesh, and therefore were the enemies of authentic life; (2) that <u>to continue to entertain those thoughts in light of who you most deeply are would be to choose to function as temporarily insane</u>? John's enthusiastic little book shouts to every "born of God"— Be what you are—golden delicious!" The Spirit makes it possible. From the pen of the Apostle John is ample evidence that the new birth is a miracle far greater than many of us have been willing to accept. It was because of this actual "*God's seed abides in us*" miracle, that **truly consistent, righteous behavior is a reasonable expectation** (1 John 3:9).

Now we look at the Apostle Paul's view of sin.
The author writes:

So much for the Apostle John. But what about Paul? What about his claim to be "the foremost" of all sinners (1 Timothy 1:15)? We dare not miss the fact that he clearly had in mind his life before he was born again. Paul could think of no sin worse than persecuting Jesus and His people, even though he had done it in ignorance. Paul's whole point was, if God's grace had reached low enough to save him, "the foremost of sinners"—after what he had done—God could save anyone! The apostle touched on the same idea in 1 Corinthians 15:9 when he said he was "the least of the apostles."
Why? Because he had "persecuted the church." Still others would argue from Romans 7:14–25 that Paul's life

continued to be marked by personal moral failure—"for I do not do the good I want, but the evil I do not want is what I do... Wretched man that I am!" If this view of Paul's perspective is correct—if this is normal, to-be-expected Christian life—we must draw two conclusions:

– First, Christians are wrong in hoping for even partial victory over sin. Instead, they should anticipate total failure. Why? Because total failure is what Romans 7:14–25 is all about. Read those verses to see if you can find even a moment of victory. In addition, we must resign ourselves to the wretchedness he described, with our only hope being that day when we will be rescued from our physical bodies.

Is this what Paul meant? Let's listen to his answers in the verses before and after Romans 7. Yes, our hope in the future redemption of our bodies is delicious to think about. And yes, in our flesh (7:18) there will be nothing but failure. That's all true—but I am sure Paul would have shouted out to those who so misuse Romans 7. "You are not in the flesh anymore! If you choose to limit God by depending on your own flesh-level resources to fulfill His law, you will make the same agonizing discovery I did. You will find yourself locked in as a captive to the law of sin. Why not see yourself as you truly are? You are not captive to sin anymore!

– (Secondly) you have been set free. The "law of the Spirit of life in Christ Jesus has set you free from the law of sin and of death." You are free to "walk" and "live" under this greater law—the law of the Spirit. So get busy and "walk by the Spirit." The result will be God's moral law actually lived out in you" (Romans 8:2-6; Galatians 5:16).[118]

Is sanctification, practically speaking, even possible? Yes! In the section titled, "Freedom from the Law of Sin and a Life Free of Sin," Needham teaches us how sanctification works.

He writes:

The freedom described in **Romans 8** is not extrinsic (the way God sees me), while all the time I am intrinsically the "wretched man" that Paul has just described. Instead, the emphasis in the verses that follow Romans 7 underline the truth of an interior miracle that has infused a new quality of life within. It is in us (8:9). Romans 6-8 are rooted in not one, but three marvelous saving acts of God:

– Justification,
– Reconciliation and
– Regeneration.

Only from these sources can sanctification (holiness) blossom. True, Paul's emphasis in Romans 3–5 was on justification by faith. But the goal of the book of Romans is not to declare our new status before God; it is about an entirely new dimension of life—risen life, eternal life God's act of justification was never intended as an end in itself. Rather, having made that external declaration on the basis of Christ's perfect life and His substitutionary death, God could then in perfect righteousness perform that marvelous internal miracle of regeneration based upon his resurrection. When our old self was crucified with him and when we recognize as a fact that we are now actually alive to God, we are declaring in a most expressive way the implications of the miracle of new birth, new life— *eternal life*. We are the new self, part of a new humanity that pulsates with life from God, Jesus' own resurrection life. Keeping in mind that God's definition of authentic life is the only definition that counts, he said "in Him was life" (John 1:4). It was to be found nowhere else. What we thought was life wasn't life at all. Actually it was a walking death. That walking death came to an end at that salvation moment when God made a marvelous interior change in you. The person you used to be was in some mysterious way crucified when Christ was crucified. In fact, you were crucified "with Christ." Try to imagine the radical change our Savior experienced. In His dying he had become all that sin was (2 Corinthians 5:21); but in His rising, this

was *exchanged* for the fullness of His own resurrection life. (Romans 6:6-11). This is what happened to you, except for one difference. At Jesus resurrection, he also received his glorified body. **We have resurrection life, but we still have our mortal bodies**. Sinning really is completely inconsistent with who we now are.[119]

In the section titles, "What Does God Expect of Us?" the author attempts to address this fundamental question. God made such a marvelous change in His children, in you and in me. Since sinning is incompatible with my spiritual Identity, how I am supposed to answer the question at the beginning of this paragraph?

Needham writes:

So what does God expect of us? You probably know my answer: genuine holiness. Is this some dreamy doctrine? I admit it sounds like it. We would all like to believe the new creation miracle described in Romans 6 automatically results in transformed lives. If "everything old has passed away" and "everything new has come" (2 Corinthians 5:17, which is the essence of Romans 6), then should we not expect all of those old sinful desires to be gone— forever?

"I used to be an alcoholic, now I hate the stuff!"
"I used to love money with a passion, now it's no problem at all!"
"I used to have homosexual desires, now they're gone!"

There are people who say such things have happened to them. But most of us have found those old sinful desires still very much around. Others remind us, "But remember, sins power has been broken," as though sin is now a powerless foe. If that were so, why did the apostle warn us, "do not let sin exercise dominion in your mortal bodies"? (Romans 6:12). We dare not deceive ourselves. Sin remains a powerful enemy to godliness. David Wenham, writing within a context of Romans 7, answers:

Paul would never admit the inevitability of defeat in the Christian life. His conviction is clear that "with the temptation God will also make a way of escape" (1 Corinthians 10:13). The power of the Spirit is the power that raised Jesus from the dead and will give us newness of life in the present as well as in the future. For Paul this is the most important reality of Christian experience, and he would not subscribe to the melancholy view that Spirit and flesh are two almost equal contestants within the Christians life. **Undoubtedly Paul would have subscribed to the view that the Christian life can be a life of victory.** If only we will recognize and appropriate the Spirits power.[120]

The next information is taken from Needham's section "You Don't Have to Sin."
He writes:

No matter how heartfelt and beautiful some of our Christian traditions are, we dare not allow them to alter God's New Covenant truth. "Does this reflect God's expectations for His miracle children—as those who "have erred and strayed as miserable offenders"—to the degree that such must be our daily confession? Has our God ordained that His resources for godliness will always be just beyond our reach? Did He give us a dream to treasure, knowing full well it was only a dream? Is this the teaching of the epistles? No matter how discouraged we may be as to the sins in our own lives, once and for all you and I must reject the idea that **sin is to be accepted as the unavoidable norm.** We must reject the teaching that says there's not too much we can do about it except to keep up-to-date on our confessions, inhale the Spirits power, and then, perhaps, enjoy a few seconds of cleanness before we start the miserable cycle all over again. What are God's expectations? The unmistakable answer is **a life of genuine holiness.**[121]

In the Chapter titled, *"The Mechanics of a Miracle Life, Part 1: Things I Must Believe,"* the author explains that it is very important for the believer to know and place his or her faith in the Word of God—to believe that He is always honoring His promises.

Needham writes:

> What is a Christian to do about sin? If this miracle of the new birth is as big as the Bible says it is, then why is it so easy to sin---and what can I do about it? If holiness is the norm for God's newly born children, what does it take to "get normal"? There are answers. Actually there are two kinds of answers: "*things I must believe*" answers and "things I must do" answers. First are those things I must believe.

1. I must make sure I am thinking rightly about God.

A.W. Tozer said it so well:

> The gravest question before the Church is always God Himself, and the most portentous fact about any man is not what he at a given moment may say or do, but what he in his deep heart conceives God to be like...There is scarcely an error in doctrine or a failure in applying Christian ethics that cannot be traced finally back to imperfect and ignoble thoughts about God.

Among many things, what you believe about God will determine:

– Whether you believe in moral absolutes;
– Where you place prayer in your list of priorities;
– How you will approach that most precious gift—His written Word.

Are you serious about living a miracle life? You will be if you are confident as to the next belief issue:

2. I must be very sure I am a Christian

"Oh, but this is an easy one to do. Do I believe Jesus died for my sins? Sure! Well, that settles it, doesn't it? It would be so nifty to say "That's it!" And it would be "it"" if becoming a Christian were something we do. But it isn't; it is something God does. Yes, we must receive the gift of His grace, but I'm afraid it is possible for a person to receive when God the Holy Spirit is not at that particular moment actively giving. **How easy it is for us to mistake psychologically conditioned emotional sincerity for the convicting, enlightening work of the sovereign Holy Spirit.** How do you know you have been born again? Praise God, he doesn't leave us in the dark over an issue this crucial. The Apostle Paul wrote, "the Spirit Himself bears witness with our spirit that we are children of God" (Romans 8:16). That sounds clear enough, but what if I don't feel that way? John wrote, "By this we know that we abide in Him and He in us, because he has given us of His Spirit" (1 John 4:13). But what if I don't sense His presence? In those times when I have my own doubts, there is one unmistakable passage that has always settled the issue for me—and I trust for you. It is this: "Therefore I want you to understand that no one... can say 'Jesus is Lord' except by the Holy Spirit" (1 Corinthians 12:3). In those darkest of times with my mind strewn with the wreckage of battered beliefs and emotions, I have forced myself to peel off all those disturbing emotions as one might tear away slimy, wilted lettuce leaves to expose its still-crisp core. "David, what is your deepest desire? What is it you desire more than anything else? I have always found the same answer— "Yes, I do want to follow Jesus. I do not want to walk away from Him. Jesus is Lord. My Lord!" It was no passing comment when Paul closed his epistle with the words, "Let anyone be accursed who has no love for the Lord" (1 Corinthians 16:22). On one hand, the proof you are a Christian is not your promise to follow Christ. Nor, on the other side, is it simply some form of "easy believism" that becoming a Christian is nothing more than affirming certain facts. Rather, the proof is in that mysterious, inner working of the Holy Spirit. He does "bear witness" that you, by his grace alone, have indeed responded to those most earnest words, "We entreat you on behalf of Christ, be reconciled to God" (2 Corinthians

5:20). Yes, you can know if you are a Christian. But you must search beneath the superficial to uncover that deep, perhaps scarcely whispered witness from your spirit that you are a child of God. Is this true of you?

3. I must be settled once and for all as to who I most deeply am and therefore where life is to be found

Like scuba divers on the floor of the sea, the apostles knew they were living in an alien environment. They were not of this world any more than Jesus was (John 17:14, 16). Life for them had to come from above—from their true home. Because of this, they looked at life through different eyes. Their awareness of their new identity automatically produced in them a revolutionary change as to why they were alive—as to who and what it was that gave purpose and significance to their existence. No longer was meaning or personal worth measured by prosperity or worldly acclaim.

…

As needs arose, Christians willingly sold their lands and houses to share with those who had less. Paul said, "I have learned to be content with whatever I have... In any and all circumstances I have learned the secret of being well-fed and of going hungry, of having plenty and of being in need" (Philippians 4:11, 12; Acts 4:34). **To whatever degree this awareness of life is missing today, to that degree holiness will be perverted.** If I wrongly assume that holiness comes in saying no to all of my desires in order to say yes to God, then, I will have to carry the added burden of my own self-pity. How radically opposite to this is Paul's declaration when he said, "I have suffered the loss of all things... that I may gain Christ." (Philippians 3:8). In view of the positive (which was his desire) he considered the loss but rubbish. He knew that to say death to the flesh was indeed saying life not only to the glory of God but also to himself as a future partaker of that glory as a joint heir with his Lord. Christians who really know this can truly be themselves without being selfish! But awareness of identity is scarcely the whole show. It rather enables you to go forward in your discovery of meaning. Once identity is a settled thing, your focus is no longer self, but on life right there in front of you. Though the initial focus is on identity, the lasting focus must be on life. "And this is eternal life," Jesus said, *"that they may know you, the only true God, and Jesus Christ whom you have sent"* (John 17:3). John later added that if we truly know God, our reaching out in love toward people would be the proof that our life indeed was from God (1 John 4:7–12). Hence, **authentic life is always relational, both vertically and horizontally**. "There was a time," Paul says, "when I thought I was alive—a good, decent, God-fearing Jew, then I made the devastating discovery that righteousness involved more than performance, more than duty, it involved desire—"Thou shalt not covet." I couldn't handle that. How could I stop wanting what I wanted? And in that moment he watched life as he knew it shrivel up and die. Happily, Paul saw the door swing wide open to authentic life as he wrote, "The law of the Spirit of life in Christ Jesus has set you free from the law of sin and death... If by the Spirit you put to death the deeds of the body, you will live" (Romans 8:2, 13). Not only had God changed his heart (*reconciliation*), but he also made the joyous discovery that he was now alive to an entirely new dimension of existence: life in the spirit by the Spirit (*regeneration*).

Then, Needham looks at another point of view:

This view appears to be built on the idea that whenever you are feeling sinful desires, you are actually encountering your fundamental nature—a sinner. In those hot, pressured times, you either follow through with those desires and do what you want, or you by God's strength resist them and end up doing what you ought. Yet whether or not you obey the *"oughts,"* you still must recon with the true nature of the kind of person you assume yourself to be—at heart, a sinful person. According to this view, the choice to go against oneself is called *"dying to self"* or to *"getting self off the throne."* Those holding this belief would say this is what Jesus meant when he said, "If any want to become my followers, let them deny themselves and take up their cross and follow me" (Matthew 16:24). How very important it is for Christians to be taught quickly that when they were saved, not only were they justified, but God also performed those interior miracles that changed the focus of their selfhood from flesh to spirit. Their deepest level of self, their truest self, never desires to sin. That "self" is always in perfect agreement with the "oughts" of God's moral law. Tragically, if in their early Christian years "justification by faith" was all they knew, they may struggle for years before discovering that the "oughts," which so often seemed opposed to their "wants," were not some nagging warnings of their conscience or God, but rather the longing cry of their own reconciled, regenerated selves We must stop believing that living a godly life is a sacrifice we should be willing to make for God.

But how do we change our beliefs?
Needham explains:

> For many of us who have been shaped by a *duty-failure-confession-forgiveness-oriented* Christianity, it is so hard to change our beliefs. We slip back so easily into those old ruts. I am faced with an impossible task of being a self-centered sinner whose purpose in life is to produce God-centered holiness. Since this is simply too painful to endure, I search for one of those threadbare counterfeits—"I know I could teach theology, the Bible. Since I can't change my nature, I can at least improve my knowledge and multiply that knowledge in my students." I visualize myself as God's "park ranger," standing—not in front of Old Faithful in Yellowstone Park, but in front of the "Fountain of Living Water"—with my students looking right past me as they observe the majesty of God's glorious fountain. God's fountain was never meant simply to be a "*look at it*," "*talk about it*," fountain, but a "*drink it*" fountain. One day in the temple, Jesus "cried out, "Let

anyone who is thirsty come to me, and let the one who believes in me drink.'"" Our Bibles end with the words *"Whoever is thirsty, let him come; and whoever wishes, let him take the free gift of the water of life"* (Revelation 22:17). There is not much space for pride when you are bending low enough to drink from the spring of Living Water. The new birth begins there. The Christian life stays there. Yes. We must know the truth. The new birth is the beginning of that life. How it grows as we continually drink in Christ's risen life will be measured by the outflow of a full meaning—significance—*love.* Actually receiving (drinking) says it all. We were saved by receiving God's love—His self-giving (John 1:12). We then respond to God's love by fulfilling his command to love Him by giving ourselves to him. How? By lifting up to Him our lives as empty dishes. Why? So that He may fulfill His heart's desire by continuing to pour His love—Himself—into us.

4. I must be convinced that God's expectation for his children is that they do not sin

We are so used to assuming that sinning is normal—that we are always failing God in one way or another. As we noted earlier, not only did John in his First Epistle repeatedly deny such an idea, but New Covenant truth in general denies it. John stated:

...

I am writing these things to you so that you may not sin. But if anyone does sin, we have an advocate with the Father, Jesus Christ, the righteous. Those who have been born of God do not sin, because God's seed abides in them, they cannot sin, because they have been born of God (1 John 2:1; 3:9).

Though John allowed that sin was possible for a child of God, **to sin would be nothing short of temporary insanity.** Rather than assuming that some measure of sin was to be expected, the epistles as a whole share in common the belief that **sin is both abnormal and irrational behavior for a child of God.**

In the section, *"When does a temptation become a sin?"* Needham explains:

> Closely related to this is the importance of being able to identify when sin is actually taking place. I hate to admit how often thoughts have burst into my consciousness that are just plain sick. I would blush to make a list—but you know them, too. My first reaction to that awareness is both shock and dismay. "How could I ever think something that bad?" This is a classic example of calling something a sin even though we are directly contradicting Scripture. James 1:14–15 is quite specific in separating the existence of a *sinful thought* from the *entertaining of a sinful thought*. What an important distinction! We have not sinned until we make the choice to entertain an evil thought. When we recognize the myriad megabytes of uncensored trash filed away in the computers of our minds, how thankful we may be that God does not measure our personal holiness by evaluating the contents of our brains. (This paragraph is worth reading again!) If in that moment of awareness, I repudiate the right of that thought to contaminate my consciousness and immediately affirm righteous thoughts, I have not sinned. Rather than those thought patterns arising from who we most deeply are, they find their source in what Paul calls "the law of sin which dwells in my members" (Romans 7:23). There is another assumption I have made regarding sin. I have assumed that personal failure was always a sin. Of course, sometimes it is. But failure as a result of poor judgment or poor memory, for example, may not have any sinful overtones. So many decisions we make and actions we take are not related to moral issues at all. They are simply matters of judgment. How encouraging it is to find Romans 14:1–6 in the Bible. Even in issues in which a lack of spiritual maturity might result in opposing opinions, God encourages us to remember that He looks at our motives and not only welcomes us, but makes us stand accepted before Him, even if our judgment is not the best. What a relief!

*5. I must be convinced a miracle life is impossible without the Holy
Spirit's power.*

"We all know it is true even if our lives are saying the
opposite. Sadly, the fact that we know a truth so well may
cause us to place it in some dusty back room of our
consciousness. Could God be saying to us, "You foolish
Galatians! Who has bewitched you?... Are you so foolish?
Having started with the Spirit, are you now ending with
the flesh? Did you experience so much for nothing?—if
it really was for nothing" (Galatians 3:1, 3–4)

In the next section, titled, *"carport Christianity,"* Needham
compares *a Christian* with *a car* conveying the main idea that the core
of a Christian is **the inmost self,** in the same way that the engine is
the core of the car. The author alerts the reader not to get
sidetracked by all the accessories and little gadgets that a car comes
equipped with, thus losing the sight the main purpose of the car to
get moving. Similarly, the Christian must remember that the main
purpose is to *receive, respond,* and *display* God's love through his or
her life.

Here is his illustration:

You've seen, perhaps, the children's books where an
automobile takes on human characteristics? The smiling
grill, the blinking headlights... get the idea? We're thinking
of a car as a person. This happens to be a Christian car.
His reason for existing is to glorify God. Remember, a
receiver, responder, and *displayer* of the life—the love of God.
How does she do this? **By moving**. She was created to
move. Of course, this car can do many other things as
well. With all those fascinating things to toy with (and
manuals to read!) one might get so wrapped up he misses
the main purpose of the car—which is to move. Though
all of these accessories get their power from the battery,
the battery is not the core of the car at all. **The core is
the engine.** For the Christian, the engine is **the inmost
self,** the deepest level of selfhood. **The battery is the
will.** Sadly, it is possible for a Christian to become so

involved in all the varied potentialities of his flesh—his moral being—that he may begin to think that life is right there, in the accessories. But where is he? Still in the carport. He has not moved at all. On the other hand, this Christian might honestly realize the reason for which God saved him. Therefore he exerts his will to roll forward. He presses on the starter with the gears meshed and—ah!— that good ol' battery comes through. The car lurches forward. How far? <u>About two inches</u>. Hmmm. Well, it's back to the turn signals or the CD—something that isn't quite so hard on the battery. Maybe someday he'll get the hang of this *moving idea*. Maybe this moving idea is something you are to take by faith. One thing for sure— the scenery hasn't changed a bit.

In the section, titled, *"Distinctive Honks and Fine–Focused Fog Lights,"* the author continues using the "car" metaphor to point out various personality differences which exists among individual Christians, that could potentially prevent him or her from moving forward in their Christian maturity and walk with the Lord.

The author writes:

> This Christian can now focus on his personhood—the distinctive honk of his horn or the fidelity of his stereo. He finds his identity as a *"pre-programmed seat adjustment"* person in contrast with someone else who happens to be a unique *"4-wheel drive"* or *"variable, intermittent-wiper"* person. Yet, even with all this, the whole thing is depressing because the battery (**his will**) keeps running down and he has to find someone to charge it up again. He may start comparing himself with someone else and either become depressed or jealous (or both) if he senses he is not nearly the car they are.

Then, he makes the point that when a Christian realizes who he really is in Christ, and decides to act (decision of his WILL), things start moving in his life. As a result—Jesus is being seen through this individual Christian.

Needham explains:

231

And then one day he stops and thinks, really thinks. Just what am I doing? Something inside me—way down deep—is crying out for action. Real action—moving action! **Who am I?** What is my identity? I am a person created by God as a receiver, responder, and displayer of the life of Jesus in the world. I was created to move! *"Oh God, I want to move!"* Quickly he turns to read his Bible, and begins to read with diligent study. Maybe, he thinks, if I knew more of what this book says, that would make me move. But is he moving? We all know that our simple wills cannot produce holiness, any more than a battery can make a car go. No, he isn't moving. **What then can produce holiness?** What does it take to get the car moving? In layman's terms, I think it happens like this: Drawing initially on the resources of my battery, I press down the clutch petal (or shift into Park), turn the ignition key to the ON position and, holding it there, turn the engine over. In so doing, fuel is drawn into the fuel injector where it is prepared to join a spark from the battery. A series of inner explosions begin, the gears are meshed... **I move.** Consider the similarities in our lives as Christians. **A Christian's will in itself does not produce holiness.** But it does initiate the circumstances in which holiness can be realized. That most important act of drawing in the fuel with the ignition key to ON and the gears disengaged parallels an essential spiritual event: one's conscious openness, dependency, and expectation of receiving the necessary risen-life energy by the Holy Spirit. That openness to him and his supernatural empowering must be an attitude of the mind, not simply a passing thought. I resolve to say *yes* to anything He might wish to do in and through my life—He is sovereign. It is then that I find myself moving into an entirely new dimension of living. The scenery is changing, I am moving. Jesus is being seen through me! The credit goes to God the Holy Spirit. He, "the Spirit of Christ," is my life! He is my strength (Romans 8:9; Philippians 1:19). This all sounds so wonderful. But still we wonder, "Paul, John—God! Is a life of victory possible? Their answer is

"Yes!" "But is it reasonable?" Their answer is still "Yes!"
122

In the chapter called, *"The Mechanics of a Miracle Life, Part 2, Things I Must Do,"* the author provides answers to the two very fundamental questions most Christians keep asking themselves.

Needham writes:

1. "Why is it so easy to sin?" and
2. "What can I do about it?"

Let's keep those two questions ... and look at the "**four crucial action steps**," which are directly connected to the things Christians must believe.

1. I must clear away the clutter in my life by drinking in God's forgiveness and freedom from guilt

From Isaiah 53, "the Lord has laid on Him the iniquity of us all" and "He bore the sins of many." Yes, Jesus took the punishment I deserved, I knew that. But he did more than that. He actually took my sins and made them His own! **He "became" my sin (2 Corinthians 5:21).** The judgment is gone, I am free—but not free. Why? Because my guilt remains. I still did those evil deeds and I will have the weight of that guilt pressing down upon me as long as I live! It is quite another thing to grasp the truth that God's kind of **forgiveness removes the *guilt* as well as the *debt.*** This is simply amazing. Somehow on the cross, Jesus became what I had been—a sinner. I—I had been crucified with Christ. Is Jesus still taking the punishment I deserved? No. He finished it. But does he still bear the guilt He took from me when he made it his own? No. He finished that, too! But how? God says, "The death he died, he died to sin, once for all; but the life that he lives, he lives to God" (Romans 6:10). When Christ arose, he not only completed the punishment, but he also left the guilt behind. What about me? Yes, the same. I, too, am risen with Christ. As new and clean and guilt-free as my risen Christ! That is Romans 6. Remember, too, that this

thirst-quenching fountain is always there, for every sin—
those past and those that may yet take place.

In the section titled, *"Acting on What You Don't Feel,"* Needham
stresses out the importance of Scriptural truth which must be applied
in our lives.

He writes:

> Remember, even deeper than our **thirst for forgiveness**
> is our *thirst for purity* and *transparency* in that relationship.
> But to believe what you may not be able to feel is so hard
> to do! **We must do that with Scripture.** It is true the
> temptations you may be feeling are totally real. The sins
> you irresponsibly permit to happen are equally real. **But
> what God has said is an overriding reality.** You must,
> as an act of trust, drink in His forgiveness. Whenever we
> have confessed some sin and received God's forgiveness,
> we face a crucial choice. We may either spend the next
> five minutes (or however long we want) groveling in the
> awfulness of what we did, meandering through our
> miseries, castigating ourselves for being such dumb jerks:
> "won't I ever learn? How could God ever put up with
> me?" Or, after we pause long enough to identify where it
> was we lost our bearings—where we lost our perspective
> and opened the door to sin—we can turn our eyes upward
> and gaze into the face of our most marvelous, forgiving,
> gracious, smiling God: "What a God! What a Savior! The
> slate is clean. I see the sunshine of your joy shining on my
> path. O, thank you, Father! Your arms are open wide and
> I run into your embrace.

2. I must actively participate in the renewing of my mind.

One of the most common answers to the question, *"Why
is there so much sin in the lives of Christians?* "Well, the devil
sure is busy these days." I believe the most powerful force
behind sin is the misuse of the most precious gift God has
given us—*our ability to think.* They have forgotten who
they are and who God is and the relational implications
of both. During those forgetful moments, their flesh

rushes in to fill up the vacuum none of us can endure. Therefore, the starting point for *"what I must do"* is simply, **I must think about what I believe.** I must repeatedly hold each marvelous truth out in front of me—turning it around in my mind to see it in all of its wonder. "To live is to think and to think is to do." We noted this back in chapter 2. Our choices and ultimately our emotions flow from this one source. And always behind our thinking is that inescapable drivenness to make some sense out of our existence. For every conscious moment of my life I must have a reason for existing. Either we fill it with life from God—the flow of love from the Father, which in turn flows out to others—or we will fill it with "all that is in the world—the desire of the flesh, the desire of the eyes, the pride in riches ["arrogant display"] (1 John 2:16). Either we fill it or we die—if not physically, at least we die inside.

In the section: *The Gift of imagination,* Needham explains how Christians can use this marvelous gift to connect with spiritual realities presented in the Bible. The author also warns of the danger of misusing the gift of imagination thus being deceived like Eve was deceived in her mind by the devil in the Garden of Eden.

Inseparable from thinking is a marvelous quality we call **imagination**—*that ability to form mental pictures or images, not simply of things, but of ideas.* Rightly used it allows "streets of pure gold" and "gates of pearls" (each gate one pearl?) to become more than words (Revelation 21:21). We actually see them. "How good of God to give us such a gift!" Yet wrongly used it can turn our lives into despair and remorse. It is in the misuse of imagination that most sin takes place. **In fact, sin becomes an empty word without imagination.** Eve imagined before she ever took one bite. Only because of this ability could the love of money be "the root of all evil." Virtually every battle we will ever fight with sin will be won or lost on the turf of our imaginations. Strange isn't it? Something so precious, so enriching and enjoyable can also be so self-destructive. This is especially true of fantasy, where we move into the world of *make believe*, where imagination reigns supreme. For a Christian, fantasy as a refreshing diversion is healthy; as a substitute for life it is sick. None of us should blame a non-Christian for this type of fantasy. Reality is dark. Life without God is futile, meaningless, a "striving after the wind." It is quite understandable for a lost world to creatively manufacture one fantasy on top of another. But for us it should be totally different. For us, reality is limited only by the infinite imagination of a God who always functions in the real world. The trouble is, too many of us who are Christians do not see ourselves as all that different. Because we don't, we have become fair game for the world's fantasy mongers.[123]

Then he ask a rhetorical question: "Is holiness getting harder?" The answer is "yes," especially in the culture in which we live. He explains:

Somehow we need to be jolted—*shaken*—into a fresh awareness that a large share of the things that claim the imaginations of the world are not simply a waste of time. They are diabolically destructive to New Covenant life and holiness. Is a truly godly life more difficult to live now than in the past? If we say yes, someone is bound to remind us of other morally monstrous pages of history. The answer is yes. Our "pure minds" (2 Peter 3:1) are more at risk now than ever in the history of the world. Never before has human imagination been so exploited, so bombarded, as in our present mechanized, media-mad electronic age. Could there be a greater paradox than to be part of an "advanced" society that proclaims so loudly its repulsion of demented human behavior, but in its place rents the videos and privately fantasizes the same brutalities while maintaining a respectable public conscience?" Even within evangelicalism we are seeing truth being bartered away for whatever stirs the heart and increases the numbers. If I am committed to holiness, I must face up to the fact that I am surrounded by an incessant bombardment from both the world and the prince of this world. Already, countless automatic, sinful, chain-reaction thought patterns have been stored away in my brain, ready for instant recall. I hope it is not too late for Christians to welcome the radical, personal disciplines that will enable the church to start behaving as strangers in Vanity Fair." (pp. 177–178)

According to Needham, the key is renewing the mind. If we don't pay attention to our thought–life, we can let the imagination run wild in order to fill moments of emptiness. What we think in those moments will pretty much determine the outcome of our lives. The author explains:

Because of all of this, it comes as no surprise when we are informed by the Apostle Paul that if a believer is ever to know a transformed life, there must be a renewing of the mind (Romans 12:2). We should thank James for telling us that genuine faith doesn't just sit there, it takes action. Therefore, I must participate in the renewing of my mind by removing myself from the circumstances that not only will add more trash to my memory bank, but will make temptations increasingly accessible. But most of the time it requires something much more difficult. **I must force myself to change the direction my thoughts are moving.**

So I do not run aimlessly, nor do I box as though beating the air; but I punish my body and enslave it, so that after proclaiming to others I myself should not be disqualified (1 Corinthians 9:26-27)

For just as you once presented your members as slaves to impurity and to greater and greater iniquity, so now present your members as slaves to righteousness for sanctification (Romans 6:19).

What part of Paul's body did he discipline the most? What member did he make his slave? Not his hand or foot or eye, but his body's control center: his brain, his mind. I fear we have been so accustomed to giving in to our thoughts, we are not sure that controlling them is possible. What about all those times when concentration is not demanded? When imagination fills the emptiness? We will think. But what will we think about? Our answer to that will determine so much." (pp. 178–179)

This requires a lot of tough decisions.
Needham continues:

We must ask ourselves, "Will these thoughts I entertain refresh me for the real world, or will they only add to my reservoir of the *"if onlys,"*the *"might have beens"* and the *"what ifs"* of my imagination? It is strange how my very active imagination can at times be my best friend or my worst enemy! Paul's expressive words, "Taking every thought captive to the obedience of Christ" are words I must live by if I am to live in the real world. <u>Let's face it. Fantasy is a little secret room you can enter at a moment's notice.</u> You are the god of that room. You create whatever you wish.

Yet the renewal of our minds is far more than simply exercising brain power. A crucial "how" of holiness is inseparable from knowing the truth of God's Word, but it must be more than simply quantitative information. It must involve a participant, relational type of knowledge, which in the Bible is inseparable from the power of its Author. Instead of simply telling us to "memorize the Bible," Paul prayed,

That the God of our Lord Jesus Christ, the Father of glory, may give to you a spirit of wisdom and revelation as you come to know Him, so that, with the eyes of your heart enlightened, you may know what is the hope to which He has called you, what are the riches of His glorious inheritance among the saints, and what is the immeasurable greatness of his power for us who believe, according to the working of his great power. (Ephesians 1:17–19).

The prayer from Ephesians 1:17–19, is crucial in the process of spiritual formation of a Christian. Is not the head knowledge of theology which transforms the inner person; it is the "supernatural enablement," which leads to such change.

And this is exactly what the author talks about in step 3:

> *3. I must repeatedly affirm my total dependence upon the Holy Spirit to enable me to express the power of Jesus' risen life.*

Why is it so easy to sin? Obviously, our flesh still has its bent toward sin. That's no surprise. It came equipped with its own built-in drivenness to fill up its own emptiness by seeking out its own meaning, significance, and love—and to do so independently from God. It also came equipped to actually fulfill (at least in some measure) the desires it feels. Normally, one's will is followed by action. Both the *desire* and the *power to sin* are resident in my flesh. But to move—to produce holiness, to produce love—requires dependence upon a power source distinct from my will. It involves dependence upon the power of another person, the Holy Spirit. Though both the desire and the power for the holiness (the Holy Spirit) are within, God has purposed that the release of that power comes only as a result of a life of active dependence upon Him—the source of our life. He did not save us to get such and such quantity of holiness produced. He saved us for love—for a dependent love relationship with him in the context of living and loving both with our brothers and sisters in Christ and the world outside. As children of the light, He greatly values our trusting Him in the dark. It is in this context as we are confronted by our own total flesh inadequacy that we cry out, "Lord I cannot live apart from your life! I have no life unless you pour your life into me. I have jettisoned all back-up systems. I will live because of you, or I will die" (John 6:57; Romans 8:6,13). We simply cannot escape the fact that the Christian life is strictly supernatural, nor should we want it any other way. And that life, above all else, is marked by supernatural love.

The Most Important Prayer in the Bible

Because of the deception of flesh-produced righteousness, it is worth our time to look at one of the most amazing, comprehensive prayers in all the Bible—the most important prayer I know to pray! It is found in Ephesians 3:14–21. Let's spread these verses out so that we take a good look at them.

For this reason
I kneel before the Father,
from whom His whole family
in heaven and on earth
derives its name.
I pray that out of his glorious riches
He may strengthen you with power
through His Spirit
in your inner being,
so that Christ may dwell in your hearts
through faith.
And I pray that you, being rooted and established in
love,
may have power, together with all the saints
to grasp how wide
and long
and high
and deep
is the love of Christ
that surpasses knowledge—
that you may be filled to the measure of all the fullness
of God.
Now to Him who is able to do
immeasurably more
than all we ask or imagine,
according to His power that is at work within us,
to Him be glory in the church and
in Christ Jesus throughout all generations,
for ever and ever!
Amen.

The kind of love God wants to give us is supernatural, beyond anything we could imagine. It involves "all the fullness of God." "Our God is the God of the impossible—able to accomplish abundantly far more than all we can ask or imagine." And how? By the Spirit's power "at work within us." Oh, what an open door! Walk through it! And then keep on walking in moment-by-moment, total dependence upon his enablement.

In the section, Holiness as Sanctified Stress, Needham discusses how all of this is possible in our lives as God's children.

"Moment by moment"—that is so easy to say but impossible to do. Life with all of its demands simply will not allow me to consciously do that. God has not asked us to exchange one kind of stress—*the stress of the world*—for another kind—*the stress of holiness.* When Paul urged us to pray without ceasing, I am sure he had in mind our living in the context of an ongoing walk with God resting in His supernatural, personal involvement right in the midst of the multitudes of activities and demands that surround us. Rather than thinking of those long spaces when duties require my total concentration as interruptions, I am sure God wishes me to assume our praying relationship has not been interrupted at all. They are simply silent times we both accept as being all right. Building on a disciplined pattern of regular times given over to nurturing our ongoing friendship with God in prayer, we begin each day affirming both our desire and expectation that the hours awaiting us will be filled with the life of Jesus. God expects us to assume He is answering our prayer until we have good reason to believe otherwise. God does not want us to live on pins and needles, worrying as to whether it is happening. Of course, the moment we are aware of entertaining sinful motives, thoughts, or actions, we must quickly drink in His cleansing and then realign ourselves with life (1 John 1:7).

The table is spread with a number of things we can do to encourage holiness in our lives.

The author describes it:

> Though by all means, the life that is now ours to live is supernatural, there are a variety of things, which in themselves initially may not be supernatural, yet are necessary in creating the context in which the life of Jesus is both fully received and displayed. As I take these actions, I place myself in a position where miracles happen.
>
> • I drink in the truth of God's Word.
> • I maintain regular times of prayer.
> • I get busy with tasks I know God wants me to do.
> • I physically remove myself from a particular circumstance where fulfilling some temptation is fostered. I don't take that second look.
> • I place myself in people–loving circumstances, some circumstances in which Jesus' life, His love, is dispensed to someone else.
> • I write that letter, make that call. I reach out, trusting that the "touch" is the actual extension of the hand of the Savior Himself.
> • I reject, as illegal aliens, any thoughts that would become sin if entertained.
> • I involve myself in doing one of the "whatsoevers" of Philippians 4:8. That opens the door of all sorts of options!"

As this happens, emptiness is replaced by fullness, even though at first I may be most conscious of my complaining flesh. Not only will I not be doing whatever sins had earlier tempted me, but I will increasingly realize that I really don't want to do them. That which my deepest level of selfhood truly desired all along—*holiness*—is now my conscious, dominant desire (Romans 7:22; 8:9, 12:1–2). Dear Christian, if you have taken God's interior miracle seriously, you must make your mind your slave.

Are you ready to confront those vile intruders, calling them what they are? I hereby choose to think of:

Whatever is true,
Whatever is honorable,
Whatever is just,
Whatever is pure,
Whatever is pleasing,
Whatever is commendable,
Anything worthy of praise
— Philippians 4:8.

It is not too late to start making your body—*that fleshy mind of yours*—your slave. Yes, it will be a tough discipline; mental discipline is the toughest one of all. But the Spirit is eager to respond to your choice (Romans 8:13). The question is, will you do it? I have found that my own need of responding to this truth is greatest during those times when my life is least structured—when the pressures are off. When I flop down in my recliner and flip on the TV, when I window shop at the neighborhood mall; those are the most dangerous times. How often do we sin simply out of boredom!" (pp. 186–188)

Our lifestyle should be of one of *being*, not of one of *doing*; that is—Being dependent upon the Spirit's power.

Needhman writes:

I'm afraid sometimes we Christians deceive ourselves into thinking we are handling this problem fairly well by packing our spare time so full of one thing or another—especially if we are either witnessing or reading our Bibles—that we're not even aware we have completely lost touch with authentic life. The answer is not in busyness, but in **making dependence our lifestyle**. Only God knows whether right around the next bend awaiting us is a surprise attack in spiritual warfare. But He does know and that is enough. Still, the Spirit must be an active participant. Otherwise, we will fall prey to those extremely subtle counterfeits of righteousness that can unknowingly slip in to fill the void. It is so hard to keep in mind that eternally significant living is not found in simply rejecting sinful things, nor is it found in coming up with wholesome alternatives; it is found only as God's life is actually received and displayed through us as a prism receives light and, in turn, produces the varied colors of the rainbow. Christianity is not simply living that ideal "eagle scout" life; it is <u>dependent resurrection life</u>. Of all spiritual disciplines, the discipline of dependence is by far the most crucial. It is not simply memorizing the manual. It is in actually *receiving, responding, and displaying* the love of God. I may push myself to perform a loving act, yet still miss expressing the fruit of the Spirit (non-Christians can do that). It is at this point that the simplest and yet most mysterious of all statements must be in sharp focus: "you in Me, and I in you" (John 14:20). Such a life is available equally to every child of God apart from all those intellectual, professional, giftedness yardsticks we wrongly use to measure a Christians worth. And as one single will arises to God, unconditionally open to Lordship, the Spirit of life places his royal impress upon our words and actions and the divine dimension of resurrection life occurs—Jesus is seen in human flesh, our flesh! God, the infinite Lover, often blesses simply because he delights in the pure pleasures of his children. Paul caught this happy thought when he wrote "God... richly provides us with everything for our enjoyment" (1 Timothy 6:17). God's love does not always have ulterior motives!

We are the crown of God's creation, and the masterpiece of His re-creation. Therefore, our time here on heart is the time of preparation, not only for this temporary life but for eternity. The truth is that we are called to reflect the invisible God, similarly to a prism which reflects the light in multiple shades. But in order to reflect God properly, our life must be shaped accordingly, in the same way the prism is cut and polished by the master glass worker.

Since you have come this far with me, the last thing I need to do is prove to you the importance of this action step, 4—"I must welcome the trial times of my life as evidences of my Father's love." This attitudinal choice each of us must make. You know it is true.

…

Perhaps right now you are experiencing some shattered dream, some fear or sense of loneliness, loss, pain, or grief. If only you might find grace to look up through to see the glory! That's the way it is with trial times. Once we see the glory, we are never the same again. (1 Peter 1:6–9) Who is a Christian? In terms of deep, spiritual personhood, he or she is God's uniquely designed prism, His ultimate spiritual masterpiece. **Our lives are the means by which the invisible God becomes visible to a world that will not see Him any other way.** Our inmost being, the prism; our flesh, the wall upon which the colors are seen. Could there be any greater purpose, any greater significance for being alive than this? But for this to happen, the Master Diamond Cutter must *progressively transform* that flawless product of His birthing by cutting multiple facets upon its surface. **The trials of our faith are this painful cutting process.** There is no other way if we are to display "His holiness the peaceful fruit of righteousness" (Hebrews 12:10,11). Can we trust our Diamond Cutter never to make a cut too deep? Remember, His intentions for us are not only for time, but forever.

Those who are wise shall shine like the brightness of the sky, and those who lead many to righteousness, like the stars for ever and ever" (Daniel 12:3). With such an important destiny, do you actually believe that God would mishandle so precious a treasure as you are to Him?[124]

Moreover, in Chapter 10 called "*The Goal of God's Miracle Children,*" David Needham explains that the Bride has been chosen before the foundations of the world to display the invisible attributes of God such as: *love* and *grace, patience* and *justice, power* and *wisdom.* Isn't this brilliant? To open the possibility for all of these to happen,

Christ had to die on the cross. Because of His supreme sacrifice now we can experience **being alive for the first time**, and not only that, but **we are going to be alive forever.** In the light of these things, what can we say, other than falling down on our faces in complete awe declaring the words of St. Paul from Romans 11:36: "from Him and through Him and to Him are all things. To Him be the glory forever Amen."

The author writes:

> You and I worship a fabulously creative God. We began this book with this truth. He tells us that creation—*the entire universe*—bears witness to his "invisible qualities—His eternal power and divine nature" (Romans 1:20). And indeed, we agree it does, no matter in which direction we might look. And all of it flowing from the unbelievably inventive mind of God! Indeed, we worship a God who is so fantastically inventive as to paint the colors and shape the forms of myriad flower petals and endless sunsets, plus mixing in the fragrances, tastes, and sounds that surround us (Genesis 1:31; 2:9; Psalm 19:1-6; 65:5–13). Yet when we stand back and attempt to evaluate the flow of human history—its tragedy and tears, its confusion and cruelty, its seemingly endless cycles—it appears to fall short of expressing the creative touch of a truly wise, powerful, and good God. Yet the Bible asks us to believe that, sprinkled about this paradoxical world, are a variety of supernatural aliens whose true home is heaven and who bear witness to a God of love and grace (Matthew 7:13–14, Luke 12:32; Philippians 3:20). It's strange, yet often true, that some of God's most beautiful masterpieces of creativity arise out of the very opposites of those masterpieces. From the dead and decaying marshlands, the lilies grow. From rotting fir needles and slimy leaves, trilliums sprout and bloom. And so it is that out of the darkness and gross evil of a justly cursed humanity, God has chosen to produce the crowning product of His new creation—His most captivating creation—*a bride for His Son* (Ephesians 5:25–27; Revelation 19:6–8). Is it not the ultimate of human folly to assume that such a God who demonstrates His

perfections in billions of momentary blossoms would approach the ultimate, eternally exhibition of his creativity—the church, the people of God—with haphazard weakness? Is it not far more reasonable to believe this remarkable God has at least an equal masterfulness of perfection in mind as he creates a bride for his Son? Though we remain humbled by the mysteries that harmonize God's sovereign will and human choice, we dare not miss his joy over every lost sheep that is found—here and around the world—each one adding a special touch to the ultimate beauty of the bride. Even now His church, His new creation, as yet physically unredeemed, continues to display itself like the late winter blossoms on some trees—unexpected, not yet overly beautiful, but still the harbinger of spring. "Not yet overly beautiful" surely is an understatement when one considers with embarrassment the mottled history of the church. Though here and there among its dark pages are sparkling examples of God's individual miracles, the overall history of the church has been more a display of his patience and grace than of the church's grand successes. This should surprise us were it not for the fact that His Bride, rather than being the goal of history, is actually *exhibit A* of God's true goal—His own glory. **What is his glory?** The displayed splendor of all of His attributes I confess that the first time I realized the goal of everything was the glory of God, my response was, "That sounds too self-centered." Why then should we be so surprised that God, the possessor of limitless qualities of infinite perfection, should so choose to display them? What rightness could there be if the possessor of absolute *love* and *grace, patience* and *justice, power* and *wisdom* never allowed them to be seen?

We should find much security and joy in the fact that his plan of creating a bride for His Son was in His mind from eternity past—"just as he chose us in Christ before the foundation of the world to be holy and blameless before Him in love" (Ephesians 1:4). He has also told us this masterpiece of his creativity is "according to his counsel and will" (Ephesians 1:11). Clearly, this captivating mystery of the Bride was no midcourse correction after his first plan in the Garden of Eden went awry. In fact, with purpose it included the cross and the resurrection, as God unfolded His own wisdom and power (1 Corinthians 1: 18–24).

When at last the moment of all moments arrives and the Son lifts up the kingdom to His Father, when at last every dazzling facet of the diamond of God's own Being is fully revealed—marvel of marvels, we will be there, standing "in the presence of his glory with rejoicing" (Jude 24). **Only then will we experience in its fullness that to be alive for the first time is to be alive forever.** Having exchanged the mortality and oft morbidity of our unredeemed flesh for the inexpressible glory of the image of the man of heaven, we will be there. With uninhibited freedom—all flesh/spirit conflicts removed—we will be there, unendingly fulfilling the destiny for which we were made as the *receivers,* the *responders,* and the *displayers* of God's love (Philippians 3:12–14). Have all our questions about the miracles of grace been answered? Far from it. Mysteries remain that stir our curiosity. But until then we must rest easy, knowing that when at last all creation beholds the Bride, you and I will be there lifting our transformed voices with emotional energies beyond our dreams, shouting "from Him and through Him and to Him are all things. To Him be the glory forever Amen" (Romans 11:36).[125]

Our highest calling is to become the best spiritual persons we can become. This requires intentionality on our part. God supplies the grace and we are supposed to supply the faith-based-obedience.

In Chapter 7 called, *"You Can't Live Beyond What You Believe,"* Dr. Anderson explains that there is a direct connection between what people believe and how people behave. Also he asserts that there is a link between human emotions and their belief system. In other words emotions are like red flags when we are pursuing goals based on erroneous beliefs.

Anderson writes:

> Your Christian walk is the direct result of what you
> believe. **If your faith is off, your walk will be off.** If your
> walk is off, you need to take a good look at what you
> believe. <u>Walking by faith simply means that you function
> in daily life on the basis of what you believe.</u> In fact, you
> are already walking by faith; you can't not walk by faith.
> People may not always live what they profess, but they
> will always live what they believe because your *misbehavior*
> is the result of your *disbelief.* The writer of Hebrews said,
> "Remember those who led you, who spoke the word of
> God to you; and considering <u>the result of their conduct,
> imitate their faith</u>" (13:7)
>
> . . .
>
> To better understand what you presently believe, take a
> few minutes to complete the following *Faith Appraisal.*
> Simply evaluate yourself in each of the eight categories by
> circling a number from one to five that best represents
> you, five being high.
>
> . . .
>
> Then complete each of the eight statements as concisely
> and truthfully as possible.

Faith Appraisal

	Low			High

1. How successful am I?

1   2   3   4   5

I would be more successful if . . .

2. How significant am I?

1   2   3   4   5

I would be more significant if . . .

3. How fulfilled am I?

1   2   3   4   5

I would be more fulfilled if . . .

4. How satisfied am I?

1   2   3   4   5

I would be more satisfied if . . .

5. How happy am I?

1   2   3   4   5

I would be happier if . . .
6. How much fun am I having?
1   2   3   4   5
I would have more fun if . . .
7 How secure am I?
1   2   3   4   5
I would be more secure if . . .
8. How peaceful am I?
1   2   3   4   5
I would have more peace if . . .

You are right now walking by faith according to what you believe. Chances are you may not have the same definitions for these eight qualities of life that God does, and therefore your walk by faith may not be achieving what you want.)

Feelings Are God's Red Flag Of Warning
"From birth, you have been developing in your mind a means for experiencing these eight values and reaching other goals in life. Consciously or subconsciously, you continue to formulate and adjust your plans for achieving these goals. Sometimes, however, your well-intended plans and noble-sounding goals are not completely in harmony with God's plans and goals for you. Must I wait until I am 45 years old or until I experience some kind of midlife crisis to discover that what I believed in these eight areas was wrong? I believe God has designed you in such a way that you can know on a moment-by-moment basis if your belief system is properly aligned with God's truth. <u>God has established a feedback system designed to grab your attention so you can examine the validity of your goals and beliefs.</u> When an experience or relationship leaves you feeling angry, anxious or depressed, those emotional signposts are there to alert you that you may be cherishing a faulty goal based on a wrong belief.

Anger Signals an Uncertain Goal
When your activity in a relationship or a project results in feelings of anger, it is usually because someone or

something has blocked your goal, something or somebody is preventing you from accomplishing what you wanted. How do you feel in a traffic jam when it is preventing you from getting to an important meeting on time? Suppose a wife and mother says, *"My goal in life is to have a loving, harmonious, happy Christian family."* Who can block that goal? Every person in her family can block that goa—not only can, they will! "Whatever is not from faith is sin" (Rom. 14:23); **therefore, an outburst of anger should prompt us to reexamine what we believe and the mental goals we have formulated to accomplish those beliefs.**

Anxiety Signals an Uncertain Goal
When you feel anxious in a task or a relationship, your anxiety may be signaling that achieving your goal may be uncertain. You are hoping something will happen, but you have no guarantee it will. **You can control some of the factors but not all of them.**

Depression Signals an Impossible Goal
When you base your future success on something that can never happen, you have an impossible, hopeless goal. Your depression is a signal that your goal, no matter how spiritual or noble, may never be reached. We can be depressed for biochemical reasons, but if there is no physical cause, then depression is often rooted in a sense of *hopelessness* or *helplessness*. You should, desire that loved ones come to Christ, pray and work to that end. When you base your sense of worth as a Christian friend, parent or child on the salvation of your loved ones, however, realize that this goal may be beyond your ability or right to control. Witnessing is sharing our faith in the power of the Holy Spirit and leaving the results to God. We can't save anyone. **Depression often signals that you are desperately clinging to a goal you have little or no chance of achieving,** which is not a healthy goal. Sometimes depression reveals a faulty concept of God. David wrote: "How long, O Lord? Will you forget me?
. . .

251

How long will my enemy triumph over me? (Ps. 13:1,2). Had God really forgotten David? Was He actually hiding from David? Of course not. David had a wrong concept of God, feeling that He had abandoned him to the enemy. The remarkable thing about David is that he didn't stay in the dumps. He evaluated his situation and realized, "Hey, I'm a child of God. I'm going to focus on what I know about Him, not on my negative feelings." With God all things are possible. He is the God of all hope. Turn to God when you are feeling down, as David did. "Why are you in despair, O my soul? And why are you disturbed within me? Hope in God, for I shall again praise Him, the help of my countenance, and my God" (Ps. 43:5).

Wrong responses to Those Who Frustrate Goals
"If our goals can be blocked or uncertain, how do we respond to someone to something that threatens our success? We may attempt to control or manipulate people or circumstances who stand between us and the achievement of our goals. It is not hard to understand why people try to control others. They believe their sense of worth is dependent on other people and circumstances. This is a false belief, as evidenced by the fact that the most insecure people you will ever meet are manipulators and controllers. **People who cannot control those who frustrate their goals will probably respond by getting bitter, angry or resentful.**[126]

Is there any way people can turn bad goals into good ones? In the section called, *"How Can I Turn Bad Goals into Good Goals?"* the author teaches us how we can do that.

Anderson writes:

Let me ask you a faith-stretching question: If God wants something done, can it be done? In other words, if God has a goal for your life, can it be blocked, or is its fulfillment uncertain or impossible? I am personally convinced that no goal God has for my life is impossible or uncertain, nor can it be blocked. I can't imagine God saying, "I've called you into existence, I've made you My child and I have something for you to do. I know you won't be able to do it , but give it your best shot." That's ludicrous! God had a staggering goal for a young maid named Mary. An angel told her she would bear a Son while still a virgin, and her Son would be the Savior of the world. When she inquired about this seemingly impossible feat, the angel simply said, *"Nothing will be impossible with God"* (Luke 1:37). You wouldn't give your children tasks they couldn't possibly complete, and God doesn't assign to you goals you can't achieve. His goals for you are possible, certain and achievable.

Goals versus Desires

To live successful lives, we need to distinguish a <u>godly goal</u> from a <u>godly desire</u>. This liberating distinction can spell the difference between <u>success</u> and <u>failure</u>, inner peace and inner pain for the Christian. <u>A godly goal is any specific orientation that reflects God's purpose for your life and is not dependent on people or circumstances beyond your ability or right to control</u>. **The only person who can block a godly goal or render it uncertain or impossible is you.** If you adopt the attitude of cooperation with God's goals as Mary did, your goal can be reached. <u>A godly desire is any specific result that depends on the cooperation of other people, the success of events or favorable circumstances you have no right or ability to control</u>. You cannot base your success or sense of worth on your desires, no matter how godly they may be, because you cannot control their fulfillment. Let's face it, life doesn't always go our way and many of our desires will not be met. We will struggle with anger, anxiety and depression when we elevate a desire to a goal in our own minds. By comparison, when a desire isn't met, you will only face disappointment. Dealing with the disappointments of unmet desires is a lot easier than dealing with the anger, anxiety and depression of goals that are based on wrong beliefs. Does God make a distinction between a goal and a desire? Yes, I think He does. "'"For I have no pleasure in the death of anyone who dies," declares the Lord GOD. "Therefore repent and

253

live"'" (Ezek.18:32). It is God's desire that everyone repent, though not everyone will. Then does God have any genuine goals—specific results that cannot be blocked? Praise the Lord, yes! For example, Jesus Christ will return and take us home to heaven to be with Him forever—it will happen. Satan will be cast into the abyss for eternity—count on it. What God has determined to do, He will do. When you begin to align your goals with God's goals and your desires with God's desires, you will rid your life of a lot of anger, anxiety and depression.

The Goal Is to Become the Person God Called You to Be
It should be obvious by now that God's basic goal for your life is character development: becoming the person God wants you to be. <u>Sanctification is God's goal for your life</u> (1 Thess.4:3). Nobody and nothing on planet Earth can keep you from being the person God called you to be. Paul teaches that the tribulations we face are actually a means of achieving our supreme goal of maturity: "We also exult in our tribulations, knowing that tribulation brings about perseverance; and perseverance, proven character; and proven character, hope; and hope does not disappoint, because the love of God has been poured out within our hearts through the Holy Spirit who was given to us" (Rom.5:3-5). The word "exult" means heightened joy. To be under tribulation means to be under pressure. Persevering through tribulations results in proven character, which is God's goal for us. <u>Trials and tribulations reveal wrong goals</u>, but they can actually be the catalyst for achieving God's goal for our lives, which is our sanctification—the process of conforming to His image. During these times of pressure, our emotions raise their warning flags, signaling blocked, uncertain or impossible goals based on our desires instead of God's goal of proven character. Is there an easier way to being God's person than through enduring tribulations? Believe me: I have been looking for one. I must honestly say, though, that it has been the dark, difficult times of testing in my life that have brought me to where I am today. We need occasional mountaintop experiences, but the fertile

soil for growth is always down in the valleys of tribulation, not on the mountaintops. Paul says, "The goal of our instruction is love" (1 Tim.1:5). Notice that if you make that your goal, then the fruit of the Spirit is love, joy (instead of depression), peace (instead of anxiety) and patience (instead of anger).[127]

When it comes to the practical aspect of walking by faith, more often than not, Christians are confused. In chapter 8, titled: *"God's Guidelines for the Walk of Faith,"* Anderson explains that there is a direct connection between *belief system* and *behavior* (or walk in life). The author suggests practical ways to fine tune our belief system and correct our walk in life.

He writes:

> When you base your sense of worth on the success of your own personal plans, your life will be one long, emotional roller-coaster ride. The only way to get off the roller-coaster is to walk by faith according to the truth of God's Word.
>
> As far as the devil is concerned, the next best thing to keeping you chained in spiritual darkness or having you live as an emotional wreck is confusing your belief system. If he can muddy your mind and weaken your faith with partial truths, however, he can neutralize your effectiveness for God and stunt your growth as a Christian. It is imperative for your spiritual maturity, though, that your beliefs about *success, significance, fulfillment, satisfaction, happiness, fun, security* and *peace* be anchored in the Scriptures. I want to review each of these belief areas from the foundation of God's Word. These descriptions may help you make some vital adjustments that will steer you back to the middle of the fairway.

1. Success. Key Concept: Goals

Note: The reader can assess his or her own score by completing the Faith Appraisal from Chapter 7, page 124–125 in the book.

Success is related to goals. If you rated yourself low in the success category, you are probably having difficulty reaching your goals in life. **If you aren't reaching your goals, it is probably because you are working on the wrong goals.** A good summary of God's goal for us is found in 2 Peter 1:2–11:

Grace and peace be multiplied to you in the knowledge of God and of Jesus our Lord; seeing that His divine power has granted to us everything pertaining to life and godliness, through the true knowledge of Him who called us by His own glory and excellence. For by these He has granted to us His precious and magnificent promises, so that by them you may become partakers of the divine nature, having escaped the corruption that is in the world by lust. Now for this very reason also, applying all diligence, in your faith supply moral excellence, and in your moral excellence, knowledge, and in your knowledge, self-control, and in your self-control, perseverance, and in your perseverance, godliness, and in your godliness, brotherly kindness, and in your brotherly kindness, love. For if these qualities are yours and are increasing, they render you neither useless nor unfruitful in the true knowledge of our Lord Jesus Christ. For he who lacks these qualities is blind or short-sighted, having forgotten his purification from his former sins. Therefore, brethren, be all the more diligent to make certain about His calling and choosing you; for as long as you practice these things, you will never stumble; for in this way the entrance into the eternal kingdom of our Lord and Savior Jesus Christ will be abundantly supplied to you.

Notice that God's goal begins with who you are on the basis of what God has already done for you. He has given you "life and godliness"; justification has already happened and sanctification has already begun. You are already a partaker of the "divine nature, having escaped" (past tense) sin's corruption. What a great start! Your primary job now is to adopt God's character goals diligently—moral excellence, knowledge, self-control, perseverance, godliness, brotherly kindness and Christian love—and apply them to your life. **Focusing on God's goals will lead to ultimate success:** *success in God's terms.* Peter promises that as these qualities increase in your life through practice, you will be useful and fruitful and you will never stumble. That is a legitimate basis for a true sense of worth and success and nobody can keep you from accomplishing it! Another helpful perspective of success is seen in Joshua's experience of leading Israel into the Promised Land (Joshua 1:7, 8). Was Joshua's success dependent on other people or favorable circumstances? Absolutely not. **Success hinged entirely on living according to God's Word.** If Joshua believed what God said and did what God told him to do, he would succeed. Joshua's success was conditional on obeying God regardless of how foolish His plan seemed. As Joshua 6 records, Joshua's success had nothing to do with the circumstances of the battle and everything to do with obedience. **Success is accepting God's goal for our lives and by His grace becoming what He has called us to be.**

2. Significance. Key Concept: Time

"Significance is a time concept. What is forgotten in time is of little significance. What is remembered for eternity is of great significance. Paul wrote to the Corinthians: "If any man's work . . . remains he shall receive a reward" (1 Cor. 3:14). He instructed Timothy: "Discipline yourself for the purpose of godliness . . . since it holds promise for the present life and also for the life to come" (1 Tim. 4:7, 8).

If you want to increase your **significance**, focus your energies on <u>significant activities</u>: those that will remain for eternity. I know some great theologians who have led very few people to Christ. If a few hundred people are believers today because of you, and they have influenced who knows how many other people for Christ, I'd call that a great work for God. <u>There is no such thing as a lowly pastor or a lowly child of God</u>. We are in the significant business of collecting treasures for eternity. What we do and say for Christ in this world, no matter how insignificant it seems, will last forever." (pp. 142–143)

3. Fulfillment. Key Concept: Role Preference
Fulfillment in life can be summarized by the simple slogan, "Bloom where you're planted." Peter said it this way: "As each one has received a special gift, employ it in serving one another" (1 Peter 4:10). Fulfillment is discovering our own uniqueness in Christ and using our gifts and talents to edify others and to glorify the Lord. God has a unique place of ministry for each of us. **It is important to your sense of fulfillment that you realize your calling in life.** The key is to discover the roles you occupy in which you cannot be replaced, and then decide to be what God wants you to be in those roles. For example, of the six billion people in the world, you are the only one who occupies your unique role as husband, father, wife, mother, parent or child in your home. God has specifically planted you to serve Him by serving your family in that environment. Furthermore, you are the only one who knows your neighbors as you do. You occupy a unique role as an ambassador for Christ where you work. These are your mission fields and you are the worker God has appointed for the harvest there. Your greatest fulfillment will come from accepting and occupying God's unique place for you to the best of your ability. Sadly, many miss there calling in life by looking for fulfillment in the world. Find your fulfillment in the kingdom of God by deciding to be an ambassador for Christ in the world (2 Cor. 5:20).

4. Satisfaction. Key Concept: Quality
Satisfaction comes from living righteously and seeking to raise the level of quality in relationships, service and product. Jesus said, "Blessed are those who hunger and thirst for righteousness, for they shall be satisfied" (Matt.5:6). Do you believe that? If you do, what are you doing? You are hungering and thirsting after righteousness, and if you aren't doing that, then you really don't believe it. **Satisfaction is a quality concern, not a**

quantity concern. You will achieve greater satisfaction from <u>doing a few things well</u> than from doing many things in a haphazard or hasty manner. The key to personal satisfaction is not found in broadening the scope of your activities but in deepening them through a <u>commitment to quality</u>. The same is true in relationships. If you are dissatisfied in your relationships, perhaps you have spread yourself too thin. Solomon wrote, "A man of many friends comes to ruin, but there is a friend who sticks closer than a brother" (Prov. 18:24). It may be nice to know a lot of people on the surface, but you need a few real good friends who are committed to a quality relationship with you. That is what our Lord modeled for us. He taught the multitudes and equipped 70 for ministry, but He invested most of His time in the 12 disciples. While suffering on the cross, Jesus committed to John, perhaps His closest friend, the care of His mother. That is a quality relationship, and we all need the satisfaction that quality relationships bring.

5. Happiness. Key Concept: Wanting What You Have
The world's concept of happiness is having what we want. When you begin to appreciate what you already have, however, you will be happy all your life. Paul wrote to Timothy, "But godliness with contentment is great gain. For we brought nothing into the world, and we can take nothing out of it. But if we have food and clothing, we will be content with that" (1 Tim.6:6-8). Actually, you already have everything you need to make you happy forever. You have Christ. You have eternal life. You are loved by a heavenly Father who has promised to supply all your needs. No wonder the Bible repeatedly commands us to be thankful (1 Thess.5:18). If you really want to be happy, learn to be content with life and thankful for what you already have in Christ." (pp. 145–146)

6. Fun. Key Concept: Uninhibited Spontaneity
Fun is uninhibited spontaneity. The secret to enjoying uninhibited spontaneity as a Christian is to remove

unscriptural inhibitors. Chief among the inhibitors of Christian fun is our fleshly tendency to keep up appearances. We don't want to look out of place or be thought less of by others, so we stifle our spontaneity with a form of false decorum. That is people pleasing, and Paul suggested that anybody who lives to please people isn't serving Christ (Gal.1:10). The joyless cry, "What will people say?" The liberated in Christ respond, "Who cares what people say?" I care what God says; I stopped playing for the grandstand a long time ago when I started playing for the coach. It is a lot more fun pleasing the Lord than trying to please people.

7. Security. Key Concept: Relating to the Eternal

Insecurity means depending upon temporal things that we have no right or ability to control. Do you realize that God is shaking the foundations of this world? Insecurity is a global problem. Some rough days are ahead for this fallen world. It doesn't take a genius to determine that. An exploding population and decreasing natural resources indicate we are fast heading on a collision course. Our security can be found only in the eternal life of Christ. Jesus said no one can snatch us out of His hand (John 10:27-29). Paul declared that nothing can separate us from the love of God in Christ (Rom.8:35-39) and that we are sealed in Him by the Holy Spirit (Eph. 1:13,14). How much more secure can you get than that? Paul said, "But whatever things were gain to me, those things I have counted as loss for the sake of Christ. More than that, I count all things to be loss in view of the surpassing value of knowing Christ Jesus my Lord, for whom I have suffered the loss of all things, and count them but rubbish in order that I may gain Christ" (Phil. 3:7,8)." (pp. 147–148)

8. Peace. Key Concept: Establishing Internal Order

Peace on earth, good will to men; that is what everybody wants. That is a great desire but a wrong goal. Nobody can guarantee external peace because nobody can control people or circumstances.

The peace of God is internal, not external. Peace with God is something you already have. (Rom.5:1). The peace of God is something you need to appropriate daily in your inner world in the midst of the storms that rage in the external world (John 14:27). A lot of things can disrupt your external world because you can't control all your circumstances and relationships. You can control the inner world of your thoughts and emotions, however, by daily allowing the peace of God to rule in your heart. Personal worship, prayer and interaction with God's Word enable us to experience the peace of God (Phil.4:6,7; Col.3:15,16).

...

Often when I share these eight critical points of the Christian's belief system, I hear people say, "Well, I suppose that's true, but I still believe . . ." Which will they live by: what they acknowledge as true or what they "still believe"? Always the latter—always! Walking by faith is simply choosing to believe what God says is true and to live accordingly by the power of the Holy Spirit.[128]

In chapter 10: *You Must be Real to be Right*, Dr. Neil T. Anderson explains that being emotionally real and transparent before God is essential for spiritual transformation. If we hide or suppress our feelings we are not real. In His love the Lord may have to make us real to become right with God. The process of mind renewal includes managing our emotions. How? By managing our thought life. When we do this we can have loving relationships with others— which is essential for our Christian living.

In the section called, *Your Emotions Reveal Your Beliefs*, Anderson writes:

Your emotions play a major role in the process of renewing our mind. In a general sense, your emotions are a product of your thought life. If you are not thinking right, if your mind is not being renewed, if you are not perceiving God and His Word properly, it will show up in your emotional life. If you fail to acknowledge your emotions appropriately, you may become spiritually vulnerable. **You are not shaped as much by your environment as you are by your perception of your environment**. Life's events don't determine who you are; God determines who you are, and your interpretation of life's events determine how well you will handle the pressures of life. We are tempted to say, "He made me so mad!" or "I wasn't depressed until she showed up!" That's like saying, "I have no control over my emotions or my will." In reality we have very little control over our emotions, but we do have control over our thoughts, and our thoughts determine our feelings and our responses. That is why it is so important that you fill your mind with the knowledge of God and His Word. You need to live from God's perspective and respond accordingly. Remember, if what you believe does not reflect truth, then what you feel does not reflect reality. The order of Scripture is to *know* the truth, *believe* it, *live* accordingly by faith, and let your emotions be a product of your trust in God and your obedience to Him.

What kind of life would you live if you believed what you felt instead of the truth? Your life would be as inconsistent as your feelings. "If you know these things, you are blessed if you do them" (John 13:17). **In other words, you don't feel your way into good behavior, you behave your way into good feelings.**

In the section titled, *Don't Ignore the Warning Signs of Your Emotions,* the author writes:

> Your emotions are to your soul what your physical feelings are to your body. **Emotions are God's indicators to let you know what is going on inside.** They are neither good nor bad; they are amoral, just part of your humanity. Just as you respond to the warnings of physical pain, so you need to learn to respond to your emotional indicators.
>
> Someone has likened emotions to the red light on the dashboard of a car indicating an engine problem. You can respond to the red light's warning in several ways. You can cover it with a piece of duct tape. "I can't see the light,

so I don't have to think about the problem." You can smash the light with a hammer. "That'll teach you for glaring in my face!" Or you can respond to the light as the manufacturer intended by looking under the hood and fixing the problem. You have the same three options in responding to your emotions. You can respond by *covering* them, *ignoring* them or *stifling* them, slow to speak. **That is called suppression.** You can respond by thoughtlessly lashing out, giving someone a piece of your mind or flying off the handle. I call that **indiscriminate expression.** Or you can peer inside to see what is going on. That is called **acknowledgment.**

What follows is *The Duct Tape of Suppression.* In this section he writes:

Suppression is a conscious denial of feelings (repression is an unconscious denial). Those who suppress their emotions ignore their feelings and choose not to confront them. **Emotional suppression may be one of the major reasons most people are sick for psychosomatic reasons.** When David kept quiet about his sins, his "vitality was drained away as with the fever heat of summer" (Psalm 32:4).You never bury dead feelings; you bury them alive and they will surface in some way that is not healthy. Suppressing our emotions leads to dishonest communication and is physically unhealthy.

The following section, called, *The Hammer of Indiscriminate* Expression, is so important.
The author writes:

Another unhealthy way to respond to emotions is to thoughtlessly express everything you feel. Indiscriminately telling anybody and everybody exactly how you feel is usually unhealthy for the other person. The apostle Peter is a great example. Peter was the John Wayne of the New Testament—a real door slammer. He had no problem telling anyone what was on his mind or how he felt. I like to refer to him as the one-legged apostle because he always had one foot in his mouth. Peter's indiscriminate expression of his emotions got him into trouble more than once. One minute he makes the greatest confession of all time: "Thou art the Christ, the son of the living God" (Matt. 16:16). A few minutes later Peter tells Jesus He doesn't know what He is doing, and Jesus has to rebuke him: "Get behind Me, Satan" (vs. 22,23). Indiscriminate expression of emotions may be somewhat healthy for you, but it is usually unhealthy for others around you. "There, I'm glad I got that off my chest," you may say after an outburst. In the process though, you just destroyed your wife, husband or children. James warned: "But let everyone be quick to hear, slow to speak and slow to anger; for the anger of man does not achieve the righteousness of God" (James 1:19,20). Paul admonished: "Be angry, and yet do not sin" (Eph. 4:26). If you wish to be angry and not sin, then be angry the way Christ was: **be angry at sin**. Turn over the tables; don't attack the money changers.

In *The Openness of Acknowledgment,* he explains:

Jesus told his disciples, "Unless your righteousness surpasses that of the scribes and Pharisees, you shall not enter the kingdom of heaven" (Matt. 5:20). **In God's eyes, if you are not real, you are not right.** <u>If necessary, God may have to make you real to make you right with Him</u>. Acknowledging your emotions as a real person is essential for intimate relationships. You shouldn't let off steam just anywhere in front of just anybody. That is indiscriminate expression, and you run the risk of hurting others more than you help yourself—and that is wrong. The biblical pattern seems to suggest you have three friends you can share with deeply. During his travels, Paul had Barnabas, Silas, or Timothy to share with. In the Garden of Gethsemane, Jesus expressed His grief to His inner circle of Peter, James and John. Psychologists tell us it is difficult for people to maintain mental health unless they have at least one person with whom they can be emotionally honest. If you have two or three people like this in your life, you are truly blessed.[129]

This is followed by *Emotional Honesty: How to Dish it Out and How To Take It.*
Dr. Anderson writes:

> One of our challenges in life is to learn how to respond to others when they honestly acknowledge their pain. We should not be listening to what people say in the midst of extreme pain. We should be responding to the pain, not the words that express it. In too many cases we ignore the feelings of hurting people, fixate on their words of despair and then react to what they said or how they said it.
>
> Although words should not be the primary focus in emotional acknowledgment, you can guard your intimate relationships by monitoring how you verbally express your emotions to others. When it comes to acknowledging emotions with your inner circle, honesty is the best policy, but be sure to speak "the truth in love" (Eph.4:15). Another important guideline for acknowledging and expressing your emotions is to know your limitations. Be aware that if you are at a seven or eight on the emotional scale—angry, tense, anxious, depressed—it is not a good time to make decisions about important matters.
>
> Realize also that a lot of physical factors will affect your emotional limits. The important process of renewing your mind includes managing your emotions by managing your thoughts and acknowledging your feelings honestly and lovingly in your relationships with others. Responding to your emotions properly is an important step in keeping the devil from gaining a foothold in your life.[130]

In chapter 11, titled: *Healing Emotional Wounds from Your Past,* Dr. Neil T. Anderson talks about how people can resolve or get healed form past traumas or emotional hurts.
Section by section, he writes:

Bad Things Do Happen to Good People

You may have grown up with a physically, emotionally or sexually abusive parent. You may have been severely frightened as a child. You may have suffered through a painful relationship in the past: a broken friendship, the untimely death of a loved one, a divorce. Any number of traumatic events in your past can leave you holding a lot of emotional baggage. Those experiences are buried in our memories and available for instant recall. Something as simple as a name can prompt an emotional response. **I call the residual effect of past traumas primary emotions.** The intensity of your primary emotions is determined by your previous life history. The more traumatic your experience, the more intense will be your primary emotion.

Notice the sequence of events:

Previous Life History
(*Determines the intensity of primary emotions*)

Present Event
(*Triggers the primary emotion*)

Primary Emotion

Mental Evaluation
(*The management stage*)

Secondary Emotion
(*The result of your thought process and primary emotion*)

The author is saying that any unresolved emotional hurts which took place in the past, (especially during the formative years of your life), have a hold on you. Therefore it is very important to process these hurts and heal past emotional wounds.

Anderson writes:

Many of these primary emotions will lie dormant within you and have little effect on your life until something triggers them. Most people try to control their primary emotions by avoiding any people or events that trigger.

The problem is, you can't isolate yourself completely from everything that may set off an emotional response. You are bound to see something on TV or hear something in a conversation that will bring to mind your unpleasant experience. **Something in your past is unresolved and therefore still has a hold on you.**

Learning to Resolve Primary Emotions
You have no control over a primary emotion when it is triggered in the present, because it is rooted in the past. Therefore, it doesn't do any good to feel guilty about something you can't control. You can, however, stabilize the primary emotion by evaluating it in light of present circumstances. For example, suppose you meet a man named Bill. He looks like the Bill who used to beat you up as a child. Although he is not the same person, your primary emotion will be triggered. So you quickly tell yourself, "This is not the same Bill; give him the benefit of the doubt." This mental evaluation produces a secondary emotion that is a combination of the past and the present. Some Christians assert that the past doesn't have any effect on them because they are new creations in Christ. I would have to disagree. Either they are extremely fortunate to have a conflict-free past or they are living in denial. Those who have had major traumas and have learned to resolve them in Christ know how devastating past experiences can be. Most don't know how to resolve those past experiences, so they have developed myriad defense mechanisms to cope. Some live in denial, others rationalize their problems or try to suppress the pain by an excess of food, drugs or sex. **Only God can set a captive free and bind up the brokenhearted.** He is the Wonderful Counselor. The answer for repressed memories is found in Psalm 139:23, 24: "Search me, O God, and know my heart; try me and know my anxious thoughts; and see if there be any hurtful way in me, and lead me in the everlasting way." God knows about the hidden hurts within you that you may not be able to see. When you ask God to search your

heart, He will expose those dark areas of your past and bring them to light at the right time.

How can I get healed you may ask. Well, according to Dr. Anderson, the process starts by re-evaluating the past and all its traumas by the reality of your present and seen the past from the prospective of your spiritual identity.

The author explains:

See Your Past in the Light of Who You Are in Christ
How does God intend you to resolve past experiences? In two ways. First, understand that you are no longer a product of your past. You are a new creation in Christ: a product of Christ's work on the cross. **People are not in bondage to past traumas. They are in bondage to the lies they believed about themselves, God and how to live as a result of the trauma.** That is why truth sets you free. As a Christian, you are literally a new creature in Christ. Old things, including the traumas of your past, "passed away" (2 Cor. 5:17). The old you in Adam is gone; the new you in Christ is here to stay. Now we can be transformed by the renewing of our minds (Rom 12:2). The flesh patterns are still imbedded in our minds when we become new creations in Christ, but we can crucify the flesh and choose to walk by the Spirit (Gal. 5:22-25). Now that you are in Christ, you can look at those events from the perspective of who you are today. <u>He is in your life right now desiring to set you free from your past.</u> That is the Gospel, the good news that Christ has come to set the captives free. Perceiving those events from the perspective of your new identity in Christ is what starts the process of healing those damaged emotions.

Another major step towards healing of damaged emotions, according to Anderson, is biblical forgiveness. The author offers us plenty of teaching regarding forgiveness.

Dr. Anderson writes:

Forgive Those Who Have Hurt You in Past

The second step in resolving past conflicts is to forgive those who have offended you. Why should you forgive those who have hurt you in the past? First, forgiveness is required by God. As soon as Jesus spoke the amen to His model prayer—which included a petition for God's forgiveness—He commented: "For if you forgive men for their transgressions, your heavenly Father will also forgive you. But if you do not forgive men, then your Father will not forgive your transgressions" (Matt. 6:14,15). Second, forgiveness is necessary to avoid entrapment by Satan. I have discovered from my counseling that unforgiveness is the number one avenue Satan uses to gain entrance to believers' lives. Paul encouraged us to forgive "in order that no advantage be taken of us by Satan; for we are not ignorant of his schemes" (2 Cor. 2:11). Third, forgiveness is required of all believers who desire to be like Christ. Paul wrote: "Let all bitterness and wrath and anger and clamor and slander be put away from you, along with all malice. And be kind to one another, tender-hearted, forgiving each other, just as God in Christ also has forgiven you" (Eph. 4:31,32).

What Is Forgiveness?
Forgiveness is not forgetting. Forgetting may be a long-term by-product of forgiving, but it is never a means to forgiveness. Forgiveness does not mean you must tolerate sin. It is okay to forgive another's past sins and, at the same time, take a stand against future sins. Forgiveness does not seek revenge or demand repayment for offenses suffered. "You mean I'm just supposed to let them off the hook?" You may argue. Yes, you let them off your hook realizing that God does not let them off His hook. **Forgiveness means resolving to live with the consequences of another person's sin.** We are all living with the consequences of Adam's sin. The only real choice is to live with those consequences in the bondage of bitterness or in the freedom of forgiveness.

After explaining what forgiveness is, the author recommends a 12-step process towards forgiveness.

Here they are:

Twelve Steps to Forgiveness

1. Ask the Lord to reveal to your mind the people you need to forgive.
2. Acknowledge the hurt and the hate. As you work through the list of people you need to forgive, state specifically for what you are forgiving them (eg., rejection; deprivation of love; injustice; unfairness; physical, verbal, sexual or emotional abuse; betrayal; neglect and so on). Remember: It is not a sin to acknowledge the reality of your emotions.
3. Understand the significance of the cross. The cross of Christ makes forgiveness legally and morally right.
4. Decide you will bear the burden of each person's sin (Gal. 6:1, 2). This means you will not retaliate in the future by using the information about their sin against them.
5. Decide to forgive. Forgiveness is a crisis of the will, a conscious choice to let the other person off the hook and to free yourself from the past.
6. Take your list to God and pray the following: "I forgive (*name*) for (list all the offenses and how they made you feel)." Stay with each person on the list until every remembered pain has been specifically addressed. That includes every sin of commission as well as omission.
7. Destroy the list. You are now free. Do not tell the offenders what you have done. Your need to forgive others is between you and God only!
8. Do not expect that your decision to forgive will result in major changes in the other persons. **Instead, pray for them** (Matt. 5:44) so they, too, may find the freedom of forgiveness (2 Cor. 2:7).
9. Try to understand the people you have forgiven, but don't rationalize their behavior. It could lead to incomplete forgiveness.
10. Expect positive results of forgiveness in you. In time you will be able to think about the people without triggering primary emotions. That doesn't mean you will like those who are abusive. It means you are free from them.

*11. Thank God for the lessons you have learned and the maturity
you have gained as a result of the offenses and your decision to forgive
the offenders* (Rom. 8:28, 29).
*12. Be sure to accept your part of the blame for the offenses you
suffered.* Confess your failure to God (1 John 1:9) and to
others (Jas. 5:16) and realize that if someone has
something against you, you must go to that person and be
reconciled (Matt. 5:23-26).[131]

Please define the spiritual identity of Christians. Please feel free
to use Bible verses, specific quotes from the materials you studied
during **Module VI,** and ideas (quotes) from other sources to sustain
your view. **Please explain why knowing our *spiritual identity*
plus *discipleship* leads to spiritual growth and maturity?** Please
elaborate. Please explain why knowing our biblical identity is
foundational to living fulfilling and victorious lives. Please elaborate.

The spiritual identity of Christians can be defined as "***Christ.***"
"Christ in you, the hope of glory. Christ is life, our life." Paul uses
one word, "*Christ*" (Colossians 1:27, 3:4). **The Holy Spirit actually
changes us by placing in us the life of Jesus (John 3:6).** "And by
this we know that He abides in us by the Spirit He has given us" (1
John 3:24, 4:13).

As we come to the realization that Christ Himself lives in us, our
true spiritual identity. It is not our efforts or works, **it is Him.** As
we allow Him full control, un-restrained by our will, our flesh. It is
Him that heals us and not our faith. **It is Him that sanctifies us,
not our efforts.** As we breathe Himself in, as we breathe ourselves
out, **allowing Him full occupancy of our spirit, all the traits of
Christ become reality in us.** This is a spiritual reality that for many
is hard to understand. I like the illustration given by A. B. Simpson.
He wrote:

> I am like the little bottle in the sea, as full as it will hold.
> The bottle is in the sea, and the sea is in the bottle; so I
> am in Christ, and Christ is in me. But, besides that
> bottleful in the sea, there is a whole ocean beyond; the
> difference is, that the bottle has to be filled over again,
> every day, evermore.[132]

Without discipleship to point, lead and guide a sincere and hungry Christian to spiritual truth such as our spiritual identity, among other key teachings, **we would find it very hard to live victorious and fulfilling lives.**

Christians who take the process of discipleship seriously, and desire to make disciples, shall be properly equipped to *"rightly divide the word of truth"* (2 Tim. 2:15, 3:16–17 NKJV). This is extremely important so a newborn follower of Christ is properly "grounded in rooted" in Christ (Ephesians 3:17, Colossians 2:7–10). Lack of discipleship is the main reason that many Christians are unable to eat solid food (Hebrews 5:12–14). This stems largely from being ignorant of their true spiritual identity. **This is exactly the reason for a solid discipleship ministry in the church today.**

If you would be required to teach others this module, **please provide a *written plan* how you would do it.**

As I said previously, if I were required to teach others this module I feel I would want to present it in much the same way it was presented to me.

7. Free in Christ—Understanding Spiritual Warfare

In a few paragraphs please provide an overall evaluation of **Module VII**. Please explain what you liked the most about this important module. Explain also what you disliked the most about this module. **How do you suggest we can make Module VII even more helpful and appealing for future disciples/students?**

Module VII: *Free in Christ—Understanding Spiritual Warfare*, was another invaluable part of the teaching. I feel it to be a necessary module in the spiritual life of Christ's disciples. It not only describes in minute detail the ***who, what, and why*** of spiritual warfare, it also **describes the tactics of the enemy** and how we can defeat him.

I also found the emphasis on forgiveness and the results of un-forgiveness in our lives, (another ploy of the enemy), extremely helpful. The writings of Dr. Neil Anderson (*Victory Over Darkness, The Bondage Breaker, Steps to Freedom in Christ*), as well as John Bevere (*The Bait of Satan*) were spot on and eye opening on this subject. Furthermore, Charles R Swindoll (*Finding Healing through Forgiveness*), and Charles F Stanley (*The Gift of Forgiveness*), **were outstanding choices for the topic of forgiveness.** Between these two last authors the subject of forgiveness was demystified, and laid bare the extreme importance of forgiveness in a healthy spiritual life.

The way this module was presented and taught was top notch and I believe Holy Spirit inspired. I could not recommend changing a thing about the module for future disciples and students.

Although there is teaching out there that upon being born again, **the battle has ended**, it is vital for the disciple of Christ to realize that this is where the real battle begins.

In his book, "The Bondage Breaker," Dr. Anderson explains:

> Instead of being victorious, productive, joy filled Christians, many Christians trudge through life under a cloud, just trying to hang on until Jesus comes… they live under the bondage of hearing voices, confusion in their daily walk, discouraged, thoughts of self-doubt. Feeling unfulfilled and unproductive. This can be due to patterns of the flesh or mental discipline problems, **but it can also reflect deception of the enemy!**[133]

Moreover, in "Victory over the Darkness," Anderson writes:

> If Satan can place a thought in your mind – and he can, it isn't much more of a trick for him to make you think it is your idea. If you knew it was Satan, you would reject the thought, wouldn't you? When he disguises his suggestions as your thoughts and ideas, however, you are more likely to accept them. That is his primary scheme or deception. If Satan can get you to believe a lie you can loose some element of control in your life.[134]

Why it is important for us as *disciples of Christ* to know that the spiritual warfare is real? Please elaborate.

Spiritual warfare is REAL because the apostles wrote about this important topic. (See Ephesians 6:11–18, 1 Peter 5:8–9, James 4:7), just to mention a few. It is extremely important for a disciple of Christ to know and understand this spiritual reality, as Paul warns in Ephesians 6:12: "For our struggle is not against flesh and blood, but against the rulers, against the powers, against the world forces of this darkness, against the spiritual forces of wickedness in the heavenly places."

Who is our real enemy? Please explain why it is important to recognize the "*character*" of our foe and his "*modus opernadi*" in the world today? Please feel free to use Bible verses, specific quotes from the materials you studied during **Module VII**, and ideas (quotes) from other sources to sustain your view.

Satan is our REAL enemy. Satan's power is in the lie. He is the father of lies (John 8:44). <u>He can do nothing about your position in Christ,</u> but if he can deceive you into accepting his lies, his strategy will be a success.

His most typical lie, used successfully from the Garden of Eden until today is "that you are capable of being the *god* of your own life." If people, including Christians, accept it as being the truth, leads them in bondage.

Anderson warns us:

> Every temptation is an endeavor by him to get you to live your life independent of God. Whenever you focus on yourself instead of Christ or prefer material over spiritual values, the tempter has succeeded.[135]

What is a "*stronghold*" and how strongholds are developed? Please feel free to use quotes from the materials studied during **Module VII** and from other sources. What are the three channels (as suggested by Neil T. Anderson) through which Satan entices Christians to act independently of God? Please elaborate.

Romans 12:2 teaches us to take hold and control what we allow in our mind! **We have learned coping mechanisms, like lying to protect ourselves early on in life.** These are what Paul calls "*strongholds,*" or what we might call defense mechanisms (2 Corinthians 10:3-5).

I like the definition of a stronghold provided by Dr. Anderson:

> Fortresses (strongholds) are fleshly patterns that were programmed into your mind when you learned to live your life independent of God... Your old fleshly habit patterns of thought weren't erased. We still battle the world, the flesh, and the devil.[136]

There are three channels that Satan entices Christians to act independently of God.

According to 1 John 2:15–17:

1. *The lust of the flesh*, or physical appetites and their gratification.
2. *The lust of the eyes*, or self-interest and testing the Word of God.
3. *The pride of life*, or self-promotion and self-exaltation.

The lust of the flesh

Satan looks for soft spots where we are weakest in our physical appetites for food, rest, comfort, and sex. **Where hunger, fatigue, and loneliness are at their peak.** Temptation is the greatest. These things in themselves with the right attitude are OK, but **when corrupted or abused they draw us from the will of God,** ignoring the truth of His Word.

The lust of the eyes

We develop a confidence in the way **we see things** rather than what God's Word teaches us. We develop a *'prove it to me'* attitude instead of trusting God. **This allows us to accept and desire what the world has to offer as a legitimate option instead and above our relationship with God.**

The pride of life

This channel leads to the destruction of your obedience to God as well as worship of God. **'Self'** is the key to this channel. Adopting a *'self knows best'* feeling that you don't need Gods help or direction, you can handle your life without consulting Him or bowing the knee to anyone versus humble obedience to God in worship. (John 15:8-10)

What is the biblical basis for standing firm and experiencing victory and freedom? Please elaborate. Why many Christians seldom experience victory and freedom in their lives. Please elaborate.

The spiritual battle field is the mind. The mind is the place where the temptation starts. It originates in your mind either by your own doing or because of temptation from Satan. Standing firm here is where you will find victory and freedom. Paul writes in 2 Corinthians 10:5 to "Take every thought captive." Before it has a chance to enter your mind we need to be ready to grab hold of the

276

thought. Then decide is this thought *true, honorable, right, pure, lovely, of good repute, excellent, or worthy of praise* (Philippians 4:8). **Does it line up with the truth?** If not, choose truth, stand firm, keep saying NO!

Anderson explains:

> When you learn to respond to tempting thoughts by stopping them at the door of your mind, evaluating them on the basis of God's Word and **dismissing those which fail the test**, you have found the way of escape that God's Word promises... We must turn to our righteous advocate and resist our perverted adversary if we are to experience victory and freedom over temptation and sin, *"submit therefore to God, resist the devil and he will flee from you"* (James 4:7).[137]

What the main schemes used by the enemy to entice, tempt, and attack us—Christians? Please elaborate. How Christians, willingly or ignorantly, (as suggested by Neil T. Anderson) can give the devil an opportunity? Please elaborate. Please feel free to use quotes from the materials studied during **Module VII** and from other sources.

According to the Bible there are several opportunities that Christians can, willingly or unwillingly, open a door to the enemy.

These are:

- Opportunity number 1—**Pride** (1 Peter5:7, James 4:7 etc.)
- Opportunity number 2—**Unresolved Anger** (Ephesians 4:24-25 etc.)
- Opportunity number 3—**Unforgiveness** (2 Corinthians 2:10-11)
- Opportunity number 4—**Lying** (Acts 5:1-11 etc.),
- Opportunity number 5—**Living in a Known Sin** (2 Timothy 2:24-26 etc.)

All of these can be used by Satan to attack Christians. Many times these five open doors actually provide opportunities for a frontal attack by the enemy. The Scripture describes the correct way to act or respond to each situation. As Christians we are advised to walk led by the Spirit, to willingly obey God, and to intentionally resist the enemy, so any doors opened by our negligence can be closed—thus shutting down the enemy's upper hand.

Let's briefly look at each opportunity we can give to the enemy.

Pride. Satan would love to take advantage of us any time we are in situations where the temptation is to take matters in our own hands—self-reliance, instead of "casting" the problem "on Him"—God-reliance, to do the work. What are we to do? The Bible tells what we should do instead. That is "submitting to God", thus defusing the opportunity for self-pride.

Unresolved Anger. This is another issue where Satan has great success in pulling Christians down. In Ephesians 4:25 we are told to "speak truth each one of you," in other words to be honest and open in our relationships. The reason for this is that "we are members of one another." If necessary, we can express our anger, but not sin in our anger. If, being under this powerful emotion, we sin (because we allowed our anger to fester), this opens the opportunity to Satan, and we play right into the enemy's hands.

Unforgiveness. This is a big one among Christians. When we willingly refuse to forgive those who have wronged us, Satan can use this against us. Second Corinthians 2:10–11, clearly states that Satan is eager to use unforgiveness as an open door to attack individuals or the church. This is a very serious matter and can result in a tremendous damage (i.e. broken relationships, church splits, broken marriages, etc.) Whatever needs be done to bring forgiveness about needs to be done without any delay.

Lying. Any form of lie, telling half-truths, or manipulating stories for personal advantage, reflects the character of Satan—the father of lies, and defame the God of Truth. The story of Ananias, and his wife Sapphira, found in Acts 5:1–11 is sobering. Satan, who is a devious person, loves to use these kind of opportunities from Christians. The story from Acts 5 clearly indicates the seriousness of lying and its deadly consequences. In fact Ananias, and Sapphira, did not lie to people but lied to the Holy Spirit.

Living in a Known Sin. This is another serious problem. When Christians live in a known sin, they can fall into Satan's trap leading to some sort of bondage. Second Timothy 2:24–26 describes exactly that. Satan traps many who are knowingly living in sin. Through the ministry of pastoral counseling, people can be assisted in getting release from the enemy's trap. This ministry involves emphatic listening and gentle correction. As the process continues, the victim held in the enemy's cage could slowly realize their status, come to their senses, repent, and, eventually, getting set free.

Please explain the biblical meaning of forgiveness? What are the three essential elements of forgiveness? Name four reasons (as suggested by Charles Stanley) why the person with an unforgiving spirit is the real loser. If our sins are already forgiven, why should we confess our sins? Please elaborate. What is the basis of continuing forgiveness? Please elaborate. **Please explain the process of forgiving others?** Please explain what to do when we are repeatedly hurt? What are the three things one can expect to happen once the forgiveness process is complete? Please elaborate and even share from your own experiences.

In 2 Corinthians 2:10,11, (as I briefly explained before), Paul warns us about the danger of **un-forgiveness because it can open the door to the enemy to attack us and torment our soul.** Many Christians are deceived in this area because they hold onto the un-forgiveness. Paul is saying that we must forgive because we have been forgiven. Any act of forgiveness is recorded in haven. Paul said that we do forgive *"in the presence of Christ."* (2 Corinthians 2:10). This means that when we don't forgive; the act of withholding forgiveness is also noticed in haven. This is exactly what Satan exploits in the lives of Christians. Un-forgiveness is part of his schemes to get access in our lives.

The biblical meaning of forgiveness, according to Charles F Stanley, is:

> Forgiveness is "the act of setting someone free from an obligation to you that is a result of a wrong done against you." For example, a debt is forgiven when you free your debtor of his obligation to pay back what he owes you.[138]

There are three essential elements of forgiveness. According to Dr. Stanly, these are: *"injury,* a *debt* resulting from the injury, and a cancellation of the debt. All three elements are essential if forgiveness is to take place."[139]

People who refuse to forgive are the one who suffer the most. There are **four reasons**, as suggested by Charles Stanley, why the person with an unforgiving spirit is the real loser.

These are:

> **1. A Wrecked and Ruined Life:** Dr. Stanley explains: "An unforgiving spirit prevents a person from being able to walk consistently in the Spirit. The only choice is to walk according to the flesh. The consequences of such a life are devastating. (Galatians 6:7,8).
>
> **2. Resentment:** A second consequence is: "resentment and other negative feelings will spill over into other relationships."
>
> **3. Rejection:** The third reason a person with an unforgiving spirit loses out on life is closely tied to the other reasons we've just discussed. When a person is wronged in some way, whether in marriage, business, friendship, or some other relationship, rejection occurs."
>
> **4. Development of fleshy patterns:** While the unforgiving person waits for the other person to make restitution and a great deal of time goes by, "**fleshly patterns of behavior and incorrect thought processes develop…**" Even if corrected the result and side effects can take years to deal with in the area of relationships especially.[140]

You may ask: "*If our sins are already forgiven, why should we confess our sins?*" This is a legitimate question. The answer is simple.

Charles F Stanley, explains:

> Confession is essential, not to receive forgiveness, **but to experience the forgiveness** God has provided through the death of Christ and to have unhindered fellowship with Him. But there is more. <u>In confession we experience release from guilt, tension, pressure, and emotional stress resulting from our sins.</u> Failure to confess our sins ensures the continuation of those unnecessary negative feelings. Failure to understand the **purpose** and **place** of confession can result in fear and uncertainty about our salvation; it takes the cutting edge off our joy; <u>it leaves us</u>

with a nagging doubt that deprives us of the peace our Lord intends for His children.[141]

The basis for continuing forgiveness is in the sacrificial substitutionary death of Jesus Christ on the cross—*the shed blood of Christ at Calvary.* We are not always aware of our sins, therefore the need for continuing forgiveness.

Let me present the process of forgiveness:

There are **five steps** involved in the process of forgiving others:

1. **Our own forgiveness:** We must recognize that we have been totally forgiven (Romans 6:10). When we understand the depths He went to forgive us, it should cause us to desire this for others.
2. **Release:** We are called to release the person for the debt we think is owed us because of the offense. A mental, emotional, as well as physical release surrendering all hostile feelings to Christ. This can be done either face-to-face or by using a substitute.
3. **Acceptance:** Forgiveness is an act of the will. When we decide to forgive, we absolve others of their responsibilities to meet our needs—we release them from our hook. Since we are releasing them from the obligation to meet our needs, now we can accept them as they are.
4. **Opportunity to grow spiritually.** We need to see those we have forgiven as tools in our life. Decide to see them as **enablers to our growth** and understanding of the grace of God. Joseph was an excellent example of this when he forgave his brothers (Genesis 50:19-21).
5. **Reconciliation:** We are encouraged to make reconciliation with those from whom we have been estranged. **Re-establish contact with those we avoided or had hostility in our heart with.**

I would like to point out that, even though we are encouraged to seek reconciliation, this may not be possible. Forgiveness is in our power to do. Reconciliation requires the collaboration and admission of fault of the other person involved in that particular conflict or dissension. If the other person doesn't want to reconcile, we cannot force it. We did our part. The fact that we release the other person from our hook it doesn't imply that they are released from God's hook.

If we are hurt repeatedly we should remember **forgiveness is an act of the will.** Stand firm on your decision to forgive, not linking the offense to past ones. Forgiving anew. **Remember it is for our benefit**. We cannot try to change their behavior. That's up to God to do it.

Forgiveness is therapeutic for our own soul. There are many benefits one can experience upon completion of the forgiveness process.

Among those benefits the most important are:

- First, negative feelings will disappear.
- Second; we will be willing to take them just the way they are.
- Finally, our concerns about the needs of others will outweigh our concerns about what they did to us.

Let me share something from my own experiences. I used to have a co-worker who for no reason mistreated me and derided me. I forgave my co-worker and the results I experienced were powerful. This person's attitude towards me changed dramatically. Also my ex-wife harbors un-forgiveness towards me because of my past behavior. I forgave her and I asked her to forgive me so we can reconcile. However, she did not want to forgive me. I left this situation in God's hands to deal with it in His timing. One thing is for sure: Because of my forgiveness, her attitude towards me visibly changed. When we are attending various family functions there is no tension or heaviness in the atmosphere anymore. Praise the Lord! This sounds unbelievable, but it is true.

Please *identify* and *discuss* the six principles for restoration or reconciliation. What happens if we have the right attitude and attempt to reconcile with someone who has sinned against us, but he or she won't listen? Please elaborate and share real life stories as the Holy Spirit leads you.

The **six principles** for restoration are:

1. Help the person <u>recognize the failure</u> and the consequences of their decision, realizing what they have done. (Psalms 5:4)
2. Help the person <u>acknowledge responsibility</u> for the sin, even if others are involved. Helping to assume personal culpability for sinful action.
3. <u>Lead</u> the person <u>to repent</u> and confess of the sin. The one who confesses and forsakes sin is the one who will prosper.
4. <u>Restitution.</u> It is the person's responsibility to restore as best as possible to those sinned against.
5. Help the fallen brother <u>receive God's message</u> to him through his failure. There may be a message God has for him in this experience not to be ignored (Proverbs 10:17).
6. <u>Guide</u> the fallen brother <u>to respond to God's chastisement</u> with gratitude (Hebrews 12:10). His willingness to accept the Father's correction is an act of thankfulness and gratitude. This can result in averting the insidious root of bitterness.

If we approach the fallen brother in love but they will not listen **we should express our love and concern**, letting them know we are there for them. **Then leave them in the Lord's hands** and continue to hold them up in prayer.

If you would be required to teach others this module, **please provide a *written plan* how you would do it.**

If I were required to teach others this module I feel I would want to present it in much the same way it was presented to me.

8. Fruits and Gifts—Developing a Genuine Intimacy with the Holy Spirit

In a few paragraphs please provide an overall evaluation of **Module VIII**. Please explain what you liked the most about this important module. Explain also what you disliked the most about this module. **How do you suggest we can make Module VIII even more helpful and appealing for future disciples/students?**

The eighth and final module in this discipleship training series, "Fruits and Gifts-Developing a Genuine Intimacy with the Holy Spirit", was a topic of vital importance in the growth and maturity of a disciple in training. There was nothing that wasn't covered or discussed about the role of the Holy Spirit in the life of the church, and also in us, as individual believers in the body of Christ. From the Holy Spirit in the early church to what is taught and experienced today, right and wrong teaching, all is examined and truth is supported and backed up by solid Scripture and reliable experiences.

The *when, how* and *why* of being filled with the Holy Spirit, the difference between the gifts of the Spirit and fruits of the Spirit, along with how to determine your gifts, all are explained in an understandable and clearly taught journey of excellent authors such as Jack Deere, Don and Katie Fortune, and John Bevere, along with an excellent DVD series by Joyce Meyer and Dr. Juan Carlos Ortiz.

I really enjoyed the different ways that each teacher had their own experiences with the Holy Spirit. All were unique, yet theologically correct.

I felt this module was complete and could find nothing I disliked about it. Would have no problem teaching it, as is for new disciples.

Please provide a biblical foundation for the *presence* and *manifestation* of the spiritual gifts in the church today. **Why God gives miraculous gifts? Provide a list of the miraculous gifts.** Use Bible verses and quotes from the materials you studied during **Module VIII** to sustain your view. **How to cultivate the gifts of the Spirit?** Please list the *five (5) guidelines* suggested by Deere. **How can a believer identify his or her gifts?** Please list and elaborate on the four (4) criteria suggested by Deere.

We can use the Gospels and the book of Acts to support the presence and manifestation of the Spiritual gifts in the church today. The Gospels, Acts, and the Epistles are the major source for our doctrine of Christology and Pneumatology. They are primary sources for the study of how the New Testament uses the Old Testament. Acts is crucial in establishing church government. Viewing the book of Acts with an anti-supernatural outlook is wrong. They are theologies in themselves. You can't pick and choose how you view Scriptures (2 Timothy 3:16). The book of Acts is the best source we have of a normal church life and what it is supposed to look like today—a miracle working church.

Why God gives miraculous gifts?

God gives miraculous gifts to strengthen the church (1 Corinthians 14:26). All of the gifts are necessary for a healthy church, in the same way as all parts are necessary for a healthy body to function correctly (1 Corinthians 12-14).

The miraculous gifts are found in 1Corinthians 12:8–10:

1. Wisdom
2. Knowledge
3. Faith
4. Healing
5. Miracles
6. Prophecy
7. Discerning spirits

8. Tongues
9. Interpretation of Tongues

The five guidelines suggested by John Deere for cultivating the gifts of the Spirit are:

1. Be sure that you believe the Bible teaches the gifts are for today, and important for all Christians (1 Peter 4:10).
2. Attempt to use the gifts on a regular basis. There is no other way to grow in anything apart from constant practice and takin the risk in this area.
3. Study the gifts, the Bible, as well as books dealing with the ministry of gifts of the Spirit, bibliographies of Christians and supernatural ministries.
4. Friendships with people who have experience with the gifts is very helpful (Proverbs 27:17). It is important to cultivate friendships with people you admire and want to be like.
5. Begin to practice the gifts of the Spirit in a non-threatening atmosphere. Small groups of ten to twenty people, home groups, give a degree of security, versus a large congregation in a formal setting.

A believer can identify his or her gifts by:

1. Your degree of success on various attempts at ministry. Where you are most successful is likely to be those areas in which are gifted.
2. Desires frequently indicate the gifts we have or the Lord wants to give us. Don't be passive, waiting to find your gift (1 Corinthians 14:13).
3. Rely on the counsel of others, especially trusted friends can save us a lot of frustration and wasted effort.
4. Gifts can be given through the laying on of hands with prophetic utterance (1 Timothy 4:14).

Please list the **seven (7) motivational gifts,** suggested by Don and Katie Fortune. Please provide the *definition* of each of the seven motivational gifts. Please explain what kind of *needs* each motivation gift meets. **In a TABLE FORMAT please explain what each gift *does*?**

The seven (7) motivational gifts indicated by Don and Katie Fortune:

GIFT	DEFINITION	NEEDS MET	WHAT IT DOES
1. Perceiver	Declares the will of God	Spiritual	Keeps us centered on spiritual principles
2. Server	Renders practical service	Practical	Keeps the work of ministry moving
3. Teacher	Researches and teaches the Bible	Mental	Keeps us studying and learning
4. Exhorter	Encourages personal progress	Psychological	Keeps us applying spiritual truths
5. Giver	Shares material assistance	Material	Keeps specific needs provided for
6. Administrator	Gives leadership and directions	Functional	Keeps us organized and increases our vision
7. Compassion Person	Provides personal and emotional support	Emotional	Keeps us in right attitude and relationships

1. *Perceiver*—one who clearly perceives the will of God. They see things the rest of us often miss completely. A clear and sound eye to detect God's truth.

2. *Server*—one who loves to serve others. The most capable in being helpful, anytime, anyplace, especially hands on involvement.

3. *Teacher*—one who loves to research and communicate truth. Intelligent to search out truth. Reliable in finding truth of Scripture.

4. *Exhorter*—one who loves to encourage others to live a victorious life. Great way with speech, counseling, and encouraging.

5. *Giver*—one who loves to give time, talent, energy, and means to benefit others and advance the Gospel. Givers are strong supporters to those who are in spiritual battle or on the front lines sharing the Gospel.

> **6. Administrator**—one who loves to organize, lead or
> direct. Carry the load of leadership.
> **7. Compassion person**—one who shows compassion,
> love and care to those in need. Care extensively,
> showing kindness concern, and mercy to others.

Knowing that each **LIVING MEMBER of the BODY** of Christ
(*the Church*) has at least **one FUNCTION** (**Romans 12:4**) and at
least **one GIFT** (**1 Corinthians 12:7**); please answer:

> **(A)** Which is your **FUNCTION?**
> **(B)** Which is your **GIFT?**

My <u>motivational gift,</u> as indicated by the self-evaluation, is
foremost that of a **compassion person**. My <u>function</u> is to take
action to remove hurts and to relieve distress in others. To keep us
in right attitudes and relationships.

Knowing that it is our **RESPONSIBILITY** to "*kindle afresh the gift*"
(**2 Timothy 1:6**) and "*to exercise*"" (**Romans 12:6**) our
FUNCTION; please answer:

> **(A)** What do you **DO** (*practically speaking*) to **KINDLE** afresh
> your GIFT?
> **(B)** How to you **get EQUIPPED** (*practically speaking*) **for your
> FUNCTION?**

It is our responsibility to "kindle afresh" your gift. Don't
become passive. Eagerly desire the spiritual gift. Pray for them. Gifts
can also be given by laying on of hands with prophetic utterances.
Get equipped for your function by constant practice and risk taking.

Please share any practical things you did, and are committed to keep
on keeping on? Please elaborate.

During the Advanced Discipleship Training, my mentor
encouraged me to practice several spiritual disciplines.

Personal Devotion

Along with daily Bible reading, study and prayer, my early morning devotions is one of the most important discipline or spiritual habit that I have implemented in my daily life. For my personal daily devotions I use "Jesus Calling,"[142] by Sarah Young, along with "My Utmost For His Highest,"[143] by Oswald Chambers. I do these devotions first thing upon waking up, usually very early. Even if that's all I have time for before leaving to work, it is still a very helpful thing to sustain me during the day. There have been many times that the Lord has spoken specific things through the words I read from these books that were directly connected to situations which happened during that day. I felt so encouraged that the Holy Spirit guided me ahead of time how to deal with these situations. Very often they have confirmed the footsteps I had taken the day before. I would hate to think of beginning a day without doing these devotions. I can confess that even a quick prayer is important to set things in motion for the day ahead of me. I highly encourage any disciple to implement the spiritual discipline of Personal Devotions in his or her life.

Centering Prayer.

Centering Prayer is a method of meditation used by Christians, placing a strong emphasis on the interior silence. It traces its roots to the contemplative prayer of the Desert Fathers. It does not replace other forms of prayers, but it helps to be more intentional and open to God.

Here are some simple guidelines:

– First, begin by finding a quiet place with less or no apparent disturbances.

– Then sit, preferably on a chair that allows you to be relaxed and fully present.

– Next, put on some spiritual worship music, (4 to 6 minutes long), having a theme similar to your desired centering prayer topic (i.e., peace, love, wisdom, care, etc.), or something that can draw you closer into the presence of the Lord. You could let the song play from the beginning to the end. This will act as your timer for the centering prayer.

– Breathe deeply through your nose. Your chest should not move. It has been scientifically proven to help the brain to calm down and relax. Hold the breath for 6-8 seconds. As you inhale, imagine taking into your heart the peace, or the love of God, or whatever the topic of your centering prayer for that time.

– Slowly breathe out through your pursed lips. It should take about 6-8 seconds to exhale. As you do this, imagine expelling anxiety, frustration, or other negative emotion you want to be removed.

– If you notice that your mind starts to wander, just let it go, and return to the word or phrase you are meditating upon (i.e., peace, love, wisdom, care, etc.)

– When the worship music is coming to an end, it signals that your centering prayer is about to end.

– Now you are ready to move into your regular prayer.

The Prayer Circle

Pastor Mark Batterson, wrote a book titled, "The Circle Maker."[144] He was inspired by the Legend of Honi the Circle Maker to take prayer to the next level. Based on this book a video curriculum was created. I watched all four session with my mentor. Batterson says that:

> Drawing prayer circles around our dreams isn't just a mechanism whereby we accomplish great things for God. It's a mechanism whereby God accomplishes great things in us.

In a nutshell the fundamental principles of the Prayer Circle are:

1. Draw a "circle" around a person, event or situation and make it the subject of your prayer for 21 days.
2. Carve four specific things, (i.e.: breakthroughs, health issues, relationships aspects, church events, family issues, etc.) on that "circle" to aid you during the 21 days of prayer.
3. Pray regularly: morning, mid-day, evening, even by reading the specifics you wrote down at the beginning of the spiritual discipline.

4. Keep a journal so you can record specific experiences
   at the end of your Prayer Circle. When done put
   together a Prayer Circle Summary.

Let me share the way I am practicing this spiritual discipline. Sometimes, I'm already aware of *what* or *whom* I am supposed to pray for, but other times I have no idea. Generally, at the beginning of the month I pray for God's given direction (person or situation) for my prayer circle. Depending on the length of each month, I start on the tenth or the eleventh of each month (except February), and continue praying for 21 days. I consider the person and situation as the center of my circle and I bring it regularly before the Lord in prayer. Again, depending on the prayer circle, I am praying for either breakthroughs, or health issues, or relationships aspects, or church events, or family issues, to be accomplished for whatever is in the center of my prayer circle.

I can confess that many times I have seen answers to prayer during the twenty-one days, but at times I see nothing not until or after I completed my prayer circle. Many times I will even feel led to return to the same prayer-subject and repeat it another month. I have found this discipline to be one of the most worthwhile and valuable of all other disciplines I am practicing. I highly encourage you to consider practicing this discipline in your discipleship journey.

Personal Retreat

Another spiritual discipline that I practiced was Personal Retreat—alone in God's presence. I found it to be extremely important for my spiritual growth and deepening my intimacy with the Lord Jesus. The personal retreat is about getting alone with the Lord for an extended amount of time, just soaking in His presence. Creating space to be alone with God allows Him to move within your spirit and transform you. It's like a modern-time Sabbath. A typical personal retreat should be a minimum of four hours of reflection, meditation, reading, and intentional listening to the voice of the Holy Spirit in your own heart.

Here are a few simple steps:

- First, before the retreat, read over the specific material and the assigned Scripture passages that will be used during the retreat.
- Second, quietly, in the background, play some worship music which concentrates on Jesus, and His complete work on the cross.
- Third, read the assigned Bible verses slowly, in a posture of deep meditation. Let God's Word penetrate your heart of hearts. Allow the Holy Spirit to speak to you or even convict you. Pause, and apply moments of intentional silence, pray short prayers using the Centering Prayer method.
- Fourth, write in your journal all impressions that the Holy Spirit brings to your attention. Record any aha moments you received during the retreat.
- Fifth, at the end of your personal retreat, be prepared to share with your mentor or with others what you experienced during the retreat, and how the Spirit of God spoke to you and transformed you.

Prayers and Proclamations

For this discipline, I am using a small book, "Prayers and Proclamations,"[145] by Derek Prince. Hebrews 4:12 tells us: "For the word of God is living and active and sharper than any two-edged sword, and piercing as far as the division of soul and spirit, of both joints and marrow, and able to judge the thoughts and intentions of the heart." Since we know the Word of God is alive, and it is powerful, when we use it in prayer, we will most likely see answers to that prayer.

Derek combined many Scriptures, which address many topics, over one hundred. These strings of related Scripture are read aloud as a prayer. I like to read them in a personal form. For example, Ephesians 3:20 would be spoken: "God is able to do exceedingly abundantly above all that Mark asks or thinks, according to the power that works in Mark."

The nice thing about it is that this small book contains plenty of Bible verses already organized by topics most Christians need to pray. This book is perfect if you have a little time to pray, but you lack the necessary time to search the Scriptures. Proclaiming God's promises, which are spoken in His written Word, is the best avenue to obtain results. I have seen great answers to my prayers and proclamations several times when using this little book. I highly recommend this spiritual discipline.

What may constitute '*surrogates*' to a genuine passion for God and to a real intimacy with the Holy Spirit? Please elaborate. **How can we develop or re-cultivate our genuine passion for God?** Please list the three steps (as suggested by Deere) and elaborate on each of them.

Some surrogates that may substitute for a genuine passion for God and a real intimacy with the Holy Spirit would be substituting a denomination or church for one's passion and love for Jesus. The Bible and passion for "it", to "know it" is not the same thing as knowing God. It is not the same as loving or hearing God. <u>External moral behavior and duty can be surrogates for a passionate love of or a longing for Christ either</u>. It is possible to put almost anything good or religious above Jesus Christ and not realize it. Anytime one begins to give more attention to one of these things (mentioned above) or pursue any of them more than one pursues the Son of God it will become an idol in my life.

We can re-cultivate our genuine passion for God by:

1. You must "know" Him. We must take the time to set at His feet and listen to Him, then we will know Him better, then we will love Him more. <u>Personal meditation in Scripture and prayer must be done in a heartfelt way</u>. If we do these things on a regular basis, expecting to meet a person, that person will not disappoint us.

2. Acquire a passion for the Lord Jesus by trusting His blood for the forgiveness of sins. <u>The guilt of sin can keep us from going into the presence of the Lord</u>. There is only one thing that will remove the wall between God and His children, that is the blood. When we sin we must go before Him in confession of our sin and trust in the power of the blood of Jesus Christ to forgive and cleanse us.

3. By placing your confidence in your discipline, good intentions, and knowledge of the Bible in order to produce

love for God, this has the danger of ending up in legalism and self-righteousness. <u>These things are good in themselves but we should never put our confidence in them</u>. We cannot earn passion for the Lord through these things. We can't allow them to deter us.

What are the **benefits of speaking in other tongues** as explained by John Bevere in his video—*"Intimacy with the Holy Spirit."* Please elaborate on all of them.

The benefits of speaking in other tongues as explained by John Bevere in his teaching video, "Intimacy With the Holy Spirit" are:

1. Communicating with God.
2. It defeats our weaknesses.
3. It edifies and builds up our spirit.
4. It strengthens our faith.
5. It enhances our ability to worship.
6. It reveals hidden council of God.
7. It gives us rest.
8. It brings refreshing.

Speaking in tongues allows for a two way conversation between our spirit and the deep things of the Spirit of God, that is in no other way possible. As we pray in tongues when struggling with weaknesses within us, the Holy Spirit the Spirit Himself "intercedes for us with groanings too deep for words" (cf. Romans 8:26); and enable us to be victorious over our weaknesses. In the same way building up our spirit and strengthening our faith.

Based on the teaching of Dr. Juan Carlos Ortiz on his video—*"Indwelt by the Beloved,"* **please explain the danger of "*negative liturgy*" when it comes to the spiritual life of a local church**. Can you think of any negative liturgy in your religious circles: church, small group, etc. Explain and elaborate.

In his video seminar, "Indwelt By the Beloved"[146], Dr. Ortiz, explains the danger of "negative liturgy" when it comes to the spiritual life of the local church. There are many subtle falsehoods in church liturgy, both ceremonial and in many music lyrics. For instance, baptism of infants, and other accepted ceremonies that have no Biblical basis or foundation. In accepted hymns, be careful with the word "feeling." For example, "Surely the presence of the Lord is in this place, I can feel His..." <u>In the new covenant church we don't feel it, we know it!</u> People who live by feelings are unstable people. **Faith is the conviction.** They are the stable people. Songs such as "Come into my heart, come in today, come in to stay". Did Jesus leave your heart? Will He leave you? (Read Hebrews 13:5–6, Matthew 28:18–20). Wrong teaching although it may sound nice and beautiful has the danger to suggest and instill incorrect doctrine. We need to be aware of what we take in! Paul warns us with these words: "Let no one deceive you with empty words, for because of these things the wrath of God comes upon the sons of disobedience" (Ephesians 5:6).

What are **the MAIN aspects** you have learned from Joyce Meyer audio Seminar *"Fruits of the Spirit:"* Please explain and elaborate on minimum ten (10) aspects.

Joyce Meyer, in her study on *"The Fruits of the Spirit"*, teaches us that we receive all Fruits of the Spirit upon our spiritual birth. They are given to us in "seed" form with no effort on our part. The Fruit doe's require effort to grow and mature. These gifts consist of *love, joy, peace, patience, goodness, kindness, faithfulness, gentleness, and self-control.*

Love is the element that is vital in **activation** and **growth** of all the other fruits. Along with *self-control* they are essential to enable the function of the fruits. **All work together and effect each other.** <u>Love is the most important of the spiritual fruits</u>. It is basically seen in how we treat people.

Moreover, *Love* is the more excellent way. Learning what love is, to walk in love. Developing that fruit of the Spirit is the most excellent way we can choose to live. <u>We can do good work for the wrong reasons.</u> God is interested not in **what we do**, but **why we do it**. If our focus is on love, we develop love. Studying it, praying about it and acting out in it. Getting your focus on what you can do to make someone else's life better is the answer to all your problems.

According to Matthew 22:36 the two most important commands are **to love God** with all we've got, and **to love our neighbor as ourselves.** The benefits of love are joy, in your soul (1 Tim. 5:6). Blessing someone else produces joy! (1 John 3:16-18). **Walking in love gives you confidence you're doing right.** Finally, love is spiritual warfare. Defeat the devil and learn to be a great lover. (Romans 12:21) overcome evil with good.

The only thing we need be concerned with is doing the will of God, **not comparing our gifts.** Many Christians are concerned with what others gifts are rather than examining the fruit. Many spend too much time being busy and not fruitful.

Life is not worth living without peace in our lives. Satan knows what buttons to push to get us upset. On the other hand the Holy Spirit can guide us and reveal to us the specific buttons that upset us the most. As these aspects are revealed, He empowers us to make the necessary changes so our actions will counteract and provide peaceful solutions. The end results are: avoiding upsetting circumstances, eliminate turmoil, experience peace in places where before we were angry.

The benefit of circumstances are what you get to practice your gifts on. Responding to them in a proper way. Using this as a tool to witness to the lost. **No peace over circumstances means no power over the enemy.**

Joyce teaches that there are three areas we need to develop peace.

These areas are:

> *Peace with God* (Psalm 32:1-5). Be quick to repent. Don't be mad at God when things don't work the way you imagine. Stop trying to figure out everything.
> *Peace with yourself* (Hebrews 12:2). Face your faults, don't focus on them. Do not compare yourself with others. Listen to what God says in His word and not what people are saying. Let go on the past and press on into the future.
> *Peace with others.* Just be at peace with yourself. Without humility (gentleness) we can never get along with

everybody. Don't try to control people. Forgive quickly
and don't be easily offended.

Hebrews 10:36 and James 1:4 promise that if we allow trials to
take their course, and endure, this will produce in us *perfection* and
completeness lacking nothing. **Receiving the promises of God.** Most
Christians never allow trials to develop gifts or the seeds through
trials and allow growth. Faith and patience work together like twins,
developing character and maturity.

Kindness and goodness are two similar fruits of the Spirit.
Kindness is the attitude that is within us. **Goodness is our actions.**
The things we do stemming from that attitude.
You are equipped with the seed of these fruits at your new birth
(spiritual birth). You need to express these seeds by watering it,
keeping the weeds out of the soil of the heart, and cultivate those
qualities on a continuous basis. We are to dress properly in the Spirit
(1 Thessalonians 5:8). How? By preparing for it mentally. **You've
got to think about it, plan ahead of time.** What you're going to
do, give away. To be kind and good. Operate in it! Colossians 3:12,
speaks of dressing accordingly. Not what you wear in the physical,
but your attitude in the spiritual realm. What should be hanging in
your spiritual closet? Christ-like behavior, kind feelings, goodness,
love. Just as you deliberately pick out and put on your clothes, set
your mind on things that are above.
Jesus is our example (Matthew 11:28). He was easy to hang out
with. We too often just go by our feelings. We need to become
nicer. **Kindness is mercy.** The greatest thing we can do in the
world as messy as it is, is to display this spiritual characteristics—
behaving like Jesus. Not to be walked on, yet not shutting people
out of your life. Sometimes you need to stand up to people, Jesus
did. It's how you handle it. Galatians 6:10, speaks of opportunity to
do good. You're whole life can change if you decide to be good to
people. Start listening to people and make a plan to meet their need!
As we learn how to do what's right and do it all the time we
become faithful and that gift of faithfulness in seed form placed
within us at new birth matures and grows. Galatians 6:9, states: "Let
us not lose heart in doing good, for in due time we will reap if we do
not grow wear." Jesus finished what He started. Paul is giving us
this assurance: "He who began a good work in you will perfect it

until the day of Christ Jesus" (Philippians 1:6). Moses spent 40 years on the backside of nowhere because God found him faithful enough to do great things in front of people. In the later years God used Moses in a great way.

The slippery slope of compromising starts with doing a little but less than what we know is right. It doe's unbelievable damage to our spirits, and we won't reap the full reward God has in mind for us. Mark 4, tells of the seed sown by the Sower which fell into the good soil produced thirty, sixty, and a hundredfold. Why not hundredfold all the way through? Because there were compromises in our lives.

The story of the ten virgins is about *compromise* versus *faithfulness.* The five virgins who brought oil in flasks along with their lamps are the faithful ones. They were fully committed and put forth effort in their faithfulness. The foolish virgins had no oil with them. That means they were compromising, did not put in any effort, and, in the end, they were found wanting. It is not what you do right one time, it's what you do over and over and over, without compromising.

Humility is the most difficult of fruits to develop. Humility is gentleness or meekness. A humble person is a happy person. Why? Because they're not trying to impress someone and don't live under the pressure of being in competition or hypocritical pretending.

In Matthew 11:28–29 Jesus said, "Come unto Me all you overburdened, heavy laden and I will give you rest." In other words, He is saying: **"If you will do what I am asking you then I am giving you the grace to do it."** The result is joy! God is not impressed by what we do; our underlining motivation counts before God. If we do things for God with the right motivation, we experience joy. Moreover, humility produces joy. The bottom line is that if our motives are wrong God is not pleased. This does not produce no joy.

Proverbs 6:16, states that God hates pride—the opposite of humility. Pride sews discord, whereas humility is freedom from pride and arrogance. We should not feel bad about our weaknesses-we all have them. God purposely leaves weaknesses in His saints. Without them we have no need for God.

I appreciate what Joyce said in one of her audio teaching seminar: "You can control yourself if you really want to." It's extremely important to know that we can do what's right with God's help. He'd never ask us to do anything without giving us the ability to do it. Pray ahead of time in areas where you know you are weak when it comes to self-control. Jesus said, "Pray that you come not into temptation." You can't walk in love and not have self-control. Love is an action not a feeling. Galatians 3:14, tells us to, "Put on love." That's why self-control is so important.

If you would be required to teach others this module, **please provide a *written plan* for how you would do it.**

As I said previously, if I were required to teach others this module I feel I would want to present it in much the same way it was presented to me.

Closing Thoughts and Conclusions

In this section please feel free to share your own thoughts, emotions, experiences related to your time spent as part of the ADT Family for over two years. I am most interested in your most significant *"aha moments"* you experienced throughout the ADT process.

Wow! How can I possibly summarize in a few paragraphs what being a part of the Advanced Discipleship Training family for the last two and a half years has meant to me. How it has changed my Spiritual walk and life.

I thank God that He cared enough for me to allow me to come to the end of myself, and led me to the ADT program. If I learned anything at all in the last two and a half years, it is that new life and growth does not come without pain and discomfort. It became obvious to me that spiritual things parallel physical things!

When it comes to the "aha moments" I experienced throughout the ADT platform there are many that I can talk about. Let me share a couple of them. One significant aha moment that I experienced in this process was the deeper meaning of the cross, which I like to call—the "two sides of the cross." In fact this is a true statement for my entire spiritual life.

This concept is based on Romans 5:9–10. In essence Paul is saying that salvation is not just getting your sins forgiven but implies living a victorious life after you are born again. I realized for the first time in my life that before I met Christ I was His enemy. In order to be saved from the wrath of God I needed Christ's blood. This is Side A of the cross. For many years of my Christian life this was the only "truth" I knew. After I received Christ, I became His friend, therefore no longer an enemy. From this point forward until I will meet my Lord in haven, I need His resurrected life for my Christian walk. This is Side B of the cross. When I finally understood the concept hidden in Romans 5:9–19, the spiritual bulb came on. It was a powerful aha moment—I felt that I was saved all over again.

Let me explain this a little bit more. The realization that not only was I saved or born again, but that Christ took residence in me—Christ in me, the hope of glory—it is the "exchanged life."

J. Hudson Taylor, that famous missionary to the inland China writes:

> I am no better than before (may I not say in a sense I do not wish to be, nor am I striving to be), but I am dead and buried with Christ-aye, and risen too and ascended and now Christ lives in me, and the life I now live in the flesh, I live by the faith of the Son of God, who loved me and gave himself to me. I now believe I am dead to sin. God reckons me so, and tells me to reckon myself so. He knows best.[147]

Once I understood and allowed that truth in my life, that I was crucified with Christ, buried with Him, and resurrected with Him, I am now able to let go and allow Him to live through me. It is His faith, power, and ability that keeps me and lives His life in me. As I learn, more and more, to keep my hands off my life, it is easier to allow His life to work through me. The result of this amazing change (or I should say—exchange) is peace and joy in all areas of my life. The fact is that I don't have to control my actions and behavior, I just have to yield my life to Him, He is the One working in me and through me.

Another life changing aha moment that I received early on in the ADT training was the realization of how greatly past emotional wounds and reactions still affect me today. Dr. Neil Anderson explains the concept of the "primary emotion" and the "secondary emotion." In other words I realized that there is a direct correlation between the negative emotions, trauma or wounds which took place in the past—*primary emotion*, and our emotional reaction to the present events—*secondary emotion*. Satan took advantage of my ignorance of these truths, and was able to cripple my spiritual walk. Therefore, it is paramount to learn how to resolve the primary emotion, by sincere acknowledgement of the past wounds, and seeking emotional healing from the One Who is able to set the captive free and bind the brokenhearted. The healing process implies inviting and allowing the Holy Spirit to examine our troubling thoughts and negative emotions, find their roots in the past, then, bringing the false belief to the Lord in prayer.

As we moved from module to module, from "The Bible" to "Fruits of the Spirit," each subject covered was of utmost importance in presenting the disciple with reliable, dependable teaching that shaped me into a well-rounded disciple of Christ.

The authors and teachers soon began to feel like old friends. Especially men like Dr. Juan Carlos, and Dr. Neil Anderson. After many months of consistent work, writing various essays, putting together book reports, doing retreats, and completing soul searching homework although hard at times, I found it all worth my time and effort. This entire process brought about a change and certainty in my faith I hadn't experienced before.

The time, dedication, love and friendship I found in my Spiritual Mentor and Life Couch-Valy, was exceptional. I could never adequately express my gratitude towards him. He was there in my dark, hard times, as well as in all the victories I have experienced during the time of my training and equipping. It felt so good to be able to share my many aha moments with the person who understood these concepts.

How do you plan to be active in making disciples? **Please OUTLINE your PLAN**. Be as specific and as detailed as possible.

I could never express the importance of being a part of the ADT family these past two years, the importance it has been to my spiritual walk and recovery, and how it has led me to freedom. The words of Jesus, "you will know the truth, and the truth will make you free" (John 8:32), kept resonating into my heart all these months.

To me the verse from 1 Peter 3:15, "always being ready to make a defense to everyone who asks you to give an account for the hope that is in you, yet with gentleness and reverence" has a tremendous value! I would love to be helpful in some way in discipling others, whether in my local church or elsewhere. Wherever the Lord opens the door and in whatever he calls me to do-my answer is predetermined-yes. If I can help one person to experience the freedom, victory, and spiritual growth the way I was helped, it would be worth it all.

At this time I don't have an exact outline or plan in place, but I am still praying and being open to the leading of the Holy Spirit in my life regarding the direction He wants me to go.

So help me God!

Upper Room Fellowship Ministry

In 1996, in response to God's calling and by the guidance of the Holy Spirit, *Upper Room Fellowship Ministry (URFM)* was formed in order to serve the body of Christ. URFM is a non-profit and non-denominational Christian organization.

VISION

Fully alive through mind renewal and spiritual transformation for God's glory.

MISSION:

Our desire at URFM is to assist believers to experience healing for the wounded heart, restoration for the soul, and spiritual growth in Christ. Our prayer and deep desire is that through the Holy Spirit you will experience Jesus Christ as your very source of life.

Through individual or small group meetings and retreats, URFM is committed to create an environment where healing, restoration, and spiritual freedom can be experienced. Under the guidance of the Holy Spirit, URFM is making disciples and equipping them for the Kingdom of God. URFM ministers for the spiritual growth of all believers.

The goal is that every member of Christ's Body would attain the Ultimate Intention—*the fullness of Christ.*

Most Christians have been taught that Jesus Christ died for their sins. Some embraced Christ as their Lord. Only a few have been taught the truth that they died with Him and experience Christ as their Life. Consequently, even fewer find victory in their lives. Although they have been set free from their sins, they have not been set free from themselves.

Our desire and fervent prayer for all of Jesus' disciples are that they all will become everything that God intends for them to become, in other words—*the fullness of Christ.*

About the Author

Mark was born and raised in Detroit, Michigan, and is currently a member of Brightmoor Christian Church in Novi Michigan. He enjoys singing in the choir and church's musical productions, as well as reading the Bible, Christian books, and having personal devotions. Mark's life journey lead him to the end of himself, therefore he needed a radical change in his life. He was directed to Upper Room Fellowship Ministry, which specializes in healing of the wounded heart, restoration of the soul, and advanced discipleship training leading to spiritual growth in Christ. Mark, went through various spiritual processes and studied several modules of spiritual formation, which radically transformed his life. This book is based on Mark's Capstones Project. He did not dream that it would turn into a book. Mark's prayer is that the pages of this book will reach out to many who are hurting and in need of healing. Mark has four adult children, and eight grandchildren, and resides in the Detroit area.

Notes:

1. The Bible—The Foundation for Spiritual Growth & Maturity

[1] https://www.goodreads.com/quotes/238236-here-then-is-the-real-problem-of-our-negligence-we (Accessed on February 28, 2018).

2. Discipleship–The Heart of the Great Commission

[2] Robert E. Coleman, *The Master Plan of Evangelism,* (Grand Rapids, MI, Revell, 1993), 9.
[3] Paul E. Billheimer, "Destined For The Throne", (Forth Washington, PA, Christian Literature Crusade, 1976), 21, 26, 27.
[4] Paul E. Billheimer, 33–34, 35–36, 39–40.
[5] Billheimer, 43–49, 52–53.
[6] Ibid, 57–58, 60–62, 65–66, 68.
[7] Ibid, 71–73, 79–80.
[8] Ibid, 83–84.
[9] Ibid, 88–91, 91–93.
[10] Ibid, 95–96, 101–102, 104–105,105–106, 112–113.
[11] Ibid, 115–116, 118, 120–121, 121, 121–123, 123–124, 126.
[12] Ibid, 131, 132, 134.

3. Maturity—The Goal of Discipleship

[13] DeVern Fromke, "The Ultimate Intention," (Sure Foundation Publishers, Sholas, IN, 1963),
[14] Miles J Stanford, "Principles of Spiritual Growth," (Back to the Bible, Lincoln, NE, 1997), 7, 9, 10.
[15] Stanford, 11, 13.
[16] Ibid, 24.
[17] Ibid, 31, 32.
[18] Ibid, 36, 37.
[19] Hannah Whitall Smit, "The Christian's Secret Of A Happy Life," (Revell Co., Old Tappan, NJ, 1952), 16–18
[20] "The Christian's Secret Of A Happy Life," 22–28, 33—34.
[21] Ibid, 45–47, 50–52.
[22] Ibid, 59–60.
[23] Ibid, 76.
[24] Ibid, 118, 124–125.
[25] Ibid, 150.
[26] Ibid, 208, 216.
[27] Ibid, 217.
[28] Dr. John E. Best, "Resolving Misunderstandings of the Exchanged Life," (Abundant Living Resources, Garland, TX, 2011), 3, 5.
[29] "Resolving Misunderstandings of the Exchanged Life," 7–8.

30 Best, 21, 22, 23. 25, 26. 29, 30, 31. 33, 34, 35. 42, 43. 51.55, 56.

31 Hannah Whitall Smit, "The Christian's Secret Of A Happy Life," (Revell Co., Old Tappan, NJ, 1952), 217.

32 J. Hudson Taylor, "The Exchanged Life," (Worldwide Missions), 1. Accessed on August 2018. https://www.wholesomewords.org/missions.biotaylor11.html.

33 Taylor, 2, 3, 4.

34 Juan Carlos Ortiz, "Accepted in the Beloved," DVD 1. www.thelifebookstore.com.

4. The Flesh—The Major Obstacle Towards Spiritual Maturity

35 Gilham, Bill, "Lifetime Guarantee," (Harvest House Publishers, Eugene, OR, 1993), 35.

36 "Lifetime Guarantee," 58–59. 60–61. 63–64.67–69.

37 Gilham, 72–73, 74–75, 75–76, 77–78, 79–80, 83–85.

38 Ibid, 87–88. 88–90. 90. 95. 96–97, 97–98. 99–100.

39 Ibid, 21. 25–26. 34. 36–37, 39, 45–46, 47–48, 52–53.

40 Ibid, 105

41 Ibid, 104–105, 105–107. 108–110.

42 Ibid, 108–112, 116, 118–119.

43 Ibid, 122–124, 125–126, 127, 130–132, 132–135, 136–137, 141–142.

44 Ibid, 147–148, 148–149, 150, 151, 153–155.

45 Ibid, 160–161, 162.

46 Ibid, 164–165.

47 Ibid, 174.

48 Ibid, 177–178, 178, 178–179, 179–180, 180–181, 181–182, 182–183, 183–184, 185–186.

49 Ibid, 186, 187–188.

50 Ibid, 190, 191, 192, 192–194.

51 Ibid, 294, 195–196.

52 Ibid, 203–204, 204–206, 208, 209.

53 Nee, Watchman, "The Normal Christian Life," (CLC Publications, Forth Washington, PA, 19034, 2012), 9.

54 "The Normal Christian Life," 9, 9–10, 12

55 Nee, 14, 21, 31, 36, 40.

56 Ibid, 42,44, 46, 48, 51, 52.

57 Ibid, 53, 58. 61–62. 65–66, 71, 73.

58 Ibid, 76–77, 78-81, 85.

59 Ibid, 88–89, 94.

60 Ibid, 95, 96, 98, 102–103, 106.

61 Ibid, 107, 112, 114, 124, 130, 132.

62 Ibid, 134, 137, 139–140, 142–143, 147, 152, 155.

63 Ibid, 155, 157, 159, 161, 162–164, 170, 171, 175–176.

64 Ibid, 184–185, 186, 18–190, 191–192, 193, 196.

65 197, 200–201, 202, 205, 208, 211–212, 216.

66 219, 220, 221–222, 225, 230, 231–232, 234.

67 240, 243, 244–245, 248–249, 252–253.

68 Best, John, "The Cross of Christ: The Center of Scripture, Your Life and Ministry," (Abundant Living Resources, Garland, TX, 2011), 1–2.

[69] "The Cross of Christ: The Center of Scripture, Your Life and Ministry," 38–39.
[70] Best, 5–6, 8, 9, 15, 16.
[71] Ibid, 26–28, 29.
[72] Ibid, 16, 17, 18, 19–21. 22–24. 26–28, 29. 30–32.
[73] Ibid, 33–34. 36–37. 37.37, 38–41.
[74] Ibid, 43, 44.
[75] Ibid, 45, 46–47.
[76] Ibid, 48–49.

5. The Cross—The Mystery of Suffering that Only a Few Embrace It

[77] Watchman Nee, "The Normal Christian Life," (CLC Publications, Fort Washington, PA 19034, 2012), 40.
[78] Charles R. Solomon, "Handbook to Happiness," (Tyndale House Publishers, Wheaton, IL, 60189, 1999), 3.
[79] Solomon, 4–5, 10.
[80] Ibid, 89-90, 91, 92, 93.
[81] Gene Edwards, "Exquisite Agony—Healing for Christians who have been hurt by other Christians," (The Seed Sowers, Jacksonville, FL, 32206, 1994), 17–19.
[82] Edwards, 41–43, 73–75.
[83] The Handbook of Happiness, 5.
[84] Paul Billheimer, "Don't Waste your Sorrows," (CLC, Fort Washington, PA, 19034, 1977), 81.
[85] Charles Stanley, "The Blessing of Brokenness," (Zondervan Publishing House, Grand Rapids, MI, 49530, 1997), 9–10.
[86] "The Blessing of Brokenness," 18–19.
[87] Stanley, 54–64.
[88] Ibid, 86–101.
[89] Ibid, 125–127.
[90] Ibid, 127–129.
[91] Ibid, 129–135.
[92] Ibid, 136–138.
[93] Solomon, "The Handbook of Happiness," 69.
[94] Stanley, "The Blessings of Brokenness," 14.
[95] Billheimer, "Don't Waste Your Sorrows," 26–27.
[96] "Don't Waste Your Sorrows," 43–45. 47–51.
[97] Billheimer, 63–64.
[98] Ibid, 67–69.
[99] Ibid, 69–70.
[100] Ibid, 73–74.
[101] Ibid, 75, 77.
[102] Ibid, 78–83.
[103] Ibid, 99–100, 101–102, 102, 104, 107–108.
[104] Ibid, 111–112, 113–114, 115–119.
[105] Ibid, 115–119.

6. Identity—Knowing Who we are in Christ—The Key to Spiritual Victory

[106] Anderson, Neil, "Victory over Darkness," (Regal Books, Ventura, CA, 93006, 2000), 32.
[107] "Victory over Darkness," 92–93.
[108] Anderson, 93–95.
[109] Ibid, 97–98.
[110] Ibid, 109–110, 110–112, 112–113, 113–114, 114–115. 117, 119.
[111] Needham, David, "Alive for the First Time," (Multnomah Books, Sisters, OR, 1995), 47–49.
[112] Needham, 52–53.
[113] Ibid, 53–61, 61–65, 66—69, 71–73.
[114] Ibid, 75–78, 79–82, 82–91, 91–92, 93–94, 95.
[115] "Victory over Darkness," 46–47.
[116] "Alive for the First Time," 64–65.
[117] Needham, 115—116.
[118] Ibid, 116–117. 117–120. 120–123. 124–126.
[119] Ibid, 126–127.
[120] Ibid, 127–129.
[121] Ibid, 129–130.
[122] Ibid, 151–152, 152–154, 155–157, 157–159, 159–161, 163, 164–165, 165–166, 166–167, 167, 168–169.
[123] Ibid, 171–172 174–175. 175–177.
[124] Ibid, 171–172, 173–174, 174–175, 175–177, 177–178, 178—179, 180–181, 181–182, 183–184, 185–186, 188–191, 192–193.
[125] Ibid, 195–199.
[126] "Victory over the Darkness," 124, 124–125, 125–126, 126–127, 127, 128–129, 129–130.
[127] Anderson, 131, 131–133, 133–135.
[128] Ibid, 139, 139–142, 142–143, 143–144, 144–145, 145–146, 146—147, 147–148, 148, 148.
[129] Ibid, 178–179.
[130] Ibid, 171–172, 173–174, 174–175, 175–176, 178–179, 180–182.
[131] Ibid, 185–187, 187–188, 188–189, 190–191, 191–192, 192–195.
[132] Simpson, A.B. "Himself," biblebelievers.com/simpson-ab_himself.html. Accessed on November 6, 2019.

7. Free in Christ—Understanding Spiritual Warfare

[133] Anderson, T. Neil, "The Bondage Breaker," (Harvest House Publishers, Eugene, OR, 97402, 2000), 18.
[134] "Victory over the Darkness," 160, 161.
[135] "The Bondage Breaker," 42.
[136] Anderson, 60–61.
[137] Ibid, 149-150.
[138] Stanley, F. Charles, "The Gift of Forgiveness," (Thomas Nelson Inc., Nashville, TN, 1991), 2.
[139] "The Gift of Forgiveness," 2.
[140] Stanley, 5, 5–6, 6, 9.
[141] Ibid, 80–81.

[142] Sarah Young, "Jesus Calling," (Thomas Nelson, Nashville, TN), 2014.
[143] Oswald Chambers, "My Utmost For His Highest," (Discovery House Publishers, Lancashire, UK, 1992.
[144] Mark Batterson, "The Circle Maker," (Zondervan, Grand Rapids, MI), 2011.
[145] Derek Prince, "Prayers and Proclamations," (Whitaker House, New Kensington, PA 15068), 2010.
[146] Juan Carlos Ortiz, "Indwelled by the Beloved," DVD 3. www.thelifebookstore.com.
[147] J. Hudson Taylor, "The exchanged life." www.wholesomewords.org. https://www.wholesomewords.org/missions/biotaylor11.html. Accessed on November 13, 2019.

Made in the USA
Monee, IL
21 January 2020

20647300R00174